the
ART
of
PROBLEM
SOLVING

Volume 1:
the BASICS
Solutions

Sandor Lehoczky
Richard Rusczyk

Cover: "Grand Canyon from South Rim" by Ansel Adams. No permissions required; National Archive photo 79-AAF-8.

Fifth Edition; printed in February, 2003.

Published by AoPS, P.O. Box 2185, Alpine, CA 91903-2185.

ISBN: 1-885875-00-2

This book was produced as camera ready copy using the TEX and LATEX typesetting systems.

Chapter 1

Exponents and Logarithms

Solutions to Exercises

1-1

    i. $3^4 = \mathbf{81}$.

    ii. $2^5 \cdot 2^2 = 2^{5+2} = 2^7 = \mathbf{128}$.

    iii. $5^{-3} \cdot 5^5 \cdot 5^{-1} = 5^{-3+5-1} = 5^1 = \mathbf{5}$.

    iv. $\dfrac{4^3}{4} = 4^{3-1} = 4^2 = \mathbf{16}$.

    v. $\dfrac{2^7}{2^2} = 2^{7-2} = 2^5 = \mathbf{32}$.

    vi. $\dfrac{3^4 \cdot 3^{-2}}{3^5 \cdot 3^{-2}} = \dfrac{3^{4-2}}{3^{5-2}} = \dfrac{3^2}{3^3} = 3^{2-3} = 3^{-1} = \dfrac{\mathbf{1}}{\mathbf{3}}$.

    vii. $2^5 \cdot 3^2 \cdot 2^{-3} = 2^{5-3} \cdot 3^2 = 2^2 \cdot 3^2 = (4)(9) = \mathbf{36}$.

    viii. $5^2 \cdot 3^{-1} \cdot 2^4 \cdot 5^{-1} \cdot 2^{-2} = 2^{4-2} \cdot 3^{-1} \cdot 5^{2-1} = 2^2 \cdot 3^{-1} \cdot 5^1 = \dfrac{4(5)}{3} = \dfrac{\mathbf{20}}{\mathbf{3}}$.

1-2

    i. $9^{3/2} = (9^{1/2})^3 = 3^3 = \mathbf{27}$.

    ii. $(\sqrt[3]{81})^{3/2} = (81^{1/3})^{3/2} = 81^{(1/3)(3/2)} = 81^{1/2} = \mathbf{9}$.

    iii. $64^{-4/3} = (64^{1/3})^{-4} = 4^{-4} = \dfrac{1}{4^4} = \dfrac{\mathbf{1}}{\mathbf{256}}$.

    iv. $\sqrt[5]{100000^3} = 100000^{3/5} = (100000^{1/5})^3 = 10^3 = \mathbf{1000}$.

v. $\left(\dfrac{4}{9}\right)^{-3/2} = \dfrac{4^{-3/2}}{9^{-3/2}} = \dfrac{(4^{1/2})^{-3}}{(9^{1/2})^{-3}} = \dfrac{2^{-3}}{3^{-3}} = \dfrac{1/8}{1/27} = \dfrac{\mathbf{27}}{\mathbf{8}}.$

vi. $\sqrt[4]{(1/16)^{-3}} = \left(\dfrac{1}{16}\right)^{-3/4} = \dfrac{1^{-3/4}}{16^{-3/4}} = \dfrac{1}{(16^{1/4})^{-3}} = \dfrac{1}{2^{-3}} = \dfrac{1}{1/8} = \mathbf{8}.$

1-3

  i. $x = (-2)^5 = (-1)^5 2^5 = \mathbf{-32}.$

  ii. $x = \sqrt[3]{-1/8} = \sqrt[3]{-1}\sqrt[3]{1/8} = \mathbf{-1/2}.$

  iii. The sixth root of 64 is 2, but -2 raised to the sixth power is also 64, so $x = \mathbf{\pm 2}$ describes all real x such that $x^6 = 64$.

  iv. The cube root of 64 is 4. Since -4 cubed is -64, it is not a solution. Thus $x = \mathbf{4}.$

  v. $x = (-27)^{-2/3} = ((-27)^{1/3})^{-2} = (-3)^{-2} = \dfrac{1}{(-3)^2} = \dfrac{\mathbf{1}}{\mathbf{9}}.$

  vi. Raising each side to the 3/5 power, we have

$$(x^{5/3})^{3/5} = x^1 = 243^{3/5} = (243^{1/5})^3 = 3^3 = \mathbf{27}.$$

Notice that we didn't have to be concerned with multiple real roots because we were taking an odd (fifth) root of 243.

1-4

  i. $\sqrt{27} = 3^{3/2} = 3^1 \cdot 3^{1/2} = \mathbf{3\sqrt{3}}.$

  ii. $\sqrt[3]{128} = 2^{7/3} = 2^2 \cdot 2^{1/3} = \mathbf{4\sqrt[3]{2}}.$

  iii. $\sqrt[4]{1600} = 2^{6/4} \cdot 5^{2/4} = 2^1 \cdot 2^{1/2} \cdot 5^{1/2} = 2(10^{1/2}) = \mathbf{2\sqrt{10}}.$

  iv. $\sqrt{9095625} = \sqrt{3^3 \cdot 5^4 \cdot 7^2 \cdot 11} = 3^{3/2} \cdot 5^{4/2} \cdot 7^{2/2} \cdot 11^{1/2} = 3^1 \cdot 5^2 \cdot 7^1 \cdot 3^{1/2} \cdot 11^{1/2} = 3(25)(7)\sqrt{33} = \mathbf{525\sqrt{33}}.$

  v. Here, we first simplify the fraction before finding the cube root: $\dfrac{36000}{243} = \dfrac{2^5 \cdot 3^2 \cdot 5^3}{3^5} = \dfrac{2^5 \cdot 5^3}{3^3}.$ Thus $\sqrt[3]{\dfrac{36000}{243}} = \dfrac{\sqrt[3]{2^5 \cdot 5^3}}{\sqrt[3]{3^3}} = \dfrac{2^{5/3} \cdot 5^1}{3^1} = \dfrac{2^1 \cdot 5^1 \cdot 2^{2/3}}{3} = \dfrac{10\sqrt[3]{4}}{3}.$

  vi. Once again, we start by reducing the fraction: $\dfrac{56}{126} = \dfrac{2^3 \cdot 7}{2^1 \cdot 3^2 \cdot 7} = \dfrac{2^2}{3^2}.$ Thus

$$\sqrt{\dfrac{56}{126}} = \sqrt{\dfrac{2^2}{3^2}} = \dfrac{\sqrt{2^2}}{\sqrt{3^2}} = \dfrac{\mathbf{2}}{\mathbf{3}}.$$

You should try to do these by inspection as well.

1-5

i. $\dfrac{3}{\sqrt{3}} \cdot \dfrac{\sqrt{3}}{\sqrt{3}} = \dfrac{3\sqrt{3}}{3} = \sqrt{3}.$

ii. $\dfrac{\sqrt{2}}{\sqrt{6}} \cdot \dfrac{\sqrt{6}}{\sqrt{6}} = \dfrac{\sqrt{12}}{6} = \dfrac{2\sqrt{3}}{6} = \dfrac{\sqrt{3}}{3}.$

iii. First, we reduce the cube root of 24, to get

$$\frac{2}{\sqrt[3]{24}} = \frac{2}{\sqrt[3]{8 \cdot 3}} = \frac{2}{2\sqrt[3]{3}} = \frac{1}{\sqrt[3]{3}}$$

Now, we simplify this:

$$\frac{1}{\sqrt[3]{3}} \cdot \frac{\sqrt[3]{3^2}}{\sqrt[3]{3^2}} = \frac{\sqrt[3]{3^2}}{\sqrt[3]{3^3}} = \frac{\sqrt[3]{9}}{3}.$$

iv. Since $1800 = 2^3 3^2 5^2$, we have

$$\frac{1}{\sqrt[4]{1800}} = \frac{1}{\sqrt[4]{2^3}\sqrt[4]{3^2}\sqrt[4]{5^2}} \cdot \frac{\sqrt[4]{2}}{\sqrt[4]{2}} \cdot \frac{\sqrt[4]{3^2}}{\sqrt[4]{3^2}} \cdot \frac{\sqrt[4]{5^2}}{\sqrt[4]{5^2}} = \frac{\sqrt[4]{2 \cdot 3^2 \cdot 5^2}}{\sqrt[4]{2^4 3^4 5^4}} = \frac{\sqrt[4]{450}}{30}.$$

v. To rationalize the denominator of this expression, we multiply by a factor which makes the exponent of 5 in the denominator an integer. To do this, we multiply by $5^{1/3}$, which will make the denominator 5^2:

$$\frac{5^{1/3}}{5^{5/3}} \cdot \frac{5^{1/3}}{5^{1/3}} = \frac{5^{2/3}}{5^2} = \frac{\sqrt[3]{25}}{25}.$$

vi. Dealing with each base separately, we have

$$\frac{3^{1/2}2^{2/3}}{3^{1/6}2^{3/2}} \cdot \frac{3^{5/6}}{3^{5/6}} \cdot \frac{2^{1/2}}{2^{1/2}} = \frac{3^{(1/2+5/6)}2^{(2/3+1/2)}}{3^1 2^2} = \frac{3^{4/3}2^{7/6}}{12} = \frac{6 \cdot 3^{1/3}2^{1/6}}{12} = \frac{6\sqrt[6]{9 \cdot 2}}{12} = \frac{\sqrt[6]{18}}{2}.$$

1-6

i. The conjugate of $\sqrt{7} + \sqrt{3}$ is $\sqrt{7} - \sqrt{3}$, so we write

$$\frac{1}{\sqrt{7}+\sqrt{3}} \cdot \frac{\sqrt{7}-\sqrt{3}}{\sqrt{7}-\sqrt{3}} = \frac{\sqrt{7}-\sqrt{3}}{7-3} = \frac{\sqrt{7}-\sqrt{3}}{4}.$$

ii. $\dfrac{6}{\sqrt{15}-\sqrt{6}} \cdot \dfrac{\sqrt{15}+\sqrt{6}}{\sqrt{15}+\sqrt{6}} = \dfrac{6(\sqrt{15}+\sqrt{6})}{15-6} = \dfrac{6(\sqrt{15}+\sqrt{6})}{9} = \dfrac{2\sqrt{15}+2\sqrt{6}}{3}.$

iii. $\dfrac{\sqrt{2}}{\sqrt{6}-2} \cdot \dfrac{\sqrt{6}+2}{\sqrt{6}+2} = \dfrac{\sqrt{2}\sqrt{6}+2\sqrt{2}}{6-4} = \dfrac{\sqrt{12}+2\sqrt{2}}{2} = \dfrac{2\sqrt{3}+2\sqrt{2}}{2} = \sqrt{3}+\sqrt{2}.$

iv. First, we multiply by $\sqrt{1+\sqrt{2}}$. This removes the outer radical from the denominator:

$$\frac{1}{\sqrt{1+\sqrt{2}}} \cdot \frac{\sqrt{1+\sqrt{2}}}{\sqrt{1+\sqrt{2}}} = \frac{\sqrt{1+\sqrt{2}}}{1+\sqrt{2}}.$$

To rationalize the denominator of this expression, we multiply by $1 - \sqrt{2}$:

$$\frac{\sqrt{1+\sqrt{2}}}{1+\sqrt{2}} \cdot \frac{1-\sqrt{2}}{1-\sqrt{2}} = \frac{(1-\sqrt{2})\sqrt{1+\sqrt{2}}}{1-2} = (-\mathbf{1}+\sqrt{\mathbf{2}})\sqrt{\mathbf{1}+\sqrt{\mathbf{2}}}.$$

v. Writing $\sqrt[4]{2}$ as $\sqrt{\sqrt{2}}$, the conjugate of $2 - \sqrt{\sqrt{2}}$ is $2 + \sqrt{\sqrt{2}}$, so we have

$$\frac{1}{2-\sqrt{\sqrt{2}}} \cdot \frac{2+\sqrt{\sqrt{2}}}{2+\sqrt{\sqrt{2}}} = \frac{2+\sqrt{\sqrt{2}}}{4-\sqrt{\sqrt{2}\sqrt{2}}} = \frac{2+\sqrt{\sqrt{2}}}{4-\sqrt{2}}.$$

Now we are in familiar territory:

$$\frac{2+\sqrt{\sqrt{2}}}{4-\sqrt{2}} \cdot \frac{4+\sqrt{2}}{4+\sqrt{2}} = \frac{(2+\sqrt{\sqrt{2}})(4+\sqrt{2})}{16-2} = \frac{8+2\sqrt{2}+4\sqrt[4]{2}+\sqrt[4]{8}}{14}.$$

Note that in this final step we have written $\sqrt{\sqrt{2}}$ as $\sqrt[4]{2}$ and $\sqrt{2}\sqrt{\sqrt{2}} = 2^{1/2} \cdot 2^{1/4} = \sqrt[4]{8}$. Make sure you understand why these are true.

1-7 In each of these, "base^{exponent} = answer" should become "$\log_{\text{base}}$ answer = exponent." Thus we obtain

    i. $\log_3 27 = 3$.

    ii. $\log_{16} 2 = 1/4$.

    iii. $\log_x y = z$.

1-8

    i. $36^{1/2} = 6$.

    ii. $3^{-2} = 1/9$.

    iii. $x^z = y$.

1-9

    i. We must find the value of x for which $5^x = 625$. Since $5^4 = 625$, $\log_5 625 = \mathbf{4}$.

    ii. $(1/2)^x = 2$. Since $1/2$ is the reciprocal of 2, the power we seek is -1. Thus $\log_{(1/2)} 2 = -\mathbf{1}$.

    iii. We wish to find the x such that $9^x = 3^{1/2}$. Writing 9 as 3^2, $(3^2)^x = 3^{2x} = 3^{1/2}$. Thus $2x = 1/2$, so $x = 1/4$. Hence, $\log_9 \sqrt{3} = \mathbf{1/4}$.

iv. Letting $\log_{\sqrt{5}} \sqrt[3]{5} = x$ and writing the result as an exponential equation, we have

$$
\begin{aligned}
\sqrt{5}^x &= \sqrt[3]{5} \\
(5^{1/2})^x &= 5^{1/3} \\
5^{x/2} &= 5^{1/3} \\
x/2 &= 1/3 \\
x &= 2/3.
\end{aligned}
$$

Thus $\log_{\sqrt{5}} \sqrt[3]{5} = \mathbf{2/3}$.

Solutions to Problems

1. The argument of the logarithm is $(125)(625)/25 = 5^3 5^4/5^2 = 5^5$. Thus we have $\log_5 (125)(625)/25 = \log_5 5^5 = \mathbf{5}$.

2. We must write the argument as a single term with base 3. Thus $27 \sqrt[4]{9} \sqrt[3]{9} = 3^3 3^{2/4} 3^{2/3} = 3^{3+(1/2)+(2/3)} = 3^{25/6}$. Hence, $\log_3 27 \sqrt[4]{9} \sqrt[3]{9} = \log_3 3^{25/6} = 25/6 = \mathbf{4\frac{1}{6}}$.

3. Rationalizing each denominator, we have

$$
2 + \sqrt{2} + \frac{1}{2+\sqrt{2}} \cdot \frac{2-\sqrt{2}}{2-\sqrt{2}} + \frac{1}{-2+\sqrt{2}} \cdot \frac{-2-\sqrt{2}}{-2-\sqrt{2}} = 2 + \sqrt{2} + \frac{2-\sqrt{2}}{2} + \frac{-2-\sqrt{2}}{2} = \mathbf{2}.
$$

4. Evaluating each term individually, then adding, we have

$$
\begin{aligned}
(-3)^{-2} + (-2)^{-1} + (-1)^0 + 0^1 + 1^2 + 2^3 + 3^4 &= \frac{1}{9} + \frac{1}{-2} + 1 + 0 + 1 + 8 + 81 \\
&= 91 + \frac{1}{9} - \frac{1}{2} \\
&= \mathbf{90\frac{11}{18}}.
\end{aligned}
$$

5. We evaluate the exponent of the expression first. Thus

$$
81^{-(2^{-2})} = 81^{-(1/4)} = (3^4)^{-1/4} = 3^{-1} = \mathbf{\frac{1}{3}}.
$$

6.   Treating each term separately, we have

$$\left(\frac{1}{2}\right)^{-1/2} + \left(\frac{3}{2}\right)^{-3/2} + \left(\frac{5}{2}\right)^{-5/2} = 2^{1/2} + \left(\frac{2}{3}\right)^{3/2} + \left(\frac{2}{5}\right)^{5/2}$$

$$= \sqrt{2} + \left(\frac{\sqrt{2}}{\sqrt{3}}\right)^3 + \left(\frac{\sqrt{2}}{\sqrt{5}}\right)^5$$

$$= \sqrt{2} + \frac{2\sqrt{2}}{3\sqrt{3}} + \frac{4\sqrt{2}}{25\sqrt{5}}.$$

Rationalizing each denominator then finding a common denominator, we have

$$\sqrt{2} + \frac{2\sqrt{6}}{9} + \frac{4\sqrt{10}}{125} = \frac{1125\sqrt{2} + 250\sqrt{6} + 36\sqrt{10}}{1125}.$$

7.   This doesn't quite fit into any of our rationalization rules. We try writing the denominator as $(\sqrt{2} + \sqrt{3}) - \sqrt{5}$, which gives us the idea of multiplying top and bottom by $(\sqrt{2} + \sqrt{3}) + \sqrt{5}$. Thus

$$\frac{\sqrt{2}}{(\sqrt{2} + \sqrt{3}) - \sqrt{5}} \cdot \frac{(\sqrt{2} + \sqrt{3}) + \sqrt{5}}{(\sqrt{2} + \sqrt{3}) + \sqrt{5}} = \frac{2 + \sqrt{6} + \sqrt{10}}{(\sqrt{2} + \sqrt{3})^2 - 5} = \frac{2 + \sqrt{6} + \sqrt{10}}{2\sqrt{6}}.$$

Now we are in familiar territory. Multiplying top and bottom by $\sqrt{6}$, we have

$$\frac{2\sqrt{6} + 6 + \sqrt{60}}{12} = \frac{6 + 2\sqrt{6} + 2\sqrt{15}}{12} = \frac{3 + \sqrt{6} + \sqrt{15}}{6}.$$

8.   Let the value of the logarithm be x. Expressing everything with a common base, 3, we have $\log_{3^{1/2}} 3^{2/3} = x$. Thus $(3^{1/2})^x = 3^{2/3}$, or $x/2 = 2/3$. Finally, $x = \mathbf{4/3}$.

9.   We need to get rid of the radicals. Squaring the equation yields $1 + \sqrt{2 + \sqrt{n}} = 4$, or $\sqrt{2 + \sqrt{n}} = 3$. Squaring again gives $2 + \sqrt{n} = 9$, or $\sqrt{n} = 7$. Squaring yet once more yields $n = \mathbf{49}$.

10.   Expressing both sides with the same base, 2, we have $2^{16^x} = 16^{2^x} = (2^4)^{2^x} = 2^{4(2^x)}$. Hence $16^x = 4(2^x)$. Again, we express these two equations with 2 as the base. Since $16^x = (2^4)^x = 2^{4x}$ and $4(2^x) = 2^2 2^x = 2^{x+2}$, we have $2^{4x} = 2^{x+2}$, so $4x = x + 2$ and $x = \mathbf{2/3}$.

11.   Writing this equation in exponential notation, we have $(2x)^x = 216 = 2^3 3^3$. Thus x must have a factor of 3 if it is an integer. Trying $x = 3$, we find $(6)^3 = 216$, as required. Since $(2x)^x$ gets larger as we try larger x and smaller as we try smaller x, $x = \mathbf{3}$ is the only solution.

12. Let the two logarithms equal x. (Introducing a new variable like this is a common technique in handling equal logarithms.) We can now write a couple of exponential equations, $A^x = B$ and $B^x = A$. Since we are seeking AB, we multiply these two equations to find $(AB)^x = AB$, or $(AB)^{x-1} = 1$. Thus either $x = 1$ or $AB = 1$. If $x = 1$, then $B^1 = B = A$, but we are given $B \neq A$. Hence, we must have $AB = \mathbf{1}$.

13. We wish to find the x for which $N = 800$. Thus $800 = 8 \cdot 10^8 \cdot x^{-3/2}$. Hence, $x^{-3/2} = 800/800000000 = 1/1000000 = 10^{-6}$. Raising each side of the equation to the $-2/3$ power (in order to have x^1 on the left), we have $(x^{-3/2})^{-2/3} = (10^{-6})^{-2/3}$, so $x = 10^4 = \mathbf{10000}$.

14. We solve for a in each of the equations and set the resulting expressions equal. In the first equation, we raise each side to the $1/x$ power, yielding $a = c^{q/x}$. Raising the second equation to the $1/z$ power, we have $a = c^{y/z}$. Thus $c^{q/x} = a = c^{y/z}$, so $q/x = y/z$, and $xy = qz$.

15. Taking logarithms base 3 of the given inequality, we have $\log_3 3^a > \log_3 2^{102}$. Thus $a > \log_3 2^{102}$. As suggested in the hint, we must now find $\log_3 2^{102}$. In fact, we will show that $\log_x y^n = n \log_x y$ in general, a fact which will be examined in greater detail in Volume 2. To do this, we start off as noted in an earlier problem, by introducing a new variable. Let $\log_x y = z$, so $n \log_x y = nz$. Thus we must show that $\log_x y^n = nz$. Writing our expression for z in exponential form gives us $x^z = y$. We raise this to the nth power to obtain an equation involving y^n. Thus $(x^z)^n = y^n$, so $x^{zn} = y^n$. Putting this in logarithmic form, we have the desired $\log_x y^n = nz = n \log_x y$. Returning to our problem, we have $\log_3 2^{102} = 102 \log_3 2 = 102(0.631) = 64.692$. Thus $a > 64.962$. The smallest integer which satisfies this is $\mathbf{65}$.

16. Our hint to the solution of this problem is that $2(3) = 6$. In fact, we will show that in general $\log_x y + \log_x z = \log_x yz$, a fact which will be examined in greater detail in Volume 2. Once again, we introduce a few new variables. Let $a = \log_x y$ and $b = \log_x z$, so $\log_x y + \log_x z = a + b$. Thus we must show $\log_x yz = a + b$. In exponential form, our expressions for a and b become $x^a = y$ and $x^b = z$. Thus $yz = x^a x^b = x^{a+b}$. Hence, $\log_x yz = \log_x x^{a+b} = a + b = \log_x y + \log_x z$ as desired. Applying this to our problem, we have $\log_6 2 + \log_6 3 = \log_6 6 = 1$. (Note we can only directly apply this identity when the bases of the logarithms are the same.)

Chapter 2

Complex Numbers

Solutions to Exercises

2-1 Since the powers of i cycle in sets of 4, we can say that $i^{17} = i^{13} = i^9 = i^5 = i^1 = i$, subtracting out 4's each time. For i^{69}, subtracting out the 4's directly is too much trouble, but we can do the same thing by finding the remainder when 69 is divided by 4. (Do you see why this is equivalent?) This remainder is 1, so $i^{69} = i^1 = i$. Similarly, since the remainder on dividing 1972 by 4 is 0, we have $i^{1972} = i^0 = 1$.

2-2 We just need to collect terms to get $(-\frac{1}{4} + 2) + (1 - \frac{3}{4})i$; then simplification yields $\frac{7}{4} + \frac{1}{4}i$.

2-3 This is the same as the previous exercise, except with variables instead of numbers. Collect the terms with i and those without to find that

$$(z_1 + z_2 i) + (w_1 + w_2 i) = (z_1 + w_1) + (z_2 + w_2)i.$$

2-4 We distribute the terms out to get

$$(-\tfrac{1}{4} + i)(2 - \tfrac{3}{4}i) = \left(-\tfrac{1}{4}\right)(2) + \left(-\tfrac{1}{4}\right)\left(-\tfrac{3}{4}\right)i + (1)(2)i + (1)\left(-\tfrac{3}{4}\right)i^2,$$

and then collecting terms as before we get $[-\frac{1}{2} - (-\frac{3}{4})] + [\frac{3}{16} + 2]i$. (Note that the minus sign in front of the $(-\frac{3}{4})$ comes from the i^2.) Simplifying then gives $\frac{1}{4} + \frac{35}{16}i$.

2-5 We repeat the same calculation with variables:

$$
\begin{aligned}
(z_1 + z_2 i)(w_1 + w_2 i) &= z_1 w_1 + z_1 w_2 i + z_2 w_1 i + z_2 w_2 i^2 \\
&= (z_1 w_1 - z_2 w_2) + (z_1 w_2 + z_2 w_1)i,
\end{aligned}
$$

where the minus sign in the first parentheses comes from the i^2.

2-6 Multiplying out, we get $z_1z_1 + z_1z_2i - z_1z_2i - z_2z_2i^2 = z_1^2 + z_2^2$.

2-7 Starting with

$$\frac{-\frac{1}{4} + i}{2 - \frac{3}{4}i},$$

we multiply top and bottom by $2 + \frac{3}{4}i$ to get

$$\frac{(-\frac{1}{4} + i)(2 + \frac{3}{4}i)}{(2 - \frac{3}{4}i)(2 + \frac{3}{4}i)},$$

and then expanding the products gives

$$\frac{\left(-\frac{1}{4}\right)(2) + \left(-\frac{1}{4}\right)\left(\frac{3}{4}\right)i + (1)(2)i + (1)\left(\frac{3}{4}\right)i^2}{4 + \frac{9}{16}} = \frac{-\frac{5}{4} + \frac{29}{16}i}{\frac{73}{16}}$$

$$= \frac{-20 + 29i}{73}.$$

2-8 We just repeat the recipe of the previous exercise to obtain

$$\frac{z_1 + z_2i}{w_1 + w_2i} = \frac{(z_1 + z_2i)(w_1 - w_2i)}{(w_1 + w_2i)(w_1 - w_2i)}$$

$$= \frac{(z_1w_1 + z_2w_2) + (-z_1w_2 + z_2w_1)i}{w_1^2 + w_2^2}$$

$$= \frac{(z_1w_1 + z_2w_2)}{w_1^2 + w_2^2} + \frac{(-z_1w_2 + z_2w_1)}{w_1^2 + w_2^2}i.$$

Whew!

2-9 Let $z = z_1 + z_2i$. Then the conjugate of z is $\overline{z} = z_1 - z_2i$. The conjugate of $\overline{z}$ is formed by negating the imaginary term again, to yield $\overline{\overline{z}} = \overline{(\overline{z})} = z_1 + z_2i = z$.

2-10 A real number a can be written $a + 0i$, so its conjugate is $a - 0i = a$. A pure imaginary bi can be written $0 + bi$, so has conjugate $0 - bi = -bi$.

2-11 Letting $z = z_1 + z_2i$ and $w = w_1 + w_2i$, we just apply the definition of the conjugate directly. We immediately see that

$$\overline{z} + \overline{w} = (z_1 - z_2i) + (w_1 - w_2i)$$

$$= (z_1 + w_1) - (z_2 + w_2)i$$

$$= \overline{z + w}.$$

Thus

$$\overline{z} + \overline{w} = \overline{z + w}$$

for all z and w.

2-12 Yet again, we just use the definition:

$$
\begin{aligned}
\overline{z}\,\overline{w} &= (z_1 - z_2 i)(w_1 - w_2 i) \\
&= (z_1 w_1 - z_2 w_2) + (-z_1 w_2 - z_2 w_1)i,
\end{aligned}
$$

which is equal to $\overline{zw}$, as you can see from looking back at previous exercises. Thus

$$\overline{z}\,\overline{w} = \overline{zw}$$

for all z and w.

2-13 For this one, we don't even need to refer to the definition of conjugate. We just let $v = 1/w$; thus, $vw = 1$. Taking conjugates of both sides of this equation gives us $\overline{vw} = 1$, and the previous exercise gives us $\overline{vw} = \overline{v}\,\overline{w} = 1$, or $\overline{v} = 1/\overline{w}$. Hence, we can again use the previous exercise to write

$$
\begin{aligned}
\overline{z}/\overline{w} &= \overline{z}\,\overline{v} \\
&= \overline{zv} \\
&= \overline{z/w}.
\end{aligned}
$$

2-14 If $z = z_1 + z_2 i$, then $\operatorname{Re} z = z_1$ and $\operatorname{Im} z = z_2$. Hence $\operatorname{Re} z + i \operatorname{Im} z = z_1 + z_2 i = \boldsymbol{z}$.

Solutions to Problems

17. We use our "rationalizing the denominator" trick to get

$$\frac{1+i}{3-i} = \frac{(1+i)(3+i)}{(3-i)(3+i)} = \frac{2+4i}{10} = \frac{1}{5} + \frac{2}{5}i.$$

18. From the last few exercises in the chapter, we can immediately see that **all three** are true.

19. Simply simplifying the simple parts one by one, we have $\sqrt{-1}\left(\sqrt{-1}\right)^2 \sqrt{(-1)^2} = (i)(i^2)(1) = (i)(-1) = -\boldsymbol{i}$.

20. To evaluate $i^{-18} + i^{-9} + i^0 + i^9 + i^{18}$, we just need to bring all the exponents down to 0, 1, 2, or 3 by repeatedly multiplying or dividing by $i^4 = 1$. Taking the remainder of each exponent when dividing by 4 accomplishes the same thing, and we quickly get $i^{-2} + i^{-1} + i^0 + i^1 + i^2 = i^2 + i^3 + i^0 + i^1 + i^2 = (-1) + (-i) + (1) + (i) + (-1) = -\boldsymbol{1}$. (Why is $i^{-1} = i^3$?)

21. We simply have $\operatorname{Re}\big((a+bi)(c+di)\big) = \operatorname{Re}\big((ac-bd) + (ad+bc)i\big) = \boldsymbol{ac - bd}$.

22. We have

$$(2+i)^3 = (2+i)(2+i)(2+i) = (4-1+2i+2i)(2+i) = (3+4i)(2+i) = 6-4+8i+3i = \mathbf{2+11i}.$$

23. We could just multiply several times, but there is a craftier way. Notice that $1+i$ and $1-i$ are conjugates. Thus, we can simplify our work by factoring a 2 out of the second term:

$$\begin{aligned}
(1+i)^4(2-2i)^3 &= 2^3(1+i)(1+i)^3(1-i)^3 \\
&= 8(1+i)\big[(1+i)(1-i)\big]^3 \\
&= 8(1+i)(1+1+i-i)^3 \\
&= 8(i+i)(8) \\
&= \mathbf{64+64i}.
\end{aligned}$$

Keep an eye out for conjugate expressions; they'll often simplify computations significantly.

24. This is equal to $(\sqrt{6}\,i)(\sqrt{2})/\sqrt{3} = i\sqrt{12}/\sqrt{3} = i\sqrt{4} = \mathbf{2i}$.

25. We have $F(x) = 3x^3 - 2x^2 + x - 3$, so $F(1+i) = 3(1+i)^3 - 2(1+i)^2 + (1+i) - 3 = 3(-2+2i) - 2(2i) + (1+i) - 3 = (-6+6i) - 4i + (1+i) - 3 = \mathbf{-8+3i}$.

26. Let's examine the choices one by one. For the first, we can use our known properties of the conjugate to get $\overline{z+3i} = \overline{z} + \overline{3i} = z - 3i$, so it is true. For the second, we have $\overline{iz} = \overline{i}\,\overline{z} = -i\overline{z}$, so this one is true as well. For the third, we have $(2+i)^2 = 3+4i = \overline{3-4i}$, so the third one is also true. **All three** choices are true.

Chapter 3

Linear Equations

Solutions to Exercises

3-1 Combining all like terms on each side of the equation yields $3y+2 = 5y-3$. Subtracting $3y$ from each side and adding 3 to each side then gives

$$\begin{aligned} 3y + 2 - 3y + 3 &= 5y - 3 - 3y + 3 \\ 5 &= 2y. \end{aligned}$$

Dividing by 2, we find $y = \mathbf{5/2}$.

3-2 Subtracting $2y/3$ from both sides gives

$$-3 = y - \frac{2y}{3} = \frac{y}{3}.$$

Multiplying both sides by 3 gives $y = \mathbf{-9}$.

3-3

  i. First we put all the variables on the left and the constants on the right, to get

$$\begin{aligned} 3x - 2y &= 5 \\ 2x - 2y &= 7 \end{aligned}$$

Subtracting the second equation from the first yields $x = -2$. Substituting this in the first equation, we have $-6 - 2y = 5$. Adding 6 to both sides yields $-2y = 11$, and dividing by -2 gives $y = -11/2$ and $(x, y) = (\mathbf{-2}, \mathbf{-11/2})$.

  ii. Multiplying the first equation by -2, our system becomes

$$\begin{aligned} -x - 6y &= -8 \\ x + 6y &= 9 \end{aligned}$$

Adding these gives $0 = 1$, which is never true. Thus there are **no solutions** to this system of equations.

iii. To eliminate y, we multiply the first equation by 3:

$$0.3x + 3y = 9$$
$$0.5x - 3y = 7$$

Adding these gives $0.8x = 16$, or $x = 20$. Substituting this in the second equation yields $10 - 3y = 7$. Thus $-3y = -3$ and $y = 1$. Hence $(x, y) = (\mathbf{20}, \mathbf{1})$ is the solution.

iv. First, we put all the variables on the left and the constants on the right:

$$-x - y = 3$$
$$x + y = 5$$

Adding these gives $0 = 8$, which means there are **no solutions** to this system of equations.

3-4 Let there be x adults and $1350 - x$ students. The total amount of money paid is then $x(3.25) + (1350 - x)(1.75) = 2700$. Expanding the left side gives $1.5x + 2362.5 = 2700$. Hence $1.5x = 337.5$ and $x = 225$, so **225** adults attended the game.

3-5 If the distance to Mom's house is D miles, it takes $D/40$ hours to get there and $D/20$ to get back, for a total time of $D(1/40 + 1/20) = 3D/40$ hours. The average speed is the total distance traveled divided by the total time used, or $2D/(3D/40) = 80/3 = 26\frac{2}{3}$ miles per hour regardless of D, which drops out of the equation.

3-6 Let the paddler's rate in still water be x. Thus while paddling upstream for 2 hours, she travels $2(x - 2) = 2x - 4$ miles upstream. Similarly, she travels $3(x + 2) = 3x + 6$ miles downstream. The result is that she travels $3x + 6 - (2x - 4) = x + 10$ miles downstream. Since we are told she travels 20 miles downstream, we have $x + 10 = 20$, or $x = 10$. Since the canoeist must travel upstream to return to her starting point, her rate is 8 mph. She must travel 20 miles, so if t is her time paddling in hours, we have $8t = 20$, so $t = \mathbf{2.5}$.

3-7 Let the amount of time which the second knight requires to storm the castle alone be x. Thus in one hour, the first knight can do $1/15$ of the job and the second can do $1/x$ of the job. Since in 10 hours, the two together can do the whole job, we have

$$10\left(\frac{1}{15} + \frac{1}{x}\right) = 1$$
$$\frac{1}{15} + \frac{1}{x} = \frac{1}{10}$$
$$\frac{1}{x} = \frac{1}{10} - \frac{1}{15}.$$

Thus $1/x = (3 - 2)/30 = 1/30$. Taking the reciprocal of each side of this equation gives $x = 30$. It would therefore take the second knight **30 hours** to storm the castle alone.

Solutions to Problems

27.   The nth boy dances with $n + 4$ girls. The last (or bth) boy dances with all g girls. Since he dances with $b + 4$ girls, $b + 4 = g$, so $b = g - 4$.

28.   Let t be the tens digit and u the units digit. The number is then $10t + u$, and we are given $t = u + 4$. The number obtained by reversing the digits is $10u + t$. From the given information we have $10t + u - 2(10u + t) = 10$, or $8t - 19u = 10$. Substituting $t = u + 4$ in this gives $8(u + 4) - 19u = 8u + 32 - 19u = 10$. Thus $-11u = -22$, so $u = 2$ and $t = 6$. The number is **62**.

29.   Let there be x nickels. Since there are a total of 16 coins, there are $16 - x$ dimes in the bank. The number of cents then is $5x + 10(16 - x) = 160 - 5x$. Since there is a total of 105 cents in the bank we find $160 - 5x = 105$, so $-5x = -55$ and $x = 11$. Thus there are **11** nickels.

30.   Let Jefferson's age in 1748 be x. Since Washington was 11 years older than Jefferson, his age in 1748 was $x + 11$. Based on this, his age in 1770 was $x + 11 + 22 = x + 33$. Based on the information in the problem, his age in 1770 was $7x + 3$. These two expressions for Washington's age in 1770 must be equal, so $x + 33 = 7x + 3$; thus $6x = 30$ and $x = 5$. Hence Jefferson was 5 in 1748, so he was 7 in 1750 and Washington was 18. The sum of their ages in 1750 was **25**.

31.   Let one number be x. The other number is then $2x + 3$, since it is three more than twice the first number. Since the sum of these is 66, we have $x + 2x + 3 = 66$, so $3x = 63$ and $x = 21$. The other number is $2(21) + 3 = 45$ and, as the larger of the two, is the answer to the problem.

32.   Let x be the cost of a pound of potatoes. From the question, a pound of string beans costs $3x$. Since we can get twice as many pounds of onions as pounds of string beans for the same price, the price of a pound of onions is half that of the string beans, or $3x/2$. From the information on onions and potatoes we have $3x/2 = 2x - 4$, so $x/2 = 4$ and $x = 8$. Thus potatoes are 8 cents a pound, string beans 24 cents a pound, and onions 12 cents a pound. Thus a pound of each together costs **44** cents.

33.   Let the smaller integer be x, so the larger is $x + 2$ (since they are consecutive odd integers). From the given information we find $(1/3)x + 2(x + 2) = x + (x + 2) + 7$. Thus $x/3 = 5$ and $x = 15$. The integers are **15** and **17**.

34.   Let the Croatian score be x, so the U. S. has $4x$ points. After the Croatians score three points, they have $x + 3$ points. The Americans have three times this, or $3(x + 3) = 3x + 9$. Since their score hasn't changed we have $4x = 3x + 9$, so $x = 9$. Thus the Americans have $4(9) = 36$ points.

35.   Let there be x slices of bread per loaf and y pieces of bologna per package. Mike, using 5 pieces of bologna per sandwich and using all of the bologna, makes $y/5$ sandwiches, which consume $2y/5$ slices of bread. Since there are still 4 slices left, $x - 2y/5 = 4$. Joey, using 4 pieces of bologna per sandwich and all the bread, makes $x/2$ sandwiches and uses

$4(x/2) = 2x$ pieces of bologna, leaving 4 left over. Thus $y - 2x = 4$. To find x, we have $y = 4 + 2x$ from the second equation. Substituting this in the first equation gives $x - 2(4 + 2x)/5 = 4$. Thus $x/5 = 28/5$ and $x = 28$. There are **28** slices of bread per loaf.

36. Let Sue have x quarters. Thus she has $x + 4$ pennies, and $x + 4 + 1 = x + 5$ nickels. Since the total is 308 cents, we have $308 = 25x + (x + 4) + 5(x + 5)$. Then $31x = 279$ and $x = 9$. Thus there are $9 + 5 = $ **14** nickels.

37. First, we get rid of the square roots by squaring, which leaves $a + \dfrac{b}{c} = \dfrac{a^2b}{c}$. Getting c out of the denominators by multiplying both sides by c, we have $ac + b = a^2b$. Thus $ac = a^2b - b$ and $c = (a^2b - b)/a = \boldsymbol{b(a^2 - 1)/a}$.

38. Beware when doing word problems: all the information given is not necessarily useful! In this question, since rate times time is distance, for K we have $(\text{Time})(x) = 30$, so K's time is $\boldsymbol{30/x}$. All the information about M is useless.

39. We are given $1 - \dfrac{1}{1 - x} = \dfrac{1}{1 - x}$; thus $2/(1 - x) = 1$. Multiplying both sides by $1 - x$ to eliminate the denominator gives $1 - x = 2$, so $x = \boldsymbol{-1}$.

40. During the first hour, the train goes the same rate, x, regardless of when the accident occurs. Over the next 80 miles, if the wreck is early, the train goes $4x/5$; otherwise, the train goes x. After these 80 miles, regardless of whether the wreck was early or late, the train goes $4x/5$. Thus the only difference between the two is the 80 mile stretch; it takes the train with an early wreck $80/(4x/5) = 100/x$ to cover it and the train with the late wreck only $80/x$ (using Time=Distance/Rate). Since the difference in these two is the overall difference in the times of the two trains, we have $100/x - 80/x = 1$. Multiplying by x, we find $x = $ **20** mph.

41. If Brenda works for 3 days alone, she does $3/15 = 1/5$ of the job. When Adam joins her, the fraction of the job they can do together each day is $\frac{1}{10} + \frac{1}{15} = \frac{1}{6}$. Let x be the number of days worked; then, since 4/5 of the job remains, $x(1/6) = 4/5$, or $x = 24/5 = $ **4.8** days.

42. During the round trip, the car goes 240 miles. The way there takes $120/30 = 4$ hours, and the way back takes 3. Thus the total trip takes 7 hours and the average speed is $240/7 = \boldsymbol{34\frac{2}{7}}$.

43. At 9 PM, the distances traveled by both cars are the same. The first car has traveled 7 hours at 40 miles per hour, so has gone 280 miles. The second car has gone this distance in 5 hours, so its speed is $280/5 = $ **56** mph.

44. Working together, each day the two complete $1/9 + 1/16 = 25/144$ of the job. Thus, in 4 days, they do $4(25/144) = 25/36$ of the job, leaving 11/36 for the father to do himself. Let x be the number of days the father works alone. Since he can do 1/9 of the job each day, we have $(1/9)x = 11/36$, so $x = 11/4 = \boldsymbol{2\frac{3}{4}}$ days.

45.   First, we determine how much of the job each woman does in one day. If the women did 1/5 of the job in 8 days, they do $(1/5)/8 = 1/40$ of the job in one day. Hence one woman alone does $(1/40)/25 = 1/1000$ of the job in a day. To answer the question, we note that the women must do the remaining 4/5 of the job in 20 days. Suppose we add x women to the 25 already there. This group can do $(x + 25)/1000$ of the job per day. Hence we must have

$$(20) \left(\frac{x + 25}{1000} \right) = \frac{4}{5}.$$

Multiplying both sides by 1000, we have $20x + 500 = 800$ and $x = 15$, so the crew needs **15** more women.

46.   At the point the rider who has the shorter distance to travel leaves the tunnel, the other still has $7/8 - 1/8 = 3/4$ of the tunnel to travel. Since at this point the train is at one end of tunnel (because the first biker has just escaped), the second biker must ride the remaining 3/4 of the tunnel in the same time that the train travels the full tunnel. Hence the biker must go 3/4 the rate of the train, or $(3/4)(40) = $ **30** mph.

47.   The train travels x meters in the 10 seconds in which it is under the light. Thus its rate is $x/10$ m/sec. When it enters the tunnel, its front proceeds to travel 300 meters and reach the end, but then must travel another x meters for the back of the train to leave the tunnel. From the time the front enters the tunnel to the time the back leaves the tunnel, the train travels $300 + x$ meters. Since it takes 20 seconds to do this, its rate is $(300 + x)/20$.

Our two calculated rates must be the same, so $(300 + x)/20 = x/10$, or $2x = x + 300$, or $x = $ **300** meters.

48.   Let x be the rate of the slower walker and y be the rate of the faster walker. When walking in opposite directions, the two men approach each other at a rate of $x + y$. Since they cover a mile at this rate in 6 minutes, or 1/10 of an hour, we have $(x + y)(1/10) = 1$. When the two men are going in the same direction, the faster man pulls away at a rate of $y - x$. Since it requires him a full hour to pull away an entire mile, $(y - x)(1) = 1$. Thus we have $x + y = 10$ and $y - x = 1$. Adding these yields $2y = 11$, so $y = 11/2$ and $x = 9/2$, so the slower walker goes at a rate of **9/2** miles per hour.

49.   Since 30 workers can build the road in 60 days, each day they finish 1/60 of the road, and each person does $(1/60)/30 = 1/1800$ of the work each day. In 10 days, the 30 workers finish $10(1/60) = 1/6$ of the road. After the change of plans, the crew must build the remaining 5/6 of the road in 20 days. Let x people be added to the crew, for a total of $x + 30$ laborers. Since each worker does 1/1800 of the work per day, $(x + 30)/1800$ of the road gets finished each day. Thus $20(x + 30)/1800 = 5/6$. Hence $20x + 600 = 1500$ and $x = 45$, so **45** people must be added to the crew.

50.   Let the hill be x units high. The rate going uphill is 8 units per minute, or $8/60$ units per second. Thus the time required to climb the hill is $x/(8/60) = 15x/2$ seconds. The time needed to tumble down is $x/8$ seconds, so the total time for the trip is $15x/2 + x/8 = 61x/8$ seconds. Since the distance traveled was $2x$ units, the average speed was

Distance/Time=$2x/(61x/8) = 16/61$ units per second. Since there are 60 seconds in a minute, their rate per minute is $60(16/61) = 960/61 = 15\frac{45}{61}$ units per minute.

51.   We know the fly's rate, so if we determine how long it flies, we can determine the distance it flies. The fly flies as long as the dogs are running toward each other. Since the dogs each travel 10 feet per second, they approach each other at a rate of 20 feet per second. Thus they cover the distance of 500 feet in $500/20 = 25$ seconds. Since the fly flies 25 ft/sec for 25 seconds, it covers $25(25) = $ **625** feet before getting crushed.

52.   Dividing each term on the left by the xy in the denominator, we have

$$\frac{1}{y} + \frac{2}{x} = \frac{11}{12}$$

$$\frac{2}{y} - \frac{3}{x} = \frac{2}{3}.$$

Instead of solving this system of equations for x and y, we solve for $\frac{1}{x}$ and $\frac{1}{y}$, since the equations are linear in these reciprocals. If we multiply the first equation by 2, we have $\frac{2}{y} + \frac{4}{x} = \frac{11}{6}$, from which we subtract the second equation to get $\frac{7}{x} = \frac{11}{6} - \frac{2}{3} = \frac{7}{6}$. Thus $\frac{1}{x} = \frac{1}{6}$. Substituting this in either of the above equations, we find $\frac{1}{y} = \frac{7}{12}$. To determine x and y, we just take reciprocals of these last two equations to find $(x, y) = (\mathbf{6}, \mathbf{12/7})$. The important concept to note here is that the equations do not need to be linear in the variables to be solved like linear equations; they can just be linear in some function, such as the reciprocal or square root.

53.   Multiplying by $\sqrt{x} + \sqrt{y}$, we have

$$3\frac{\sqrt{x}}{\sqrt{y}} + 3 - \frac{\sqrt{y}}{\sqrt{x}} - 1 = 2$$

$$3\frac{\sqrt{x}}{\sqrt{y}} - \frac{\sqrt{y}}{\sqrt{x}} = 0$$

$$3\frac{\sqrt{x}}{\sqrt{y}} = \frac{\sqrt{y}}{\sqrt{x}}$$

Thus multiplying by $\sqrt{xy}$ gives $3x = y$ and $x/y = \mathbf{1/3}$.

54.   Let the numbers be x, y, and z. We are given $x + y = 29$, $x + z = 46$, and $y + z = 53$. This is a set of three linear equations, something new. If we note that each variable appears twice on the left, we see that adding the three equations yields $2(x + y + z) = 29 + 46 + 53 = 128$. Thus the sum of the numbers is **64**. Furthermore, we could use this to find the variables quite easily. For example, since $x + y + z = 64$ and $x + y = 29$, $29 + z = 64$ and $z = 35$; the same method works for the other variables. Remember this method of solution! It is very effective in solving "symmetric" systems. The method wouldn't work on a system where the variable expressions were $2x + y$, $y - 2z$, and $3x + z$, but it does work on the given problem where the expressions have symmetry: $x + y$, $y + z$, $x + z$. Do you see why? Symmetric systems and functions will be examined in detail in Volume 2.

55.   Let a be the time for valve A to fill the tank alone, b the time for valve B, and c the time for valve C. Thus in one hour valve A can fill $1/a$ of the tank and so on. With all three valves open, we have $1\left(\frac{1}{a} + \frac{1}{b} + \frac{1}{c}\right) = 1$, since it only takes 1 hour for the three valves together to fill up the tank. With A and C open we have $1.5\left(\frac{1}{a} + \frac{1}{c}\right) = 1$, and with B and C open, $2\left(\frac{1}{b} + \frac{1}{c}\right) = 1$. Letting it take x hours for A and B to fill the tank, we have $x\left(\frac{1}{a} + \frac{1}{b}\right) = 1$. To get a nice symmetric set of equations, we divide by the coefficients on the left side, 1.5, 2, and x. Thus our equations are

$$
\begin{aligned}
\frac{1}{a} + \frac{1}{b} + \frac{1}{c} &= \frac{1}{1} \\
\frac{1}{a} + \frac{1}{c} &= \frac{1}{1.5} \\
\frac{1}{b} + \frac{1}{c} &= \frac{1}{2} \\
\frac{1}{a} + \frac{1}{b} &= \frac{1}{x}.
\end{aligned}
$$

As we saw in the prior example, we can relate the first equation to the final three by adding the last three equations together. Thus we have

$$
\begin{aligned}
2\left(\frac{1}{a} + \frac{1}{b} + \frac{1}{c}\right) &= \frac{1}{3/2} + \frac{1}{2} + \frac{1}{x} \\
2(1) &= \frac{2}{3} + \frac{1}{2} + \frac{1}{x} \\
2 &= \frac{7}{6} + \frac{1}{x}.
\end{aligned}
$$

Thus $1/x = 5/6$, and $x = 6/5 = 1.2$, so it takes **1.2** hours for valves A and B to fill the tank.

Chapter 4

Proportions

Solutions to Exercises

4-1 We have points/games $= 124/4 = 31/1$. Thus,

$$\frac{\text{points}}{\text{games}} = \frac{x}{6} = \frac{31}{1}.$$

Solving for x, we find that in the next 6 games, Jordan should score **186** points.

4-2 The Yankees lose 16 out of every $16 + 15 = 31$ games. Thus losses/games$= 16/31$. Since they have lost 64 out of x games, $16/31 = 64/x$, so $x = 124$. Thus, they have played **124** games.

4-3 More hens means more eggs, so hens and eggs are directly proportional. More days also means more eggs, so days and eggs are directly proportional. Thus, both the ratio of eggs to hens and the ratio of eggs to days are constant. Hence, we have the relation

$$\frac{\text{eggs}}{(\text{hens})(\text{days})} = \frac{24}{(5)(5)} = \frac{24}{25}.$$

To determine the number x of days needed for 8 hens to lay 20 eggs, we use this relation:

$$\frac{\text{eggs}}{(\text{hens})(\text{days})} = \frac{20}{8x} = \frac{24}{25}.$$

Solving for x, we find $x = \mathbf{125/48}$ days are necessary.

4-4 We wish to have a ratio involving only x and y, so we multiply the ratios to eliminate the z's. Our desired ratio has y in the numerator, so we multiply the factors accordingly:

$$\left(\frac{y}{4z}\right)\left(\frac{3z}{x}\right) = 2(1/3)$$

$$\frac{3y}{4x} = \frac{2}{3}.$$

This doesn't quite get us there, as we want $2y/x$. We find y/x by multiplying the above equation by $4/3$, yielding $y/x = (2/3)(4/3) = 8/9$; then $2y/x = \mathbf{16/9}$.

4-5

    i. $35\% = \mathbf{0.35} = \dfrac{35}{100} = \dfrac{\mathbf{7}}{\mathbf{20}}.$

    ii. $175\% = \mathbf{1.75} = \dfrac{175}{100} = \dfrac{35}{20} = \dfrac{\mathbf{7}}{\mathbf{4}}.$

    iii. $66\dfrac{2}{3}\% = \mathbf{66.\overline{6}\%} = \mathbf{0.\overline{6}} = \dfrac{6}{9} = \dfrac{\mathbf{2}}{\mathbf{3}}.$

    iv. $16\dfrac{2}{3}\% = 16.\overline{6}\% = \mathbf{0.1\overline{6}} = \dfrac{16-1}{90} = \dfrac{15}{90} = \dfrac{\mathbf{1}}{\mathbf{6}}.$

4-6

    i. Dividing 6 into 5 gives $\dfrac{5}{6} = 0.8\overline{3} = 83.\overline{3}\% = \mathbf{83\dfrac{1}{3}\%}.$

    ii. Since $3/4 = 0.75$, we have $2\dfrac{3}{4} = 2.75 = \mathbf{275\%}.$

    iii. $0.\overline{1} = 11.\overline{1}\% = \mathbf{11\dfrac{1}{9}\%}.$

    iv. $3.5 = \mathbf{350\%}.$

4-7   Let the original price be x. After the decrease, the price is $(1-0.4)x = 0.6x$. Upon increasing this by 50%, the price is $(1+0.5)(0.6x) = (1.5)(0.6x) = 0.9x$. Since we are given that this final price is \$360, we have $0.9x = 360$. Multiplying both sides by 10 (to remove the decimal) then dividing both sides by 9, we find $x = 400$. Thus, the original price of the ring was **\$400**.

4-8   The price has been decreased \$1000. Since the original price was \$8000, the percent decrease is

$$\frac{1000}{8000} = \frac{1}{8} = 0.125 = \mathbf{12.5\%}.$$

4-9   The U.S. wishes to charge France 0.5 million dollars interest on a 1.5 million dollar loan. This represents an interest rate of

$$\frac{0.5}{1.5} = \frac{1}{3} = 0.\overline{3} = \mathbf{33\dfrac{1}{3}\%}.$$

4-10   Since the 80 ml solution is 20% acid, it has $80(0.20) = 16$ ml acid. Let the total volume of solution removed be x. In this removed solution, there is $0.20x$ ml acid. Since the entire x ml of added solution is acid, the amount of acid in the final solution is $16 - 0.2x + x =$

$16 + 0.8x$. Since the total volume of the final solution is still 80, we have

$$\frac{16 + 0.8x}{80} = \frac{40}{100} = \frac{2}{5}.$$

Thus we find $5(16 + 0.8x) = 80(2)$. Solving for x gives $x = 20$. Hence, **20 ml** of the existing solution must be removed and replaced with pure acid to make a 40% solution.

Solutions to Problems

56.   Since $13/20 = 0.65$, 13 is **65**% of 20.

57.   Let the population of the town at the beginning of 1991 be x. At the end of 1991, the population is $1.25x$ because the population increases by 25%. In the following year, the population then falls from $1.25x$ back to x, a difference of $0.25x$. This represents a change of $(0.25x)/(1.25x) = 0.20$, or 20%. Thus, the population must fall **20**% to return to the level it was at in the beginning of 1991.

58.   Let the initial number be x. After increasing by 50%, the number is $1.5x$. After decreasing this by 40%, we have $1.5x(1 - 0.4) = 1.5(0.6)x = 0.9x$. For this to equal 8 less than the original number, we must have $0.9x = x - 8$. Thus, $x = $ **80** is the original number.

59.   First we convert 4 metric months, 5 metric weeks, and 8 metric days to metric days. Four metric months have 40 metric weeks, which have 400 metric days. Five metric weeks have 50 metric days. Thus, our total is 458 metric days. There are 1000 metric days in a year, so we have 1000 metric days = 365 calendar days. Hence,

$$458 \text{ metric days} \cdot \frac{365 \text{ calendar days}}{1000 \text{ metric days}} = \frac{167170}{1000} \text{ calendar days} \approx \textbf{167} \text{ calendar days.}$$

60.   Just use algebra. Since $(2x - y)/(x + y) = 2/3$, we have $3(2x - y) = 2(x + y)$. Rearranging this yields $4x = 5y$, so $x/y = $ **5/4**.

61.   We have 0.5 inches = 8 quarters. Thus,

$$1 \text{ foot} = 12 \text{ inches} \cdot \frac{8 \text{ quarters}}{0.5 \text{ inches}} = \textbf{192} \text{ quarters.}$$

Note we have used conversion factors to tackle this proportion problem.

62.   Since y^2 varies inversely as x^3, the product y^2x^3 is constant. From our given information, this product is $3^2 \cdot 2^3 = 72$. Thus, when $x = 9$, we have $(9^3)y^2 = 72$, so $y^2 = 8/81$. Since $y > 0$, we take the positive square root, yielding $y = \mathbf{2\sqrt{2}/9}$.

63.   Let the price be x. Since the discount is $69 and is 15% of the price, we have $0.15x = 69$, or $x = $ **$460**.

64. We multiply the ratios to get rid of the y's since the desired ratio includes only x and z. Thus, $(x/y)(y/z) = (2/3)(3/2)$, so $x/z = \textbf{1}$.

65. Let the test have x points. To average 90%, the student must get $0.90x$ points on the test. The first part, 60% of the test, is worth $0.60x$ points, of which the student gets $0.60x(0.95) = 0.57x$ points. Thus, to get $0.90x$ total points, the student needs only $0.90x - 0.57x = 0.33x$ points on the second part. The second part is worth $0.40x$ points, so $0.33x$ is $(0.33x)/(0.40x) = 0.825 = \textbf{82.5\%}$ of the last part. If you don't follow this, use 100 in place of x and go through the solution.

66. Let x be the total number of Gummy Bears. Thus, Jessica gets $x/2$ and Jana gets $x/3$ of them. In all, Jennifer gives away $\frac{x}{2} + \frac{x}{3} + 15$. Since this represents all x of the Gummy Bears, we have $\frac{x}{2} + \frac{x}{3} + 15 = x$, which yields $x = \textbf{90}$ Gummy Bears total.

67. Let w be the number of yards he runs. Then, since distance and time are directly proportional, we have

$$\frac{x \text{ feet}}{y \text{ seconds}} = \frac{w \text{ yards}}{z \text{ minutes}}.$$

To solve for w, multiply both sides by z minutes, then convert the feet to yards and the seconds to minutes. Thus,

$$w \text{ yards} = (z \text{ minutes})\left(\frac{x \text{ feet}}{y \text{ seconds}}\right) \cdot \frac{1 \text{ yard}}{3 \text{ feet}} \cdot \frac{60 \text{ seconds}}{1 \text{ minute}} = (z \text{ minutes})\left(\frac{20x \text{ yards}}{y \text{ minutes}}\right).$$

Hence, the man can run $\textbf{20xz/y}$ yards in z minutes.

68. We are given that xz/y is invariant (constant). From the data given we have $xz/y = (1/2)(2/3)/(3/4) = 4/9$. Substituting $y = 7/8$ and $z = 7/9$, we get $x(7/9)/(7/8) = 4/9$, so $x = \textbf{1/2}$.

69. Let x be the amount invested at 4%. The return on this investment is then $0.04x$. The amount invested in the other venture is $4500 - x$, and the return on this is $0.06(4500 - x)$. These returns are equal, so $0.04x = 0.06(4500 - x)$. Solving gives $x = 2700$. To get the interest on both investments together, we find first the total return, which is $2(0.04x)$. (Remember, the return on the two investments is the same.) So the total return is \$216, and the average rate of interest is $216/4500 = 0.048$, or $\textbf{4.8\%}$.

70. More men means more money, so men and money are directly proportional. Similarly, more weeks means more money, so these are also directly proportional. Hence (men)(weeks)/(money) is invariant. From the given information, the invariant value equals $(3)(4)/108 = 1/9$. For the new amounts of money and men, we have

$$\frac{5(x \text{ weeks})}{135} = \frac{1}{9}.$$

Solving for x, we find that the men will work for $\textbf{3}$ weeks.

71. We'll let Vantage's earnings be x and determine everyone else's earnings in terms of x; then we can set the total amount in terms of x equal to the given \$3150. From Smash:Vantage $= 32{:}15$, Smash earns $32x/15$. From the relation Love:Smash $= 3{:}4$, Love earns $(3/4)(32x/15) = 8x/5$. From Lob:Love $= 17{:}12$, Lob earns $(17/12)(8x/5) = 34x/15$. Thus, we have

$$x + \frac{32x}{15} + \frac{8x}{5} + \frac{34x}{15} = 7x = 3150.$$

So $x = 450$, and Love's salary is $8(450)/5 = \mathbf{\$720}$.

72. Let p and V be the initial pressure and volume, respectively, of the container. Increasing the pressure by 25% makes it $1.25p$. Letting the new volume be xV, we have $1.25xpV$ as the product of the pressure and volume. Since this must equal the original product, pV, we must have $1.25x = 1$, or $x = 0.8$. Hence, the new volume is $0.8V$, which is a decrease of $0.2V$, or $0.2V/V = 0.2 = \mathbf{20\%}$.

73. Let the total number of votes be x. Expressing each individual's number of votes in terms of x, we have

$$A + B + C + D = \frac{x}{3} + \frac{9x}{20} + \frac{2x}{15} + 75 = \frac{11x}{12} + 75.$$

This must equal the total number of votes x, so $11x/12 + 75 = x$, so $x = 75(12) = \mathbf{900}$.

74. Since A sees a 10% profit on the first deal, she sells the house for $(\$10000)(1.1) = \$11000$. If B then sells his \$11000 house at a loss of 10%, the selling price must be $(\$11000)(0.90) = \$9900$. Thus, A sells a house for \$11000 and buys it back for \$9900, for a profit of $\mathbf{\$1100}$.

75. We are asked to find clicks per second. We know there are 30 feet per click. Since there are 5280 feet in a mile, there are then $5280/30 = 176$ clicks per mile. Thus, we can express x miles per hour as clicks per second as follows:

$$x \, \frac{\text{miles}}{\text{hour}} = \frac{x \text{ miles}}{1 \text{ hour}} \cdot \frac{1 \text{ hour}}{3600 \text{ seconds}} \cdot \frac{176 \text{ clicks}}{\text{mile}} = \frac{176x \text{ clicks}}{3600 \text{ seconds}}.$$

Since $176 \approx 180$, we have $x \, \text{miles/hour} \approx 180x \, \text{clicks}/3600 \, \text{seconds} = x \, \text{clicks}/20 \, \text{seconds}$. Hence there are x clicks in 20 seconds, so the number of clicks in **20** seconds is approximately equal to the speed in miles per hour of the train.

76. Let the original population be x. After the increase, it's $x + 1200$. Decreasing this by 11%, we have $(x + 1200)(.89)$. Since this is 32 less than the original population x, we have $.89(x + 1200) = x - 32$; solving, we find $x = \mathbf{10000}$.

77. Let the cost of living at the beginning of the year be x. At the end of the first quarter, it is $1.02x$. At the end of the second quarter, it increases another 2% to $(1.02)^2 x$. Continuing in this manner, at the end of four quarters, the cost of living is $(1.02)^4 x \approx 1.082x$. Thus, the increase of 2% per quarter corresponds to an annual increase of approximately **8.2%**.

78. We are given that xz^2/y is invariant. From the given information we find $xz^2/y = (10)(196)/4 = 490$. For $y = 16$ and $z = 7$ we have $x(49)/16 = 490$, so $x = \mathbf{160}$.

79. After 24 seconds, the first runner has covered $24/56 = 3/7$ of the track. Since the other runner meets the first after 24 seconds, that runner must have covered $4/7$ of the track in 24 seconds. Since length run and time run are directly proportional, we have $24/(4/7) = x/1$, where x is the amount of time required to run the entire track. Thus, $x = 42$ and it takes **42 seconds** for the second runner to run the whole track.

80. We are given that the quotients x/y^3 and $y/z^{1/5}$ are invariant. We wish to find an n such that x/z^n is invariant. Returning to our given invariant quotients, any power of these quotients is also invariant. Thus, we can raise $y/z^{1/5}$ to the third power and multiply by x/y^3 to cancel the y's. Since all quotients in the product are invariant, the resulting product is also invariant:

$$\left(\frac{x}{y^3}\right)\left(\frac{y}{z^{1/5}}\right)^3 = \frac{x}{y^3}\cdot\frac{y^3}{z^{3/5}} = \frac{x}{z^{3/5}}.$$

Hence, x varies as $z^{\mathbf{3/5}}$. Make sure you understand why we chose to cube the second equation to cancel the y's.

81. Let the time now be 10 hours and x minutes. Thus, six minutes from now, the minute hand will be pointing at $x + 6$ minutes. We must find out what *minute* the hour hand was pointing at three minutes ago. At that time, the minute hand was at $x - 3$. The hour hand then was $(x - 3)/60$ of the way from hour 10 to hour 11, or from minute 50 to minute 55. Thus, it was at minute $50 + 5(x - 3)/60$. Make sure you follow this. Since this is exactly opposite the minute $x+6$ as described by the problem, the minute $50 + 5(x-3)/60$ is exactly 30 minutes after the minute $x + 6$. Thus, $50 + 5(x - 3)/60 = (x + 6) + 30$. Solving for x, we find $x = 15$, and the time now is **10:15**.

82. We are given $p = 0.5q$ and $r = 0.4q$. Dividing these two equations, we cancel the q's and have the desired expression in terms of only r and p. Thus $p/r = 0.5/0.4 = 1.25$, so $p = 1.25r$ and p is **125%** of r.

83. Let the overall population be x and the overall wealth be y. Thus, in country A, there are $cx/100$ people who share $dy/100$ equally. Hence, each person has $(dy/100)/(cx/100) = dy/cx$. Similarly, in country B, each citizen has fy/ex. The ratio of the wealth of a citizen in A to that in B is then $(dy/cx)/(fy/ex) = \mathbf{de/cf}$.

84. Let $DE = x$ and find the length of each short segment in terms of x: $CD = DE/2 = x/2$; $BC = CD/4 = x/8$; $AB = BC/3 = x/24$. Thus, $AC = AB + BC = x/24 + x/8 = x/6$. Similarly, $BE = BC + CD + DE = x/8 + x/2 + x = 13x/8$. Hence,

$$\frac{AC}{BE} = \frac{x/6}{13x/8} = \frac{\mathbf{4}}{\mathbf{39}}.$$

85.   Let the population be x. At time $t = 1$, the population is $x(1+i/100)$. At time $t = 2$, the population is then $x(1 + i/100)(1 + j/100)$. Expanding this yields

$$x\left(1 + \frac{i}{100} + \frac{j}{100} + \frac{ij}{10000}\right)$$

The last three terms in the parentheses describe the overall increase. To determine this as a percent, we multiply by 100, just as $1.2x$ is a $100(0.2) = 20\%$ increase of x. Thus, the overall percent increase from $t = 0$ to $t = 2$ is

$$100\left(\frac{i}{100} + \frac{j}{100} + \frac{ij}{10000}\right) = i + j + \frac{ij}{100}.$$

86.   We can solve this using the clever manipulations discussed in the section on proportion manipulations:

$$\frac{x}{y} = \frac{(y) + (x + y) + (x)}{(x - z) + (z) + (y)} = \frac{2(x + y)}{x + y} = 2.$$

Note that we have set one of the proportions, x/y, equal to a ratio in which the numerator is the sum of the numerators of the fractions and the denominator is the sum of the denominators. This fact is always true, and we think to use it when the ratio we are asked to find is one of the ratios in a given equation.

Chapter 5

Using the Integers

Solutions to Exercises

5-1 Since 20 is divisible only by the primes 2 and 5, we need only try numbers made up of factors of 2 and 5. These are 2, which is a divisor, 4, which is, 5, which is, 8, which isn't, 10, which is, 16, which isn't, and 20, which is. We also need to include 1. The divisors are thus **1, 2, 4, 5, 10, and 20**.

5-2 For 11, we try the possible divisors 2, 3, 5, 7; none of them work, so it is prime. (We didn't have to try 4 or 6 since they have 2 and 3 as factors; we can stop at 7 because $2 \cdot 7 = 14$, which is too large.) 12 is even, so can't be prime, as it is divisible by 2. For 13, again nothing works; it is prime. 14 is even. 15 has divisors 3 and 5. 16 is even. For 17, trying 2, 3, 5, 7, and 11 shows that none divide, so 17 is prime. 18 has factors 3 and 6. 19, prime. 20, even. The primes are **11, 13, 17, and 19**.

5-3 Any prime greater than 2 cannot be divisible by 2, so cannot be even. Thus **2 is the only even prime**.

5-4 The base 8 number 47 equals $4 \cdot 8 + 7 = 32 + 7 = \mathbf{39}$ in base 10. The base 9 number 47 equals $4 \cdot 9 + 7 = \mathbf{43}$, and the base 16 number equals $4 \cdot 16 + 7 = \mathbf{71}$.

5-5 To find the base 10 number 47 in base 8, we note that no multiple of $8^2 = 64$ can be there, since it is too big. Thus the first digit will represent $8^1 = 8$. The number of 8's is given by dividing 8 into 47 to get a quotient of 5 and remainder 7. The 5 is how many 8's we can take out, and the 7 is what's left over, so the base 8 equivalent is **57**.

For the base 9 equivalent, we similarly use $47 = 9 \cdot 5 + 2$, so the number is **52**.

For the base 16, we divide 16 into 47 to get 2, with remainder 15. What can we do with this 15? It can't be broken down into 16's, since it is less than 16. We are forced to conclude that this is a digit larger than 10! If you look a few paragraphs down in the text, you'll see that this base-16 digit is called F. Thus the base 16 number is the odd-looking **2F**.

5-6   We convert the B to an 11 and the E's to 14's to get $BEE_{16} = (16^2(11) + 16(14) + (14))_{10} = (256 \cdot 11 + 16 \cdot 14 + 14)_{10} = \mathbf{3054_{10}}$. Similarly, $DEF_{16} = (16^2(13) + 16(14) + (15))_{10} = (256 \cdot 13 + 16 \cdot 14 + 15)_{10} = \mathbf{3567_{10}}$. And again: $A1 = 16 \cdot 10 + 1 = \mathbf{161_{10}}$.

5-7   This question can be answered best with another question: how do you multiply a number by 10 in base 10? You add a zero. Similarly, in base 2, the number

$$\underline{b_n}\,\underline{b_{n-1}} \cdots \underline{b_0} = b_n 2^n + b_{n-1} 2^{n-1} + \cdots + b_0 2^0$$

becomes

$$b_n 2^{n+1} + b_{n-1} 2^n + \cdots + b_1 2^1 = \underline{b_n}\,\underline{b_{n-1}} \cdots \underline{b_0}\,\underline{0}$$

when multiplied by 2.

5-8   Let's do one: 99. The largest power of 2 less than 99 is $64 = 2^6$, so the number will have seven digits. Taking out the 64, we are left with 35, which does contain a 32, so the second digit is a 1. Taking out the 32, we are left with only 3, which contains no 16, 8, or 4, but does contain a 2 and a 1. Thus the number is **1100011**, where the first two 1's correspond to 64 and 32, the middle 0's to 16, 8, and 4, and the last two 1's to 2 and 1.

5-9   The last digits of 34 and 17 are 4 and 7, respectively. Thus the last digits of the product and sum should be the last digits of $4 \cdot 7 = 28$, or 8, and $4 + 7 = 11$, or 1. Multiplying and adding the numbers themselves, they are 578 and 51, with last digits 8 and 1 as advertised.

5-10   The squares of the single digits are $0^2 = 0$, $1^2 = 1$, $2^2 = 4$, $3^2 = 9$, 16, 25, 36, 49, 64, and 81, with last digits 0, 1, 4, 9, 6, and 5. Since any integer must have a number 0 through 9 as the last digit, it must have one of these last digits. Thus the excluded digits are **2, 3, 7, and 8**.

5-11   The easiest way to write some down is to just keep adding 5's: 3, 8, 13, 18, ... To be more interesting, we can add large multiples of 5, like 25, 50, or 5555, to get 28, 53, or 5558.

5-12   Clearly 103 is congruent to 3 (mod 5), but 103 is too big. If we subtract 5, however, we get **98**, which is both congruent to 3 (mod 5) and less than 100. There can obviously be none greater.

5-13   We first find the smallest and the largest numbers congruent to 1 (mod 7). To find the smallest, we just take a multiple of 7 which is close and well-known, like 49. The corresponding number which is congruent to 1 (mod 7) is $49 + 1 = 50$. (Or we could have started with 71, another easy candidate, and subtracted: 71, 64, 57, 50.) We can find the largest in a similar way. Since 280 is 4 times 70, it is a multiple of 7, and 281 is thus congruent to 1 (mod 7). Subtracting sevens, we get 274, 267, 260, 253, 246. The smallest is $50 = 7 \cdot 7 + 1$ and the largest is $246 = 7 \cdot 35 + 1$. Thus the total number is $35 - 7 + 1 = \mathbf{29}$.

5-14   The obvious place to start is at 0. From there, we just add 5's: 5, 10, 15, 20, ... The numbers congruent to 0 (mod 5) are just the multiples of 5!

5-15 We could try to subtract out all the 4's: 123, 119, 115.... However, the easiest way is to get rid of all the 4's at once, dividing by 4 and keeping only the remainder. Long dividing 123 by 4 gives 30, with remainder **3**.

Similarly, long dividing 321 by 7 gives 45, with remainder **6**.

5-16 Every number is congruent to 0, 1, 2, 3, 4, 5, 6, or 7 (mod 8). The squares are thus congruent to either 0, 1, 4, $9 \equiv 1$, $16 \equiv 0$, $25 \equiv 1$, $36 \equiv 4$, or $49 \equiv 1$. We don't need to try higher numbers because all higher numbers can be modded out before squaring. For example, $19^2 \equiv 3^2 \equiv 1$ (mod 8).

5-17 Clearly any multiple of 5 ends in either 5 or 0: 5, 10, 15, 20, ...

5-18 While 10 is not divisible by 4, 100 is, so a number is divisible by 4 if and only if its last two digits form a number which is divisible by 4. For example, 10174 has last two digits 74, and 74 is not divisible by 4, so neither is 10174.

Divisibility by 8 works the same way, but we have to consider the last *three* digits, since 8 does not divide 100 but does divide 1000 ($1000 = 8 \cdot 125$). Let's try it on $13216 = 13000 + 216$. Since 13000 is automatically divisible by 8 (since is is a multiple of 1000), we discard it. Thus 13216 is divisible by 8 if and only if 216 is. (Is it?)

Since 20 divides 100, we consider the last two digits: they must be 20, 40, 60, 80, or 00.

5-19 Since all these numbers are made up of only 2's and 5's, they all divide relatively small powers of 10. Thus we can throw out all but the last few digits. On the other hand, 3 doesn't divide any power of 10, so we have to take all digits into account when determining if a number is divisible by 3.

5-20 For 1717, 3451, and 173451, the sums of the digits are 16, 13, and 21, so **only the last** should be divisible by 3. (Neither 16 nor 13 is divisible by 3, but 21 is.) Direct division confirms this.

5-21 In the same way as for 3, we find that a number is divisible by 9 if and only if the sum of its digits is. For example, $7965841 = 7(999999 + 1) + 9(99999 + 1) + \cdots + 1$. Modding out by 9 gets rid of all the numbers of the form $99 \cdots 9$, since they are divisible by 9, so we are left with $7 + 9 + 6 + 5 + 8 + 4 + 1$, which must be divisible by 9 if 7965841 is.

5-22 The sums of the digits of 4995, 4996, 4997, 4998, and 4999 are 27, 28, 29, 30, and 31. Of these numbers, both 27 and 30 are divisible by 3, but 27 is divisible by 9 as well. Thus 30 is the sum we want, and **4998**, the number which generated it, is the answer.

5-23 We just need to write down the alternating sums. For 11, the sum is $1 - 1 = 0$, so 11 is indeed divisible by itself. For 111, the alternating sum is $1 - 1 + 1 = 1$, so no. For 1111, $1 - 1 + 1 - 1 = 0$, so yes. For 1716, $1 - 7 + 1 - 6 = -11$, so yes. For 1761, $1 - 7 + 6 - 1 = -1$, so no. For 152637, $1 - 5 + 2 - 6 + 3 - 7 = -12$, so no.

5-24 Let the number be $\underline{a}\,\underline{b}$. The alternating sum is $a - b$. If $a = b$, this is 0, and the number is divisible by 11. If not, the largest it can be is $9 - 0 = 9$, and the smallest is $1 - 9 = -8$. It cannot reach the 11 or -11 it would need in order to be divisible by 11. Thus the only way $\underline{a}\,\underline{b}$ can be divisible by 11 is if $a = b$.

5-25 Trial and error quickly gives results: 2 is prime, 3 is prime, $4 = 2^2$, 5 is prime, $6 = 2 \cdot 3$, 7 is prime, $8 = 2^3$, $9 = 3^2$, $10 = 2 \cdot 5$, 11 is prime, and $12 = 2^2 \cdot 3$.

5-26 Clearly 256 is even, so we immediately factor out a 2 to get $2 \cdot 128$. 128 is also even, so we can factor out another 2 to get $256 = 2 \cdot 2 \cdot 64$. But $64 = 2^6$, so $256 = 2 \cdot 2 \cdot 2^6 = \mathbf{2^8}$.

5-27 First, 141. We go upward through the primes. (This is why it is important to know the primes up to about 20 by heart.) Clearly 2 won't work, because it is even. However, since the sum of the digits is 6, which is divisible by 3, 141 itself is divisible by 3. It factors into $3 \cdot 47$ by direct division. We then turn our attention to 47. Neither 2 nor 3 nor 5 will work. But the next prime, 7, is too large, since $7^2 = 49 > 47$. Thus 47 is prime, and the complete factorization is $\mathbf{3 \cdot 47}$.

For 1441, we immediately eliminate 2, 3 (since the sum of the digits is 10), and 5. 7 doesn't go by straight division. The next prime is 11. The alternating sum is $1 - 4 + 4 - 1 = 0$, so 11 does divide: $1441 = 11 \cdot 131$. 11 doesn't divide 131 by the test, and 13 is too big ($13^2 = 169 > 131$), so 131 is prime. Thus the factorization is $\mathbf{11 \cdot 131}$.

For 14441, we can immediately eliminate 2, 3, and 5. 7 does work, though; by long division, $14441 = 7 \cdot 2063$. Trying 7 again, it does not divide into 2063. 11 does not work, from the alternating sum test. Now we begin to get into deep water. If 2063 turns out to be prime, we will have to go all the way up to about 45 to find out. We have to grind: 13 doesn't work, and neither do 17, 19, 23, 29, 31, 37, 41, and 43. The next prime, 47, is too big, because $47^2 = 2209 > 2063$. Thus 2063 is prime, and the complete factorization is $\mathbf{7 \cdot 2063}$. Sometimes we don't get the breaks.

5-28 We factor. Using the usual methods, we have $117 = 3^2 \cdot 13$ and $165 = 3 \cdot 5 \cdot 11$, so that $(117, 165) = \mathbf{3}$. Again: $102 = 2 \cdot 3 \cdot 17$ and $119 = 7 \cdot 17$; 17 is the only common factor so the GCF is $\mathbf{17}$. For the third, $96 = 2^5 \cdot 3$ and $36 = 2^2 \cdot 3^2$; the GCF is the product of the two 2's and one 3 which are in common, or $2^2 \cdot 3 = \mathbf{12}$.

5-29 It is self-evident that a number must be less than or equal to a number which it divides. Since the GCF divides a and b, then, it is clearly less than or equal to both. Moreover, if we let the GCF be g, then we can show g is a divisor of $a - b$:

$$a - b \ (\mathrm{mod}\ g) \equiv a \ (\mathrm{mod}\ g) - b \ (\mathrm{mod}\ g) \equiv 0 \ (\mathrm{mod}\ g).$$

Thus g divides $a - b$, so must be less than or equal to it. (Note how we used the fact that $a \equiv b \equiv 0 \ (\mathrm{mod}\ g)$, which is true because g divides both a and b.)

5-30 We have already factored these pairs, so we can read the LCMs directly off. For the first pair, we need two 3's, a 5, an 11, and a 13, for an LCM of $9 \cdot 5 \cdot 11 \cdot 13 = \mathbf{6435}$. For the second we need a 2, a 3, a 7, and a 17, for an LCM of $\mathbf{714}$. For the third we need five 2's and two 3's, for an LCM of $2^5 \cdot 3^2 = 32 \cdot 9 = \mathbf{288}$.

5-31 Just doing the multiplications directly, we easily verify $3 \cdot 6435 = 19305 = 117 \cdot 165$, $17 \cdot 714 = 12138 = 102 \cdot 119$, and $12 \cdot 288 = 3456 = 36 \cdot 96$.

5-32 Consider any prime p. It enters the factorization of m as p^e and of n as p^f (e and f could be zero). Without loss of generality let's say that $e \leq f$. When we take the GCF of m

and n, we need e p's, since any more factors of p will not divide m. Similarly, when we take the LCM, we need f p's, since f factors of p are required if n is to divide the LCM. Thus, in the product of the GCD and LCM all factors of p will come together as p^{e+f}. But this factor p^{e+f} is the same power of p which enters into the prime factorization of mn! Since this argument applies to any prime p, the prime factorizations of $(m, n)[m, n]$ and mn must be the same, so $(m, n)[m, n]$ and mn must be equal.

5-33   This proof is only slightly more complicated than the last one. For any prime p let p^d be in the factorization of l, p^e in that of m, and p^f in that of n. (Some of d, e, and f may be zero.) Without loss of generality, let us assume that

$$d \le e \le f, \tag{$*$}$$

so that p^d is the p-term in the factorization of (l, m, n). Now p divides lm $d + e$ times, mn $e + f$ times, and nl $f + d$ times. Since from $(*)$ we have

$$d + e \le d + f \le e + f,$$

the p-term in the factorization of $[lm, mn, nl]$ is p^{e+f}. Thus p comes into the product $(l, m, n)[lm, mn, nl]$ as a $d + e + f$ power, which is the same power as that with which it appears in the product lmn. Since this argument holds for all primes, we're done.

If you like playing with these things (and who doesn't?) try to find more complex identities of this type. Two possibilities to chew on are the "dual" of the one you just proved, or

$$(lm, mn, nl)[l, m, n] = lmn,$$

and ones with nested GCD's and LCM's, like

$$[(l, m), (m, n), (n, l)] = lmn.$$

Are either of these true? Can you find more complex ones, or even ones which generalize to arbitrarily many variables?

Solutions to Problems

87.   Since $36 = 2^2 \cdot 3^2$, $27 = 3^3$, and $45 = 3^2 \cdot 5$, the three numbers have two 3's in common, so the GCF is $3^2 = \mathbf{9}$.

88.   The smallest multiple of 7 in the given range is $7(15) = 105$ and the largest is $7(28) = 196$, so 7 times any number from 15 to 28 is between 100 and 200. Thus, there are $28 - 15 + 1 = \mathbf{14}$ multiples of 7 in the given range.

89.   The units digit of 19^{93} is the same as that of 9^{93}. Since $9^2 = 81$, $9^{92} = (9^2)^{46}$ ends in 1. Thus, 9^{93} ends in $1 \cdot 9 = \mathbf{9}$.

90. The sequence repeats in cycles of 8. Thus we should take all the 8's out of 1275 to find a term equivalent to the 1275th term. In the new language of mods (which you would do well to become fluent in), this is exactly the same as 1275 (mod 8). In any case, a simple way to find it is by dividing 8 into 1275 and taking the remainder, which turns out to be 3. Thus the 1275th term is equivalent to the 3rd term, which is **5**.

A slightly more clever approach saves us from the long division. That is to realize that 8 divides 1200, since it divides $400 = 8 \cdot 50$, so we can subtract 1200 from the 1275 with no effect. We can then subtract off $72 = 8 \cdot 9$ from the 75 which remains, and immediately be left with 3. This method has the advantage of feeling more understandable and less mechanical than just doing the division and taking the result.

91. To get used to the notation, we can think of this as the set of 10 simultaneous congruences

$$
\begin{aligned}
x &\equiv 9 \quad (\text{mod } 10) \\
x &\equiv 8 \quad (\text{mod } 9) \\
&\vdots \\
x &\equiv 1 \quad (\text{mod } 2).
\end{aligned}
$$

We still need an insight, though. The insight is to add 1 to both sides of all the congruences, to get

$$
\begin{aligned}
x + 1 &\equiv 10 \equiv 0 \quad (\text{mod } 10) \\
x + 1 &\equiv 9 \equiv 0 \quad (\text{mod } 9) \\
&\vdots \\
x + 1 &\equiv 2 \equiv 0 \quad (\text{mod } 2).
\end{aligned}
$$

Thus all we need is for $x + 1$ to be divisible by all numbers from 2 to 10. We let x have a factor of 2 for 2, a factor of 3 for 3, a factor of 2 for 4 (one was already taken care of by the 2), a 5 for 5, nothing for 6 (we already have a 2 and a 3), a 7 for 7, a third 2 for 8 (we need three and already have two), a 3 for 9 (we've got one already), and nothing for 10 (already have 2 and 5). Then $x + 1 = 2^3 \cdot 3^2 \cdot 5 \cdot 7 = 2520$, so $x = \mathbf{2519}$.

92. Since we want $12A3B$ to be divisible by 9, the sum of the digits, $A + B + 6$, must also be divisible by 9. Since this sum cannot equal 0, it must be 9 or 18, since 27 is too high even if A and B are both 9. So $A + B = 3$ or $A + B = 12$.

Since we want $12A3B$ to be divisible by 4, the number $3B$ formed by taking the last two digits must be divisible by 4. This can only be if B is 2 or 6. If $B = 6$, then by the restrictions on $A + B$, A must equal -3 (an impossibility) or 6, which is banned because A cannot equal B. Thus $B = 2$, so $A = 1$ or $A = 10$, another impossibility. The only solution is $\boldsymbol{A = 1, B = 2}$.

93.   The units digit of the difference $3^{1986} - 2^{1986}$ will be the same as the units digit of the difference of the units digits of 3^{1986} and 2^{1986}. (Got that?) We thus compute the two units digits separately. For powers of 3, the units digits go 3, 9, 7, 1, 3, ..., repeating in cycles of 4. Since the sequence repeats in cycles of 4, the 1986th term will be the same as the 2nd term (dividing by 4 and taking the remainder, or 2), which is 9. For the powers of 2, the units digit goes 2, 4, 8, 6, 2, 4, ..., again repeating in fours. Modding out by 4, the 1986th digit is the same as the 2nd, which is 4. The difference is $9 - 4 = \mathbf{5}$.

94.   The easy way to think of this is as simply counting the possible numbers of \$5 bills. There cannot be zero \$5's, since \$69 is odd and cannot be formed of all \$2's; similarly there can't be any even number of \$5's. There can, however, be only one \$5, with \$64 worth of \$2 bills. The greatest number of \$5 bills will similarly be when the first \$65 is made of \$5's and the remaining \$4 of \$2's. In this case there are 13 \$5's. Since we can have any odd number of \$5's from 1 to 13, the total number is **7**.

95.   We immediately simplify the problem by noticing that any number divisible by 8 and 9 must also be divisible by 2, 3, 4, and 6. Now a number of the form $4AB8$ is divisible by 9 if and only if the sum of its digits, $12 + A + B$, is divisible by 9; in this case, the condition forces $A + B = 6$ or $A + B = 15$, since $A + B$ must be positive and less than 18.

To consider divisibility by 8, we write the number as $4000 + 100A + 10B + 8$. Clearly we can wipe out the 4000 and the 8, so the number $10(10A + B)$ must be divisible by 8. The multiplier of 10 contains one factor of 2, so $10A + B$ (or the two-digit number AB) must contain the other two factors of 2: it must be divisible by 4. This immediately forces B to be even since $10A + B$ is odd otherwise.

With these restrictions, we can make the trial-and-error portion of the solution short and sweet. With the first possibility, $A + B = 6$, the only candidates are $A = 0$, $B = 6$; $A = 2$, $B = 4$; $A = 4$, $B = 2$; $A = 6$, $B = 0$. The first and third don't work because 06 and 42 are not divisible by 4. However, 24 and 60 are, so the second and fourth do work, yielding the solutions 4248 and 4608. With the second possibility, $A + B = 15$, the candidates are 78; 96. Only the second is divisible by 4, yielding the solution 4968. The sum of the three solutions is $4248 + 4608 + 4968 = \mathbf{13824}$.

96.   This is really a rehash of an earlier problem. We just note that if we call the number of markers x, then $x + 2$ must be divisible by 4, 5, and 7, so the smallest nonzero value is $4 \cdot 5 \cdot 7 = 140$, and $x = 140 - 2 = \mathbf{138}$.

97.   If we rewrite the question in the language of modular arithmetic, it becomes very simple: If $n \equiv 1 \pmod{5}$, what is the smallest positive integer congruent to $3n \pmod{5}$? We know that $3n \equiv (3)(n) \equiv (3)(1) \equiv 3 \pmod{5}$, and we're done.

98.   Let the three-digit number be r; then the composite number can be written $1000r + r = 1001r$. Thus **1001** must divide our number. Since r can be anything, it contributes nothing further.

99.   Three times the number equals two times the number plus one times the number.

Two times the number just adds a zero at the end of the number, so the sum will look like

$$11@ \qquad \text{(15 digits total)}$$
$$+ \; 11@0 \qquad \text{(16 digits total)}$$

where @ is a string of thirteen 1's. When we do the sum, only the leftmost digits will add to the number of digits of the sum. Since the first digit on the top, a 1, goes with the second on the bottom, another 1, there will definitely be a 1 carried over to the leftmost column. This 1 will combine with the first digit on the bottom and spill a 1 over into the next column. Thus there will be one more digit than there is in the bottom number, or **17** digits. For practice, do the entire addition; it's only 1's and 0's, after all.

100. The largest three-digit base 5 number is 444_5, which in base 10 becomes $4 \cdot 25 + 4 \cdot 5 + 4 = 100 + 20 + 4 = \mathbf{124}$, or $5^3 - 1$ (since $5^3 = 1000_5$).

101. The three digit numbers in base 12 range from $100_{12} = 1 \cdot 12^2 = 144$ to $1000_{12} - 1 = 12^3 - 1 = 1728 - 1 = 1727$. (The latter is because the largest three digit number must be 1 smaller than the smallest four digit number. Do you see why?) The smallest four-digit number in base 9 is $1000_9 = 1 \cdot 9^3 = 729$. Thus the numbers from 729 to 1727 satisfy the problem, and there are $1727 - 729 + 1 = \mathbf{999}$ of them.

102. We have $531{,}441_{10} = 9^6 = 1000000_9$, so that $531{,}440_{10} = 9^6 - 1 = \mathbf{888888_9}$.

103. If n is the number, then $n - 1$ is divisible by 2, 3, 4, 5, 6, 7, 8, and 9. It suffices to be divisible by 8, 9, 5, and 7, since numbers divisible by 8 are clearly divisible by 2 and 4, numbers divisible by 9 are also divisible by 3, and numbers thus divisible by 2 and 3 are also divisible by $2 \cdot 3 = 6$. The smallest positive number divisible by 8, 9, 5, and 7 is $8 \cdot 9 \cdot 5 \cdot 7 = 2520 = n - 1$, so $n = \mathbf{2521}$.

104. We wish the five-digit number $a679b$ to be divisible by $72 = 2^3 3^2$. It must first be divisible by $2^3 = 8$, and using our divisibility rule, this means that the three digit number $79b$ is divisible by 8. But 800 is divisible by 8, so $800 - 8 = 792$ is also. This is the only number of the desired form which is divisible by 8, and thus $b = 2$. The number $a679b$ must next be divisible by 9, so the sum of the digits, $22 + a + b = 24 + a$, must also. The only way this can be is if $a = 3$. Thus $a + b = 3 + 2 = \mathbf{5}$.

105. This seems to be getting a little tough. However, our basic divisibility rules should still win out. We factor: $84 = 4 \cdot 21 = 4 \cdot 3 \cdot 7$. Thus our number must be divisible by 4, 3, and 7. First think about divisibility by 4. The number formed by the last two digits, which is either 66, 67, 76, or 77, must be divisible by 4; only 76 works. We use the other digits to satisfy the restriction that the sum of the digits be divisible by 3, and test the results for divisibility by 7 using straight division. Since every digit of 6 is divisible by 3, only the 7's matter. There must be three 7's (or six or nine or...) for divisibility by 3. The immediate prospect is thus 7776, but this is not divisible by 7 since it is one less than 7777. The next three candidates are 77676, 76776, and 67776. Testing all three for divisibility by 7, we find that 77676 and 67776 are not, but **76776** is.

Don't despair—88 is easier. The number must only be divisible by 8 and 11. Using the 8, the last three digits can only be 776, and we can immediately make the alternating sum go to 0 for divisibility by 11 by making the first digit 6. The answer is **6776**.

106.   Using the base b representation, we see that $n = b(b-2)+2$. To convert this to base $(b-1)$, we need to break down the expression $b(b-2)+2$ in terms of powers of $(b-1)$. We write $b(b-2)+2$ as $(b-1)(b-2)+(b-2)+2$, or $(b-1)(b-1)-(b-1)+b = (b-1)^2+1 = 101_{b-1}$.

107.   We can write $\sqrt[a]{10000_a} = \sqrt[a]{a^4} = a^{4/a}$, and this must equal $10_a = a$. Thus $a^{4/a} = a$, so $4/a = 1$ and $a = \mathbf{4}$.

108.   We write $p_1 p_2 \cdots p_k + 1 = m^2$, so that $p_1 p_2 \cdots p_k = m^2 - 1 = (m-1)(m+1)$. Now comes the clever part. Since $p_1 = 2$, the product $p_1 p_2 \cdots p_k$ must be even, so $p_1 p_2 \cdots p_k + 1$ is odd, and m must also be odd. Then $(m-1)$ and $(m+1)$ are both even, and the product $(m-1)(m+1)$ is thus divisible by 4. But this product is supposed to equal the product $p_1 p_2 \cdots p_k$, which *can't* be divisible by 4 because it only has one 2 among its factors. Thus there can be no such m.

109.   Let the squares be $(x-1)^2$, x^2 and $(x+1)^2$. The sum of these is $3x^2 + 2$. This number is congruent to 2 mod 3 since it is two more than a multiple of 3. Since a number can only end in a 0, 1, or 2 in base 3, a square ends in $0^2 = 0$, $1^2 = 1$, or $2^2 = 4 \equiv 1$. Thus all squares end in 0 or 1 base 3. Since no square can be congruent to 2 mod 3, our aforementioned sum, $3x^2 + 2$, cannot be the square of an integer. (Why do we only try 0, 1, and 2 when finding what the last digit of a square can be in base 3?)

Chapter 6

Quadratic Equations

Solutions to Exercises

6-1 Write $(x + y)^3$ as $(x + y)(x + y)(x + y)$. Thus we have

$$
\begin{aligned}
(x + y)^3 &= [x(x + y) + y(x + y)][x + y] \\
&= [x^2 + 2xy + y^2][x + y] \\
&= (x^2 + 2xy + y^2)x + (x^2 + 2xy + y^2)y \\
&= x^3 + 3x^2y + 3xy^2 + y^3.
\end{aligned}
$$

6-2

    i. Rearranging so that all terms are on the left yields $x^2 + 5x + 6 = 0$. Now, we seek two positive numbers whose sum is 5 and product is 6. A little thought yields 2 and 3 as the numbers, so our factored equation is $x^2 + 5x + 6 = (x + 2)(x + 3) = 0$, and the solutions are $x = \mathbf{-2}$ and $x = \mathbf{-3}$.

    ii. We seek two numbers whose product is -40 and sum is -3. Since the product is negative, the numbers have different signs. Since the sum is -3, they differ by 3 in magnitude. Thus the numbers are -8 and 5 (not -5 and 8 because $8 - 5 = 3$, not -3). Thus $x^2 - 3x - 40 = (x - 8)(x + 5) = 0$, so the solutions are $x = \mathbf{8}$ and $x = \mathbf{-5}$.

    iii. First, we get rid of the fractions by multiplying the whole equation by 3, leaving $6x^2 + x - 2 = 0$. We know that the factorization is of the form $(sx + u)(tx + v)$. Since $uv = -2$, we try $u = 1$ and $v = -2$. It doesn't take long to decide that there is no pair (s, t) which will, when combined with $u = 1$ and $v - 2$, satisfy the required $tu + vs = 1$ and $ts = 6$. Our other option for u and v is $u = -1$, $v = 2$. By trial and error, we find that

$(s, t) = (3, 2)$ fits the conditions. Thus our equation factors as

$$6x^2 + x - 2 = (3x + 2)(2x - 1) = 0.$$

Hence the solutions are $x = -\mathbf{3/2}$ and $x = \mathbf{1/2}$.

iv. Since the constant term is positive and the coefficient of x is negative, u and v are negative in the factorization $(sx + u)(tx + v)$. Since $st = 49$, we have two possibilities; $(s, t) = (49, 1)$ and $(s, t) = (7, 7)$. Playing with the second, we find that there is no pair (u, v) such that $uv = 132$ and $7u + 7v = -316$. For the former pair, however, we find the factorization $(49x - 22)(x - 6) = 49x^2 - 316x + 132 = 0$. Thus the solutions are $x = \mathbf{6}$ and $x = \mathbf{22/49}$.

v. Multiplying both sides by $x - 3$, we have $x(x - 3) = 28$. Rearranging yields $x^2 - 3x - 28 = 0$. To factor this, we seek two numbers whose product is -28 and sum is -3. The numbers -7 and 4 fit this description, so $x^2 - 3x - 28 = (x - 7)(x + 4) = 0$. Thus the solutions to the original equation are $x = \mathbf{7}$ and $x = -\mathbf{4}$.

6-3   Let $u = p/q$, where p and q have no common divisors except 1. We show that u is an integer by showing that q must be 1. Since $(x + u)(x + v) = x^2 + bx + c$, $x = -u$ must be a solution to $x^2 + bx + c = 0$. Thus $u^2 - bu + c = 0$. Substituting $u = p/q$, we find

$$\frac{p^2}{q^2} - \frac{bp}{q} + c = 0.$$

Multiplying by q^2 to get rid of the fractions, we have

$$p^2 - bpq + cq^2 = 0.$$

We rewrite this as $p^2/q = bp + q^2$, which implies that q divides p^2 evenly since $bp + q^2$ is an integer. Since p and q have no common divisors besides 1, the only way q can divide p is if it is 1. Hence $u = p/q$ must be an integer, as must v.

6-4

i. $3x^2 + 5x = x(3x + 5) = 0$. Thus the solutions are $x = \mathbf{0}$ and $x = -\mathbf{5/3}$.

ii. First divide both sides by 3, leaving $x^2 + 2x + 1 = 0$. As the constant term is the square of half the coefficient of x $((2/2)^2 = 1)$, the expression on the left side is the square of $(x + 1)$. Thus $x^2 + 2x + 1 = (x + 1)^2 = 0$. The only solution is $x = -\mathbf{1}$.

iii. First divide by 5, leaving $x^2 - 9 = 0$. This is clearly the difference of two squares: $x^2 - 9 = (x - 3)(x + 3) = 0$. Hence the solutions are $x = \mathbf{3}$, $-\mathbf{3}$.

iv. First, multiply both sides by 3 to get rid of the fractions. This gives $x^2 - 6x + 9 = 0$. Since the constant term is the square of half the coefficient of x $((-6/2)^2 = (-3)^2 = 9)$, this quadratic is the perfect square of $(x - 3)$. Thus $x^2 - 6x + 9 = (x - 3)^2 = 0$, and the only solution is $x = \mathbf{3}$.

v. First put all the terms on the left, leaving $4x^2 - 5x = x(4x - 5) = 0$, which has solutions $x = \mathbf{0},\ \mathbf{5/4}$.

vi. The expression $36 - 25x^2$ is the difference of the squares of 6 and $5x$. Thus $36 - 25x^2 = (6 - 5x)(6 + 5x) = 0$. The solutions are then $x = \mathbf{6/5},\ \mathbf{-6/5}$.

6-5 Let the quadratic equation be $at^2 + bt + c = 0$, where $a > 0$. By the quadratic formula, the roots are

$$t = \frac{-b \pm \sqrt{b^2 - 4ac}}{2}.$$

Since $x + y\sqrt{z}$ is one of these roots, we have

$$x + y\sqrt{z} = -\frac{b}{2} + \frac{\sqrt{b^2 - 4ac}}{2}.$$

(Do you see why we took the + from the ± in this case?) Equating radical parts of both sides and radical-free parts of both sides, we obtain $x = -b/2$ and $y\sqrt{z} = \sqrt{b^2 - 4ac}/2$. The other root is

$$\left(-\frac{b}{2}\right) - \left(\frac{\sqrt{b^2 - 4ac}}{2}\right) = x - y\sqrt{z},$$

proving our assertion.

6-6 By the quadratic formula, the two roots of the equation $ax^2 + bx + c = 0$ are

$$\frac{-b + \sqrt{b^2 - 4ac}}{2} \qquad \text{and} \qquad \frac{-b - \sqrt{b^2 - 4ac}}{2}.$$

The sum of these is

$$\frac{-b + \sqrt{b^2 - 4ac}}{2a} + \frac{-b - \sqrt{b^2 - 4ac}}{2a} = \frac{-2b + (\sqrt{b^2 - 4ac} - \sqrt{b^2 - 4ac})}{2a} = -\frac{b}{a}.$$

The product of these is

$$\left(\frac{-b + \sqrt{b^2 - 4ac}}{2a}\right)\left(\frac{-b - \sqrt{b^2 - 4ac}}{2a}\right) = \frac{b^2 - b\sqrt{b^2 - 4ac} + b\sqrt{b^2 - 4ac} - (b^2 - 4ac)}{4a^2}$$

$$= \frac{4ac}{4a^2}$$

$$= \frac{c}{a}.$$

6-7

i. A straightforward application of the quadratic formula yields

$$x = \frac{-3 \pm \sqrt{9 - 4}}{2} = \frac{-3 \pm \sqrt{5}}{2}.$$

ii. Once again, plug into the quadratic equation:

$$x = \frac{-(-1) \pm \sqrt{1 - 4(4)(7)}}{2(4)} = \frac{1 \pm \sqrt{-111}}{8} = \frac{1 \pm i\sqrt{111}}{8}.$$

iii. Multiply by 3 to get rid of the fraction, then rearrange to get $3z^2 - 3z - 4 = 0$. Applying the quadratic formula yields

$$z = \frac{-(-3) \pm \sqrt{9 - 4(3)(-4)}}{2(3)} = \frac{3 \pm \sqrt{57}}{6}.$$

iv. Multiply by 10 to remove the decimals, then rearrange to get $z^2 + 10z - 2 = 0$. Applying the quadratic formula gives

$$z = \frac{-10 \pm \sqrt{100 - 4(1)(-2)}}{2} = \frac{-10 \pm 6\sqrt{3}}{2} = -5 \pm 3\sqrt{3}.$$

6-8   We solve this problem using a method similar to the "completing the square" method we used to prove the quadratic formula. Since $x^3 + 3x^2 + 3x + 1 = (x + 1)^3$, we add 1 to both sides of the given equation to get

$$\begin{aligned} x^3 + 3x^2 + 3x + 1 &= 1 + 1 \\ (x + 1)^3 &= 2. \end{aligned}$$

Taking the cube root, we find $x + 1 = \sqrt[3]{2}$, so $x = \sqrt[3]{2} - 1$. Note that we have "completed the cube" by adding 1 to both sides.

6-9   Squaring this as it is would be rather messy, so we first move one term to the right side of the equation, then square the result:

$$\begin{aligned} (\sqrt{5z + 5} - \sqrt{3 - 3z})^2 &= (2\sqrt{z})^2 \\ 5z + 5 - 2\sqrt{(5z + 5)(3 - 3z)} + 3 - 3z &= 4z \\ 8 + 2z - 2\sqrt{15(1 - z^2)} &= 4z. \end{aligned}$$

Now we just put the radical expression on a side by itself (after dividing everything by 2; it is always useful to remove such factors if possible) and square one more time:

$$\begin{aligned} (z - 4)^2 &= \left(-\sqrt{15(1 - z^2)}\right)^2 \\ z^2 - 8z + 16 &= 15 - 15z^2. \end{aligned}$$

Rearranging gives $16z^2 - 8z + 1 = (4z - 1)^2 = 0$; thus the only possible solution is $z = 1/4$. Substituting this back into the original equation gives $5/2 - 3/2 = 1$, so $z = \mathbf{1/4}$ 'checks' and thus is a solution.

6-10 Here, our expression is $\sqrt{x^2 + 1}$ and its square is $x^2 + 1$. Letting $y = \sqrt{x^2 + 1}$, so that $y^2 = x^2 + 1$, the equation becomes $y + y^2 = 90$, a quadratic! Rearranging and factoring yields $y = 9$ and $y = -10$ as the solutions. Substituting back into our expression for y, we get $\sqrt{x^2 + 1} = 9$ or $\sqrt{x^2 + 1} = -10$. The latter is impossible, since square roots are always positive unless specified otherwise. Squaring the former yields $x^2 + 1 = 81$, so $x = \pm 4\sqrt{5}$. The trickiest part of this is the initial substitution $y = \sqrt{x^2 + 1}$. With experience, you'll learn to spot a trick like this immediately.

6-11

i. First we try $x + y\sqrt{10}$. $(x + y\sqrt{10})^2 = x^2 + 10y^2 + 2xy\sqrt{10} = 35 - 10\sqrt{10}$. Thus $xy = -5$. Our options for (x, y) are $(-5, 1)$ and $(-1, 5)$. We find that $(-5, 1)$ works, since $(-5)^2 + 10(1)^2 = 35$, as required. However, $-5 + \sqrt{10}$ is a negative number. Since a square root should be positive, $\mathbf{5 - \sqrt{10}}$ is the answer.

ii. Trying $x + y\sqrt{10}$, we have $x^2 + 10y^2 + 2xy\sqrt{10} = 55 - 10\sqrt{10}$. As in the previous question, $xy = -5$, so our choices for (x, y) are $(-5, 1)$ and $(-1, 5)$. Both of these fail, so we are forced to try $x\sqrt{2} + y\sqrt{5}$. Squaring yields $(x\sqrt{2} + y\sqrt{5})^2 = 2x^2 + 5y^2 + 2xy\sqrt{10} = 55 - 10\sqrt{10}$, and our choices here are the same as before, $(x, y) = (-5, 1)$ or $(-1, 5)$. Since $2(-5)^2 + 5(1)^2 = 55$, we have $(-5\sqrt{2} + \sqrt{5})^2 = 55 - 10\sqrt{10}$. As in the previous problem, $-5\sqrt{2} + \sqrt{5}$ is negative (because $(5\sqrt{2})^2 > (\sqrt{5})^2$). Since we must have a positive answer, $\mathbf{5\sqrt{2} - \sqrt{5}}$ is the desired square root.

iii. $(a + bi)^2 = a^2 - b^2 + 2abi = 15 + 8i$. The imaginary terms give us the equation $2ab = 8$, so $b = 4/a$. Substituting this into the equation we get from the real parts, $a^2 - b^2 = 15$, yields the equation $a^2 - 16/a^2 = 15$, which can be factored as a quadratic: $a^4 - 15a^2 - 16 = (a^2 - 16)(a^2 + 1) = 0$. Taking the real values for a, we get $a = \pm 4$. Using this to find $b = \pm 1$, the square roots are $\pm(\mathbf{4 + i})$. (What would have happened if we took the imaginary values for a?

Solutions to Problems

110. From the quadratic formula, the roots are $\dfrac{7 \pm \sqrt{85}}{2}$. The positive difference is given by the '+' root minus the '−' root, or

$$\frac{7 + \sqrt{85}}{2} - \frac{7 - \sqrt{85}}{2} = \sqrt{\mathbf{85}}.$$

111. First we get $\sqrt{x + 10}$ out of the denominator by multiplying everything by $\sqrt{x + 10}$, yielding $x + 10 - 6 = 5\sqrt{x + 10}$, or $x + 4 = 5\sqrt{x + 10}$. Squaring then yields

$$(x + 4)^2 = 25(x + 10)$$

$$x^2 + 8x + 16 = 25x + 250.$$

Rearranging gives $x^2 - 17x - 234 = 0$; factoring, we have $(x + 9)(x - 26) = 0$, which has roots $x = -9$ and $x = 26$. Substituting these back into the original equation, we find that $x = -9$ gives $1 - 6 = 5$, which isn't true; thus $x = -9$ is an extraneous root. $x = \mathbf{26}$ is OK, and is our only answer.

112.   Combining the two in one fraction and factoring yields

$$\frac{2x^2 - x - (4 + x)}{(x + 1)(x - 2)} = \frac{2x^2 - 2x - 4}{(x + 1)(x - 2)}$$
$$= \frac{2(x^2 - x - 2)}{(x + 1)(x - 2)}$$
$$= \frac{2(x + 1)(x - 2)}{(x + 1)(x - 2)} = \mathbf{2}.$$

113.   To get the variables out of the denominator, we multiply both sides by $z(z - 1)$, yielding $z^2 = (z + 1)(z - 1) - 2z(z - 1)$. Expanding gives $z^2 = z^2 - 1 - 2z^2 + 2z$, so $2z^2 - 2z + 1 = 0$. Applying the quadratic formula yields

$$z = \frac{2 \pm \sqrt{4 - 8}}{4} = \frac{\mathbf{1 \pm i}}{\mathbf{2}}.$$

114.   First, we note that $-27 + 36i = 9(-3 + 4i)$, so $\sqrt{-27 + 36i} = 3\sqrt{-3 + 4i}$. Now, let $\sqrt{-3 + 4i} = a + bi$, so $a^2 - b^2 = -3$ and $ab = 2$. Letting $b = 2/a$, we have $a^2 - 4/a^2 = -3$ and $a^4 + 3a^2 - 4 = (a^2 + 4)(a^2 - 1)$. Since we want a to be real, $a = \pm 1$. Finding b, our solutions are $\mathbf{\pm 3(1 + 2i)}$.

115.   Since the coefficient of n^2 is 9, the expression squared is of the form $(3n + a)$. Since the coefficient of n in $(3n + a)^2$ is $6az$, we have $6a = -30$, or $a = -5$. Thus the constant term, $c = a^2$, is $\mathbf{25}$. Note that the expression squared could also be $-3n + 5$, but this doesn't change the answer.

116.   Solving the equation $2a + b = 12$ for b in terms of a, we have $b = 12 - 2a$; substituting this into $ab = 3$ yields $a(12 - 2a) = 3$. Rearranging this gives $2a^2 - 12a + 3 = 0$. Factoring won't get you far with this equation, so we instead apply the quadratic formula, yielding

$$a = \frac{12 \pm \sqrt{144 - 4(2)(3)}}{4} = \frac{6 \pm \sqrt{30}}{2}.$$

When $a = (6 + \sqrt{30})/2$, $b = 12 - (6 + \sqrt{30}) = 6 - \sqrt{30}$. When $a = (6 - \sqrt{30})/2$, $b = 12 - (6 - \sqrt{30}) = 6 + \sqrt{30}$. Thus the solution pairs are

$$(a, b) = \left(\frac{\mathbf{6 + \sqrt{30}}}{\mathbf{2}}, \mathbf{6 - \sqrt{30}} \right) \text{ and } \left(\frac{\mathbf{6 - \sqrt{30}}}{\mathbf{2}}, \mathbf{6 + \sqrt{30}} \right).$$

117.   Since the plane travels 2000 km in 10 hours when there is no wind, its rate in still air is $2000/10 = 200$ km/hr. With the tailwind blowing at speed k, its effective speed becomes $200 + k$, and the trip thus takes $1000/(200 + k)$. On the way back, its speed is reduced to $200 - k$, and the trip takes $1000/(200 - k)$. Since the overall trip with wind is $10\frac{25}{60} = 10\frac{5}{12}$ hours, we have

$$\frac{1000}{200 + k} + \frac{1000}{200 - k} = 10\frac{5}{12} = \frac{125}{12}.$$

Multiplying by all the factors in the denominator to get rid of them and dividing everything by 125, we have

$$8(200 - k)(12) + 8(200 + k)(12) = (200 - k)(200 + k).$$

Thus $40000 - k^2 = 38400$, so $k^2 = 1600$ and $k = \mathbf{40}$.

118.   First, we square and rearrange:

$$\left(\sqrt{40 - 9x} - 2\sqrt{7 - x}\right)^2 = \left(\sqrt{-x}\right)^2$$
$$40 - 9x + 4(7 - x) - 4\sqrt{(40 - 9x)(7 - x)} = -x$$
$$-4\sqrt{9x^2 - 103x + 280} = 12x - 68.$$

Dividing by four, then squaring again, we have $9x^2 - 103x + 280 = 9x^2 - 102x + 289$, so $x = -9$. We plug this back into the original equation to make sure it is not extraneous, and it isn't. Thus $2x + 5 = \mathbf{-13}$.

119.   Adding $7/(x - 3)$ to both sides leaves $x = 3$. However, this root is extraneous, because the terms $7/(x - 3)$ in the equation are undefined when $x = 3$. Thus there are **no solutions** to this equation.

120.   Start by multiplying by x^2 to get the variables out of the denominator. This leaves $-x^2 + x + 2 = 0$, or $x^2 - x - 2 = 0$. Factoring gives $(x - 2)(x + 1) = 0$, so the roots are 2 and -1 and their sum is **1**. Remember, we can also find the sum of roots without actually finding the roots. In this case, we have $-(-1/1) = \mathbf{1}$ as the sum.

121.   Since the discriminant is zero, we can neglect the square root portion of the quadratic formula. There is only one distinct root, which has value $2\sqrt{2}/2a = \sqrt{2}/a$. Since a is real, $\sqrt{2}/a$ is real. We cannot, however, say whether this expression is rational or irrational. For example, if $a = 1$, the root is irrational, whereas if $a = \sqrt{2}$, the root is rational. Thus we can only say the root must be **real**.

122.   Even though the coefficients are imaginary, the quadratic formula is still valid ((D) is true), as are the expressions we derived for the sum and product of roots. Just like quadratics with real coefficients, quadratics with imaginary coefficients can be factored. For example, the given quadratic factors as $ix^2 - x + 2i = (ix + 1)(x + 2i)$, so the roots are

$x = i$ and $-2i$. (Thus (C) and (E) are true.) The sum of these is $-i$, not 2, so (A) is false. Finally, the discriminant is $(-1)^2 - 4(i)(2i) = 1 + 8 = 9$, so (B) is true and (**A**) is the only false statement.

123. Writing all expressions with a common base, 3, and simplifying the left side, we have $3^{x^2 - 3x} = 3^{-2}$. Since the bases are the same, these expressions are equal only if the exponents are equal. Thus $x^2 - 3x = -2$, so $x^2 - 3x + 2 = (x - 1)(x - 2) = 0$, and the solutions are $x = 1$ and $x = 2$.

124. Since the product of the roots is the constant term divided by the coefficient of x^2, we have $2k^2 - 1 = 7$, so $k = \pm 2$. The roots are then given by the quadratic formula as

$$x = \frac{3k \pm \sqrt{(-3k)^2 - 4(1)(2k^2 - 1)}}{2}.$$

Since $k = \pm 2$, $k^2 = 4$ regardless of whether k is positive or negative. Thus the roots are

$$x = \frac{3k \pm \sqrt{9k^2 - 4(7)}}{2} = \frac{3k \pm \sqrt{8}}{2} = \frac{3k \pm 2\sqrt{2}}{2}.$$

Since k is rational, the two roots are **irrational**.

125. Let Janet's initial speed be x. Thus it takes $2/x$ minutes to cover the first 2 miles. She increases her speed and then it takes $8/(x + 0.5)$ minutes to cover the remainder of the course. Had she gone the whole race at this increased speed, it would have taken her $10/(x + 0.5)$ minutes. Since this is 2 minutes less than it actually took her, we have

$$\frac{2}{x} + \frac{8}{x + 0.5} = \frac{10}{x + 0.5} + 2.$$

Dividing by 2 and rearranging, we have $\frac{1}{x} = \frac{1}{x+0.5} + 1$. Multiplying both sides by $x(x+0.5)$ to get rid of the denominators, we have $x + 0.5 = x + x(x + 0.5)$. Expanding, rearranging, and multiplying by 2 to get rid of the 0.5's, we are left with $2x^2 + x - 1 = (2x - 1)(x + 1) = 0$. Since Janet's initial rate must be positive, it is 0.5 miles per minute rather than -1 miles per minute. To determine her average speed for the whole race, we find the time she rode for the whole race, or $2/x + 8/(x + 0.5) = 4 + 8 = 12$ minutes. Since she travels 10 miles in 12 minutes, her average speed is $10/12 = $ **5/6** miles per minute.

126. Square both sides:

$$\left(\sqrt{x + \sqrt{x + 11}} + \sqrt{x - \sqrt{x + 11}} \right)^2 = 16$$

$$x + \sqrt{x + 11} + x - \sqrt{x + 11} + 2\sqrt{(x + \sqrt{x + 11})(x - \sqrt{x + 11})} = 16$$

$$2x + 2\sqrt{x^2 - x - 11} = 16.$$

Divide by 2, rearrange to isolate the radical expression, and square again:

$$\left(\sqrt{x^2 - x - 11}\right)^2 = (8 - x)^2$$
$$x^2 - x - 11 = x^2 - 16x + 64.$$

Thus $15x = 75$, and $x = \mathbf{5}$. As always, we check that this works to ensure that it is not extraneous.

127. Write both sides with the same base; 2 is the best choice:

$$\left(2^3\right)^{x^2 + 3x + 10} = \left(2^2\right)^{x^2 - x}$$
$$2^{3(x^2 + 3x + 10)} = 2^{2(x^2 - x)}.$$

Since the bases are the same, the exponents must be the same in order for these two expressions to be equal. Thus $3(x^2 + 3x + 10) = 2(x^2 - x)$. Expanding and rearranging yields $x^2 + 11x + 30 = 0$. The sum of the roots is $-\mathbf{11}$. (Remember how we can find the sum of the roots without actually finding the roots.) One warning about this shortcut to find the sum of roots is that you should *not* use it when the roots may be extraneous, i.e. in problems involving radicals or variables in denominators. This is because we want the sum of the valid roots only, not including the extraneous ones.

128. Make the substitution $y = x^2 - 3x$. Thus we have $4 = (x^2 - 3x)^2 - 3(x^2 - 3x) = y^2 - 3y$. Rearranging and solving for y, we find $y^2 - 3y - 4 = (y - 4)(y + 1) = 0$, so $y = 4$ and $y = -1$ are the solutions. The answer is not 3, however, because we want the values for x. For $y = 4$, we have $x^2 - 3x - 4 = (x - 4)(x + 1) = 0$, so 4 and -1 are solutions. For $y = -1$, we have $x^2 - 3x + 1 = 0$, the sum of whose solutions is $-(-3)/1 = 3$. Thus the sum of all possible values of x is $4 - 1 + 3 = \mathbf{6}$.

129. The student who found $\{-6, 1\}$ as the roots solved the equation $x^2 + 5x - 6 = 0$, while the student who obtained the solutions $\{2, 3\}$ solved the equation $x^2 - 5x + 6 = 0$. The first student had the right constant term and the second had the right coefficient of x. Thus the proper equation was $x^2 - 5x - 6 = 0$, which factors as $(x - 6)(x + 1)$, so the roots are $x = \mathbf{6}$ and $x = -\mathbf{1}$.

130. Isolating the square root and squaring yields $x - 2 = x^2 - 8x + 16$. Thus $x^2 - 9x + 18 = (x - 3)(x - 6) = 0$, and the roots are 3 and 6. Since $x = 6$ is extraneous (test for yourself), the only solution to the initial equation is $x = \mathbf{3}$.

131. Let the factored form be $(sx + t)(ux + v)$. Thus s, t, u, and v are all factors of 21 and hence are all odd. The coefficient of x in the expansion of this factored form is $tu + sv$. Since tu and sv are products of pairs of odd numbers, they are odd, so their sum, $a = tu + sv = a$, is even.

132. Since 15 factors as $3 \cdot 5$, there are two possibilities to try: an answer of the form $x + y\sqrt{15}$, or an answer of the form $x\sqrt{3} + y\sqrt{5}$. On a hunch, we try the second. Squaring it, we have $53 - 8\sqrt{15} = 3x^2 + 5y^2 + 2xy\sqrt{15}$, so we have $3x^2 + 5y^2 = 53$ and $-8 = 2xy$. The second equation yields the possibilities $(2, 2)$, $(1, 4)$, and $(4, 1)$ for $(|x|, |y|)$; we'll consider the signs of x and y in a moment. Trying these possible pairs in the first equation, we find that $(4, 1)$ is the right one. Since exactly one of x and y must be negative, the two square roots are thus $4\sqrt{3} - \sqrt{5}$ and $-4\sqrt{3} + \sqrt{5}$. The positive square root is $\mathbf{4\sqrt{3} - \sqrt{5}}$, since $4\sqrt{3} > \sqrt{5}$.

133.   First, we write the equation using a common base for the exponential expressions: $(3^2)^{z-1} - 3^{z-1} - 2 = 3^{2z-2} - 3^{z-1} - 2 = 0$. Thus

$$3^{2z-2} - 3^{z-1} - 2 = 3^{2z}3^{-2} - 3^z 3^{-1} - 2 = \frac{3^{2z}}{9} - \frac{3^z}{3} - 2 = 0.$$

Making the substitution $x = 3^z$, so $x^2 = 3^{2z}$, we have $\frac{x^2}{9} - \frac{x}{3} - 2 = 0$. Multiplying by 9 gives $x^2 - 3x - 18 = (x - 6)(x + 3)$. Thus $3^z = -3$ or $3^z = 6$. The first has no real solution, but the second has solution $z = \log_3 6$.

134.   Factoring the quadratic as shown in the beginning of the chapter, we have, where r_1 and r_2 are the roots,

$$ax^2 + bx + c = a(x - r_1)(x - r_2) = a\left(x^2 - (r_1 + r_2)x + r_1 r_2\right).$$

Comparing coefficients of x, we have $b = -a(r_1 + r_2)$. Thus $r_1 + r_2 = -b/a$. Similarly, comparing constant terms yields $c = ar_1 r_2$, so $r_1 r_2 = c/a$. Challenge: Can you extend this argument to equations of the form $ax^3 + bx^2 + cx + d$? How about higher degree expressions?

135.   Rather than actually finding the roots, we'll use what we know about the sum and product of the roots of a quadratic. The given equation, upon rearrangement, is $x^2 + (-6 - 2i)x + 11 + 10i = 0$. Thus the sum of the roots is $-(-6 - 2i) = 6 + 2i$ and the product is $11 + 10i$. If the roots are $a + bi$ and $c + di$, the above yields $a + c + (b + d)i = 6 + 2i$ and $(a + bi)(c + di) = ac - bd + (ad + bc)i = 11 + 10i$. The roots of the new equation are $a - bi$ and $c - di$. Thus their sum is $a + c - (b + d)i$ and their product is $ac - bd - (ad + bc)i$. Comparing the new sum and product to the expressions above, we find that they are the conjugates of the sum and product of the roots of the original equation. Make sure you see why they are conjugates. (Compare $(a + c) + (b + d)i$ and $(a + c) - (b + d)i$.) Thus the sum of the new roots is $6 - 2i$ and the product is $11 - 10i$. Since the coefficient of x^2 in the new quadratic is 1, the constant must be $11 - 10i$ and the coefficient of x must be $-(6 - 2i)$. Hence the new quadratic is $\mathbf{x^2 - (6 - 2i)x + 11 - 10i}$.

136.   An imaginary number with irrationals…this gets pretty messy. We know that the answer is of the form $a + bi$, where either (1) one of a and b contains a $\sqrt{6}$, or (2) one has $\sqrt{3}$ and the other $\sqrt{2}$. We'll try (1) first, looking at roots of the form $x\sqrt{6} + yi$ and $x + yi\sqrt{6}$. The first yields $6x^2 - y^2 = 10$ and $xy = -2$, which has no rational solution, and the second yields $x^2 - 6y^2 = 10$ and $xy = -2$, which also has no rational solution (we just have to try

$(x, y) = (-2, 1)$ and $(-1, 2)$ to check these). Thus we move on to $x\sqrt{3} + yi\sqrt{2}$, which yields $3x^2 - 2y^2$ and $xy = -2$. Since $(-2, 1)$ satisfies these, we have $-2\sqrt{3} + i\sqrt{2}$ as a solution. Since we are working with imaginary numbers, we take both $\pm(-\mathbf{2}\sqrt{\mathbf{3}} + i\sqrt{\mathbf{2}})$ as solutions.

137. First, get rid of the denominators by multiplying by $a + b$ and a. This yields $(a + b)^2 = ab$, so $a^2 + ab + b^2 = 0$. Using the quadratic formula to find a in terms of b, we have

$$a = \frac{-b \pm \sqrt{b^2 - 4b^2}}{2} = \frac{-b \pm \sqrt{-3b^2}}{2}.$$

If b is real, $\sqrt{-3b^2}$ is imaginary (as the square root of a positive number) and so is $(-b \pm \sqrt{-3b^2})/2$. Thus if b is real, a is imaginary, so a and b cannot both be real.

Chapter 7

Special Factorizations and Clever Manipulations

Solutions to Exercises

7-1 Expanding the product $(a + b)(a^2 - ab + b^2)$ using the distributive property, we have

$$
\begin{aligned}
(a + b)(a^2 - ab + b^2) &= a(a^2 - ab + b^2) + b(a^2 - ab + b^2) \\
&= a^3 + b^3.
\end{aligned}
$$

7-2 The key here is to note that $\sqrt[3]{1} + \sqrt[3]{2} + \sqrt[3]{4}$ is a factor of $2 - 1$! How can this be? Expand $2 - 1$ as a difference of cubes:

$$
2^{3/3} - 1^{3/3} = \left(2^{1/3} - 1^{1/3}\right)\left(2^{2/3} + 2^{1/3}1^{1/3} + 1^{2/3}\right) = \left(\sqrt[3]{2} - \sqrt[3]{1}\right)\left(\sqrt[3]{4} + \sqrt[3]{2} + \sqrt[3]{1}\right).
$$

Hence, if we multiply top and bottom of $1/(\sqrt[3]{4} + \sqrt[3]{2} + \sqrt[3]{1})$ by $\sqrt[3]{2} - \sqrt[3]{1}$, we have

$$
\frac{1}{\sqrt[3]{4} + \sqrt[3]{2} + \sqrt[3]{1}} \cdot \frac{\sqrt[3]{2} - \sqrt[3]{1}}{\sqrt[3]{2} - \sqrt[3]{1}} = \frac{\sqrt[3]{2} - \sqrt[3]{1}}{\left(\sqrt[3]{4} + \sqrt[3]{2} + \sqrt[3]{1}\right)\left(\sqrt[3]{2} - \sqrt[3]{1}\right)} = \frac{\sqrt[3]{2} - \sqrt[3]{1}}{2 - 1}.
$$

Similarly, $\sqrt[3]{4} + \sqrt[3]{6} + \sqrt[3]{9}$ is a factor of $(3 - 2)$, and $\sqrt[3]{9} + \sqrt[3]{12} + \sqrt[3]{16}$ is a factor of $(4 - 3)$. Multiplying these terms top and bottom by $\sqrt[3]{3} - \sqrt[3]{2}$ and $\sqrt[3]{4} - \sqrt[3]{3}$, respectively, we have

$$
\frac{1}{\sqrt[3]{1} + \sqrt[3]{2} + \sqrt[3]{4}} + \frac{1}{\sqrt[3]{4} + \sqrt[3]{6} + \sqrt[3]{9}} + \frac{1}{\sqrt[3]{9} + \sqrt[3]{12} + \sqrt[3]{16}}
$$

$$= \frac{\sqrt[3]{2} - \sqrt[3]{1}}{2 - 1} + \frac{\sqrt[3]{3} - \sqrt[3]{2}}{3 - 2} + \frac{\sqrt[3]{4} - \sqrt[3]{3}}{4 - 3}$$

$$= \sqrt[3]{2} - 1 + \sqrt[3]{3} - \sqrt[3]{2} + \sqrt[3]{4} - \sqrt[3]{3}$$

$$= \mathbf{\sqrt[3]{4} - 1}.$$

7-3 Following the hint, we square $z + \dfrac{1}{z}$:

$$\left(z + \frac{1}{z} \right)^2 = z^2 + 2 + \frac{1}{z^2} = 14 + 2 = 16.$$

Thus $z + \dfrac{1}{z} = \pm 4$. Since $z > 0$, $z + \dfrac{1}{z} = 4$. Now, we need 5th powers. We can get there in two steps. First, we cube the relation we have just learned.

$$\left(z + \frac{1}{z} \right)^3 = z^3 + 3z^2 \left(\frac{1}{z} \right) + 3z \left(\frac{1}{z} \right)^2 + \frac{1}{z^3}$$

$$4^3 = z^3 + \frac{1}{z^3} + 3 \left(z + \frac{1}{z} \right)$$

$$64 = z^3 + \frac{1}{z^3} + 12$$

Thus $z^3 + \dfrac{1}{z^3} = 52$. To get 5th powers from perfect cubes, we multiply by perfect squares; since we know $z^2 + \dfrac{1}{z^2}$, this seems like a logical choice:

$$\left(z^3 + \frac{1}{z^3} \right) \left(z^2 + \frac{1}{z^2} \right) = 52(14)$$

$$z^5 + z^3 \left(\frac{1}{z^2} \right) + \left(\frac{1}{z^3} \right) z^2 + \frac{1}{z^5} = 728$$

$$z^5 + \frac{1}{z^5} + z + \frac{1}{z} = 728$$

$$z^5 + \frac{1}{z^5} + 4 = 728.$$

Thus $z^5 + \dfrac{1}{z^5} = \mathbf{724}$.

7-4 Employing our strategy from the previous problem, we find $a + b$ as $(a + b)^2 = a^2 + 2ab + b^2 = 4 + 2(4) = 12$. Thus $a + b = \pm 2\sqrt{3}$. First we try $a + b = 2\sqrt{3}$. Cubing this equation gives

$$(a + b)^3 = a^3 + 3a^2 b + 3ab^2 + b^3$$

$$(2\sqrt{3})^3 = a^3 + b^3 + 3ab(a+b)$$
$$24\sqrt{3} = a^3 + b^3 + 3(4)(2\sqrt{3}).$$

Thus we come to the somewhat surprising result that $a^3+b^3 = 0$! When we try $a+b = -2\sqrt{3}$, we come to the same conclusion. Thus, **0** is the only possible value.

Solutions to Problems

138. $9877^2 - 9876^2 = (9877-9876)(9877+9876)$. Hence $9877^2 = (1)(19753)+97535376 = $ **97555129**.

139. We could pound out 2^{16} and go from there, but it is much easier to factor first. We have

$$2^{16} - 1 = (2^8 - 1)(2^8 + 1) = (2^4 - 1)(2^4 + 1)(2^8 + 1) = 15(17)(257) = 3(5)(17)(257).$$

(Make sure you see that 257 is prime.) The sum of the factors is **282**.

140. We know from our discussion on quadratic equations that the sum of the roots is $-(-3/2) = 3/2$ and the product of them is $4/2 = 2$. Thus, letting a and b be the roots, we have $a + b = 3/2$ and $ab = 2$ and we are asked to find $a^2 + b^2$. We write

$$(a+b)^2 = a^2 + b^2 + 2ab$$
$$\frac{9}{4} = a^2 + b^2 + 4.$$

Thus, $a^2 + b^2 = -\mathbf{7/4}$.

141. We can factor b^2 out of the first three terms and c^2 out of the last three, leaving

$$b^2(-a^2 + 2ab - b^2) + c^2(a^2 - 2ab + b^2).$$

The first term in parentheses is $-(a-b)^2$, and the second is $(a-b)^2$. Thus, the expression is

$$-b^2(a-b)^2 + c^2(a-b)^2 = (c^2 - b^2)(a-b)^2 = \mathbf{(c-b)(c+b)(a-b)^2}.$$

142. As in the previous problem, we recognize $2mn - m^2 - n^2$ as $-(m-n)^2$. Thus, $x^2 + 2mn - m^2 - n^2 = x^2 - (m-n)^2$. This we can factor as a difference of squares:

$$x^2 - (m-n)^2 = \big(x - (m-n)\big)\big(x + (m-n)\big) = \mathbf{(x - m + n)(x + m - n)}.$$

143. We factor as the difference of squares when possible, and as the difference or sum of cubes otherwise:

$$\begin{aligned}
x^{12} - y^{12} &= (x^6 - y^6)(x^6 + y^6) \\
&= (x^3 - y^3)(x^3 + y^3)(x^2 + y^2)(x^4 - x^2y^2 + y^4).
\end{aligned}$$

Thus we have

$$x^{12} - y^{12} = (x - y)(x^2 + xy + y^2)(x + y)(x^2 - xy + y^2)(x^2 + y^2)(x^4 - x^2y^2 + y^4).$$

144. We factor everything to get

$$\left(\frac{(a - 1)(a^2 + a + 1)}{(a - 1)(a + 1)} \right) \left(\frac{(a + 1)^2}{(a + 1)(a^2 - a + 1)} \right) \left(\frac{a^2 - a + 1}{a + 1} \right).$$

Canceling like crazy, we're left with $(a^2 + a + 1)/(a + 1)$.

145. First factor out an x, then repeatedly apply the difference of squares:

$$\begin{aligned}
x^9 - x &= x(x^8 - 1) = x(x^4 - 1)(x^4 + 1). \\
&= x(x^2 - 1)(x^2 + 1)(x^4 + 1) = x(x - 1)(x + 1)(x^2 + 1)(x^4 + 1)
\end{aligned}$$

Thus, there are **5** factors with integral coefficients.

146. Let the two numbers be x and y, so that $x + y = 1$ and $xy = 1$. Cubing the first equation, since we want $x^3 + y^3$, we have

$$\begin{aligned}
(x + y)^3 &= x^3 + y^3 + 3xy(x + y) \\
1^3 &= x^3 + y^3 + 3(1)(1).
\end{aligned}$$

Thus, $x^3 + y^3 = -\mathbf{2}$.

147. To get fourth powers, we square $x - \dfrac{1}{x}$ twice. Since $\left(x - \dfrac{1}{x} \right)^2 = x^2 + \dfrac{1}{x^2} - 2 = 5^2$,

we have $x^2 + \dfrac{1}{x^2} = 27$. Squaring this to get our fourth powers, we find $\left(x^2 + \dfrac{1}{x^2} \right)^2 =$

$x^4 + \dfrac{1}{x^4} + 2 = 27^2 = 729$. Thus, $x^4 + \dfrac{1}{x^4} = \mathbf{727}$.

148. First, as a difference of squares,

$$\begin{aligned}
x^8 - y^8 &= (x^4 - y^4)(x^4 + y^4) \\
&= (x^2 - y^2)(x^2 + y^2)(x^4 + y^4) \\
&= (x - y)(x + y)(x^2 + y^2)(x^4 + y^4).
\end{aligned}$$

We look done, but we're not; we can factor $x^4 + y^4$ further. Recall that we can use $a^2 + b^2 = (a + b)^2 - 2ab$ if it leads to further factorization. Thus, $x^4 + y^4 = (x^2 + y^2)^2 - 2x^2y^2$. Factoring this as the difference of squares yields $(x^2 + y^2 - \sqrt{2}\,xy)(x^2 + y^2 + \sqrt{2}\,xy)$. Note that we don't apply this method to $x^2 + y^2$ because it would lead to $\sqrt{xy}$ terms, which are inadmissible. Thus,

$$x^8 - y^8 = (x - y)(x + y)(x^2 + y^2)(x^2 + y^2 - \sqrt{2}\,xy)(x^2 + y^2 + \sqrt{2}\,xy).$$

149.   Noting that two of the terms in the parentheses, a^2x^2 and b^2y^2, are in both pairs of parentheses, we have

$$\frac{bx(a^2x^2 + b^2y^2) + bx(2a^2y^2) + ay(a^2x^2 + b^2y^2) + ay(2b^2x^2)}{bx + ay}.$$

Collecting terms, we get

$$\frac{(bx + ay)(a^2x^2 + b^2y^2) + 2a^2bxy^2 + 2ab^2x^2y}{bx + ay}.$$

Factoring $2abxy$ out of the final two terms in the numerator then yields

$$\frac{(bx + ay)(a^2x^2 + b^2y^2) + 2axby(bx + ay)}{bx + ay}.$$

Thus, we can factor $(bx + ay)$ from each term in the numerator, to get

$$\frac{(bx + ay)(a^2x^2 + b^2y^2 + 2axby)}{bx + ay}.$$

Canceling $bx + ay$ and noting that the other term in the numerator is the square of $ax + by$, we find that our fraction, reduced as much as possible, is $(ax + by)^2$.

150.   First, we write the given expression with bases 2 and 3 rather than 8 and 27, to get $8^{2x} - 27^{2y} = 2^{6x} - 3^{6y}$. We factor this as the difference of squares, then factor each of the resulting terms as the difference or sum of cubes:

$$
\begin{aligned}
2^{6x} - 3^{6y} &= \left(2^{3x}\right)^2 - \left(3^{3y}\right)^2 \\
&= (2^{3x} - 3^{3y})(2^{3x} + 3^{3y}) \\
&= (2^x - 3^y)(2^{2x} + 2^x3^y + 3^{2y})(2^x + 3^y)(2^{2x} - 2^x3^y + 3^{2y}).
\end{aligned}
$$

151. To get sixth powers, we cube then square the equation $x + y = 4$. Cubing, we have

$$\begin{aligned} (x+y)^3 &= x^3 + y^3 + 3xy(x+y) \\ 4^3 &= x^3 + y^3 + 3(2)(4), \end{aligned}$$

so $x^3 + y^3 = 40$. Squaring, we then find

$$\begin{aligned} (x^3 + y^3)^2 &= x^6 + y^6 + 2x^3 y^3 \\ (40)^2 &= x^6 + y^6 + 2(2)^3, \end{aligned}$$

and $x^6 + y^6 = 1600 - 16 = \mathbf{1584}$.

152. Isolating the square root, we find $2\sqrt{x} = x - 2$. Squaring this gives $4x = x^2 - 4x + 4$, so $x^2 - 8x + 4 = 0$. Thus, $x = \frac{8 \pm \sqrt{48}}{2} = 4 \pm 2\sqrt{3}$. Now we must check these to make sure they're not extraneous. Since $\sqrt{4 + 2\sqrt{3}} = 1 + \sqrt{3}$, $4 + 2\sqrt{3}$ works fine. However, $\sqrt{4 - 2\sqrt{3}} = \sqrt{3} - 1$, so substituting $4 - 2\sqrt{3}$ in the equation gives $0 = 4 - 4\sqrt{3}$; thus $4 - 2\sqrt{3}$ is extraneous. The only solution is $\mathbf{4 + 2\sqrt{3}}$.

153. Letting S be the sum, we rationalize each denominator by multiplying by the conjugate:

$$\begin{aligned} S &= \left(\frac{1}{\sqrt{15} + \sqrt{13}}\right)\frac{\sqrt{15} - \sqrt{13}}{\sqrt{15} - \sqrt{13}} + \cdots + \left(\frac{1}{\sqrt{7} + \sqrt{5}}\right)\frac{\sqrt{7} - \sqrt{5}}{\sqrt{7} - \sqrt{5}} \\ &= \frac{\sqrt{15} - \sqrt{13}}{2} + \cdots + \frac{\sqrt{7} - \sqrt{5}}{2} \\ &= \frac{1}{2}\left(\sqrt{15} - \sqrt{13} + \sqrt{13} - \sqrt{11} + \cdots + 3 - \sqrt{7} + \sqrt{7} - \sqrt{5}\right) \\ &= \frac{\sqrt{15} - \sqrt{5}}{2}. \end{aligned}$$

Make sure you see how the other terms cancel.

154. To solve the problem, we'll find $x + \frac{1}{x}$ and cube it. To find $x + \frac{1}{x}$, we square it and use $x^2 + \frac{1}{x^2} = 7$:

$$\left(x + \frac{1}{x}\right)^2 = x^2 + \frac{1}{x^2} + 2 = 9.$$

Thus $x + \frac{1}{x} = \pm 3$. We'll treat the $+$ and $-$ cases separately. We try $x + \frac{1}{x} = 3$ first to find

$$\begin{aligned} \left(x + \frac{1}{x}\right)^3 &= x^3 + \frac{1}{x^3} + 3\left(x + \frac{1}{x}\right) \\ 3^3 &= x^3 + \frac{1}{x^3} + 3(3). \end{aligned}$$

Thus, $x^3 + \dfrac{1}{x^3} = 18$ in this case. Similarly, if we let $x + \dfrac{1}{x} = -3$, we find that $x^3 + \dfrac{1}{x^3} = -18$. Hence the possible values of $x^3 + \dfrac{1}{x^3}$ are $\pm\mathbf{18}$.

155. We recall from our discussion of quadratic equations that $r + s = -p$ and $rs = q$; all four parts can be solved with these two equations and some sweat.

i. $(r + s)^2 = r^2 + s^2 + 2rs$, so $r^2 + s^2 = (r + s)^2 - 2rs = \mathbf{p^2 - 2q}$.

ii. Since we know $r^2 + s^2$ and rs, we can evaluate $(r - s)^2$; hence $(r - s)^2 = r^2 + s^2 - 2rs = p^2 - 2q - 2q = p^2 - 4q$. Taking the square root, we find $r - s = \pm\sqrt{\mathbf{p^2 - 4q}}$.

iii. Factoring the desired expression, we have $r^2 s + rs^2 = rs(r + s) = -\mathbf{pq}$.

iv. Since we know $r^2 + s^2 = p^2 - 2q$, we can square this to get fourth powers:

$$
\begin{aligned}
(r^2 + s^2)^2 &= r^4 + s^4 + 2r^2 s^2 \\
(p^2 - 2q)^2 &= r^4 + s^4 + 2q^2 \\
p^4 - 4p^2 q + 4q^2 &= r^4 + s^4 + 2q^2.
\end{aligned}
$$

Hence $r^4 + s^4 = \mathbf{p^4 - 4p^2 q + 2q^2}$.

156. Writing everything with 2's and 3's as bases, we have $2^{16} + 2^8 3^8 + 3^{16}$. Since $2^{16} + 3^{16} = \left(2^8 + 3^8\right)^2 - 2\left(2^8 3^8\right)$, we have

$$2^{16} + 2^8 3^8 + 3^{16} = \left(2^8 + 3^8\right)^2 - \left(2^8 3^8\right).$$

Factoring this as a difference of squares, we have

$$(2^8 + 3^8 + 2^4 3^4)(2^8 + 3^8 - 2^4 3^4) = \mathbf{(8113)(5521)}.$$

157. Factoring the expression, we have $n^3 - n = n(n^2 - 1) = n(n - 1)(n + 1)$, so $n^3 - n$ is the product of three consecutive integers. One of these must be even, and one (maybe the same one) must be divisible by 3. Thus $n^3 - n$ must be divisible by **6**. We can say no more about the number.

158. $(a + b)^2 = a^2 + b^2 + 2ab$, so $a^2 + b^2 = 4 - 2ab$. Squaring this to get to our relation involving fourth powers gives

$$
\begin{aligned}
(a^2 + b^2)^2 &= a^4 + b^4 + 2a^2 b^2 \\
(4 - 2ab)^2 &= 16 + 2a^2 b^2 \\
16 - 16ab + 4a^2 b^2 &= 16 + 2a^2 b^2.
\end{aligned}
$$

Thus $2a^2 b^2 - 16ab = 2ab(ab - 8) = 0$, so the possible values of ab are **0 and 8**.

159. This one's pretty tricky. Since $(a+b)^2 = a^2 + b^2 + 2ab$, we can find $a+b$ if we find $a^2 + b^2$ and ab. To get ab, we cube $a - b = 2$ (so we can use the equation involving cubes).

$$
\begin{aligned}
(a-b)^3 &= a^3 - 3a^2 b + 3ab^2 - b^3 \\
8 &= a^3 - b^3 - 3ab(a-b) \\
8 &= 24 - 3ab(2)
\end{aligned}
$$

So $ab = 8/3$. We now square $a - b$ to find $a^2 + b^2$:

$$
(a-b)^2 = a^2 + b^2 - 2ab = a^2 + b^2 - \frac{16}{3}.
$$

Thus $a^2 + b^2 = 28/3$. Finally,

$$
(a+b)^2 = a^2 + b^2 + 2ab = \frac{44}{3},
$$

and $(a+b) = \pm\sqrt{44/3} = \pm 2\sqrt{33}/3$.

160. Start with the difference of squares, then factor the sum and difference of cubes:

$$
\begin{aligned}
3^{18} - 2^{18} &= (3^9 - 2^9)(3^9 + 2^9) \\
&= (3^3 - 2^3)(3^6 + 3^3 2^3 + 2^6)(3^3 + 2^3)(3^6 - 3^3 2^3 + 2^6) \\
&= (19)(729 + 216 + 64)(35)(729 - 216 + 64) \\
&= 5(7)(19)(577)(1009).
\end{aligned}
$$

161. Let $q = a^2 + b^2$. We wish to show that there is some pair of integers whose squares sum to $2q = 2a^2 + 2b^2$. The best way to do this is to find the integers. Indeed, $(a-b)^2 + (a+b)^2 = (a^2 - 2ab + b^2) + (a^2 + 2ab + b^2) = 2a^2 + 2b^2$, so, since a and b are integers, $a - b$ and $a + b$ are the desired integers. How did we think to use these? Since we needed expressions whose squares included a^2 and b^2, $a - b$ and $a + b$ were natural guesses. Upon writing their squares down, we realized that they were the right numbers.

We employ the same strategy on $5q = 5a^2 + 5b^2$. Once again we need a^2 and b^2 to be in the expansions, but $(a-b)$ and $(a+b)$ aren't large enough. Thus we try letting one number be $2a - b$. We have

$$
\begin{aligned}
5q - (2a-b)^2 &= 5a^2 + 5b^2 - (4a^2 - 4ab + b^2) \\
&= a^2 + 4ab + 4b^2 = (a+2b)^2,
\end{aligned}
$$

so $(2a - b)$ and $(a + 2b)$ are the desired integers.

Chapter 8

What Numbers Really Are

Solutions to Exercises

8-1 The nonnegative integers are all those which are not negative, or $\{0, 1, 2, \ldots\}$; the positive integers must be greater than zero, so they are $\{1, 2, 3, \ldots\}$.

8-2 Since the decimal terminates, it must be writable in the form

$$\frac{\text{numerator}}{10^{\text{power}}}.$$

Taking the fraction into lowest terms, we may divide all 2's and 5's out of the top and bottom, but the bottom will continue to consist solely of 2's and 5's no matter what. To be precise, we can have any fraction with denominator $2^a 5^b$, where a and b are nonnegative integers.

8-3 For the first, we long divide and find $3/11 = 0.272727\ldots = \mathbf{0.\overline{27}}$.

For the second, we just write $x = 0.345$, so that $1000x = 345$, and $x = 345/1000 = \mathbf{69/200}$.

For the third, we can either long divide or just notice that $4/8 = 1/2 = \mathbf{0.5}$.

For the fourth, we first write

$$x = 0.\overline{345}.$$

Multiplying through by 1000, we get

$$1000x = 345.\overline{345},$$

and subtracting the first from the second yields $999x = 345$, so that $x = 345/999 = \mathbf{115/333}$.

8-4 Using the same argument as in the text, we get down to $7 \cdot 19 = 133 < 153 = 9 \cdot 17$, so we have $7/17 < 9/19$.

8-5   In either case, we divide the inequality $a < b$ by ab (which is positive in either case), from which we find $1/a > 1/b$. Thus we must reverse the sign when we take reciprocals if a and b have the same sign. (Examples: $2 < 3$, but $1/3 < 1/2$; $-3 < -2$, but $-1/2 < -1/3$.)

8-6   Take reciprocals of both to find $x + (y/a)$? $x + (y/b)$. Since $y/a > y/b$ (because $a < b$ implies $1/a > 1/b$), the question mark becomes a $>$, and $x + (y/a) > x + (y/b)$. Taking reciprocals to get back where we started, we have to reverse the inequality, so $a/(ax + y) < b/(bx + y)$.

8-7   All of these should be easy modifications of the text's argument.

8-8   If p/q is in lowest terms, there can be no common factor between the top and the bottom. After squaring, there still can be no common factor, since squaring simply repeats the factors that were already there. Thus the square must be in lowest terms. However, adding a constant to the top and the bottom does not necessarily preserve lowest terms; for example, $7/9$ is in lowest terms, but $(7 + 3)/(9 + 3) = 10/12$ is not.

8-9   Call the square root of our fraction p/q, since we are told that it is rational. Assume p/q is in lowest terms. Then the square is equal to p^2/q^2 in lowest terms. The only change that can be made to get back to the original fraction is to multiply the top and bottom by some constant, to get ap^2/aq^2.

8-10   The last term we were given was $41/29$. Thus $p = 41$ and $q = 29$, so the next term is $(p + 2q)/(p + q) = (41 + 58)/(41 + 29) = 99/70$, which as a decimal equals 1.4142857. Squaring this, we get 2.00020, which is already really close. We can repeat the process to get $\frac{239}{169} = 1.414201 = \sqrt{1.99996}$; $\frac{577}{408} = 1.41421568 = \sqrt{2.000005}$. We're getting pretty close.

8-11   What do you think this is, a book of philosophy? You'll have to figure this one out yourself.

Solutions to Problems

162.   The numbers are equal to π, $\sqrt[3]{8}/\sqrt[3]{10} = 2/\sqrt[3]{10}$, $\sqrt[4]{16}/\sqrt[4]{10000}\sqrt[4]{10} = 2/10\sqrt[4]{10}$, and $\sqrt[3]{-1}\sqrt{100/9} = (-1)(10/3) = -10/3$. Thus only the last is rational.

163.   We have $x = 0.0038888\ldots$; then $10x = 0.038888\ldots$, and, subtracting, $9x = .035$. Thus $9000x = 35$, so $x = 35/9000 = 7/1800$. The sum of the numerator and denominator is **1807**.

164.   For this one we have to be careful, because we are in base 5. We will do most of the problem in base 5, to avoid conversion problems. We have

$$x = 0.\overline{31}_5,$$

and to move the decimal back by two places, we have to multiply by $5^2 = 25 = 100_5$, to get

$$100_5 x = 31.\overline{31}_5.$$

Subtracting, we get

$$44_5x = 31_5.$$

(Do you see why $100_5 - 1_5 = 44_5$? If not, look back at the sections on number bases.) Dividing, we find that as a base-5 fraction, $x = 31/44$. Is this in lowest terms? Converting to base 10 (because it is too hard to factor in base 5), $x = 16/24 = \mathbf{2/3}$.

165. We have $1/x > 4/49$, so $x < 49/4$ (reversing the inequality when we take reciprocals). The largest such x is **12**.

166. For the repeating fraction, we have $x = 0.363636\ldots$; $100x = 36.363636\ldots$; $99x = 36$; $x = 36/99 = 12/33 = 4/11$. For the terminating fraction, we have $x = 0.36$; $100x = 36$; $x = 36/100 = 9/25$. The difference is $4/11 - 9/25 = (100 - 99)/(11 \cdot 25) = \mathbf{1/275}$.

Chapter 9

An Introduction to Circles

Solutions to Exercises

9-1 Since the area is 8π, the radius is $\sqrt{8} = 2\sqrt{2}$, and the circumference is $2(2\sqrt{2})\pi = 4\pi\sqrt{2}$.

9-2 Let r be the radius of circle C and s the radius of circle B. Segment BX, as a radius of circle B, has length s. Thus $AX = 6 + s$. Similarly, $AY = 5 + r$. Since these are both radii of the same circle, $AX = AY$, so $6 + s = 5 + r$, or $r - s = 1$. Combining this with $BC = r + s = 9$ and solving for r, we find $r = 5$. Hence the radius of the largest circle is $5 + r = \mathbf{10}$.

9-3 The two pieces have length 36 and are made into circumferences of circles of diameter $36/\pi$. These circles each have radius $18/\pi$ and area $(18/\pi)^2\pi = 324/\pi$. Hence, the total area of the two is $\mathbf{648/\pi}$.

9-4 Let circles A, B, and C have radii r, s, and t, respectively, and let $a = BC$, $b = AC$, and $c = AB$. Thus $a = s + t$, $b = r + t$, and $c = s + r$. We are asked to find r in terms of a, b, and c. As discussed in the chapter on linear equations, we add the three equations, yielding $a + b + c = 2(r + s + t)$. We then subtract $s + t = a$ from $r + s + t = (a + b + c)/2$ to cancel s and t, yielding $r = (\boldsymbol{b + c - a})/\mathbf{2}$.

Chapter 10

Angles

Solutions to Exercises

10-1 Let the interior angles be A, B, and C. By the Exterior Angle Theorem, the exterior angles are $A+B$, $A+C$, and $B+C$. Their sum then is $2A+2B+2C$. Since the sum of the interior angles of a triangle is $180°$ $A+B+C = 180°$, and the sum of the exterior angles is $2A+2B+2C = 2(180°) = 360°$.

10-2 As an angle formed by two secants, $\angle P = (\overarc{BD} - \overarc{AC})/2$. As an inscribed angle, $\angle Q = \overarc{AC}/2$. Thus $\angle P + \angle Q = \overarc{BD}/2 = (\overarc{BQ} + \overarc{QD})/2 = (42° + 38°)/2 = \mathbf{40°}$.

10-3 Let $\overarc{TA} = x$. Then $\overarc{TXA} = 360° - x$. Since $\angle TPA = (\overarc{TXA} - \overarc{TA})/2 = (360 - 2x)/2$, we have $180 - x = 42$, so $x = 138$. Since $\angle TXA$ is an inscribed angle, its measure is half that of $\overarc{TA}$. Thus $\angle TXA = \mathbf{69°}$.

Chapter 11

Triangles, a.k.a. Geometry

Solutions to Exercises

11-1 We use in the diagram a fact we proved in an example earlier in this chapter: the center of the circle is the midpoint of the hypotenuse. Clearly AO is both a circumradius of $\triangle ABC$ and half the hypotenuse. Thus the circumradius of a right triangle is half the hypotenuse.

11-2 Referring to the diagram in the previous solution, we see that the median CO to the hypotenuse of the right triangle is also a radius of the circumcircle of the right triangle. Thus the median to the hypotenuse of a right triangle is half the hypotenuse.

11-3 If the median CO from vertex C to AB equals $AB/2$, then $AO = BO = CO$. Since the vertices of the triangle are equidistant from O, there is a circle with center O and radius OC which passes through all three vertices as shown. Since the midpoint of AB is the center of the circle, AB is a diameter. Thus $\overset{\frown}{AB} = 180°$. Since $\angle C$ is an inscribed angle, $\angle C = 180°/2 = 90°$. Thus the triangle is right.

11-4 We must choose the three numbers so that the sum of any two exceeds the third. Thus we cannot choose 1 as a side length. If we choose 2 as a side length, the possible pairs for the other two sides are $(3, 4)$ and $(4, 5)$. Finally, we may choose $(3, 4, 5)$ as the three side lengths. Thus there are **three** ways we can choose distinct numbers from the given set to form a nondegenerate triangle.

11-5 The altitude from the vertex of an isosceles triangle bisects the base. Thus, drawing the altitude to the base forms two right triangles as shown. Using the Pythagorean Theorem, we determine the altitude length as $\sqrt{10^2 - 8^2} = \mathbf{6}$.

11-6 The triples which can be sides of a triangle which has perimeter 11 are $(2, 4, 5)$; $(3, 3, 5)$; and $(3, 4, 4)$. A triangle is obtuse if the sum of the squares of the two smallest sides is less than the square of the largest. Since $2^2 + 4^2 < 5^2$, $3^2 + 3^2 < 5^2$, and $3^2 + 4^2 > 4^2$, the first two triples represent obtuse triangles but the third does not. Thus there are **2** such triangles.

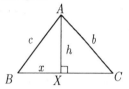

11-7 We approach this just as we did the similar example involving obtuse triangles. Drawing altitude AX, we let $BX = x$, so $CX = a - x$. From right triangle AXC, we have $b^2 = h^2 + (a - x)^2$. From right triangle AXB, we have $h^2 = c^2 - x^2$. Thus $b^2 = (c^2 - x^2) + (a - x)^2 = a^2 + c^2 - 2ax$. Since ax is a positive quantity, $b^2 = a^2 + c^2 - 2ax$ implies $b^2 < a^2 + c^2$. Since we have placed no restrictions on the side lengths (i.e., we have not mandated which is largest, a, b, or c), this proves that in an acute triangle, the sum of the squares of any two sides exceeds the square of the third.

11-8 From the Pythagorean Theorem, the top of the ladder was originally $\sqrt{25^2 - 7^2} = 24$ feet from the base. After sliding, it is 20 feet from the base, so the foot of the ladder is $\sqrt{25^2 - 20^2} = 15$ feet from the base of the wall. Thus the foot of the ladder slid **8** feet.

11-9 The legs are in ratio $3 : 4$. Thus we know the sides have ratio $3 : 4 : 5$. Since the legs are $3(3\sqrt{3})$ and $4(3\sqrt{2})$, the hypotenuse is $5(3\sqrt{2}) = \mathbf{15\sqrt{2}}$.

11-10 Since the ratio of the given leg to the hypotenuse is $49 : 175 = 7 : 25$, we recall the Pythagorean triple $7 : 24 : 25$. Since one leg is $7(7)$ and the hypotenuse is $25(7)$, the other leg is $24(7) = \mathbf{168}$.

11-11 Recall from our discussion of "if and only if" that this proof actually requires two parts. (If you don't understand why, read the discussion of "if and only if" in the chapter entitled "Prove It!") First, if $AB \perp CO$ in the diagram, then since $BO = AO$ as radii of the same circle, $\triangle AXO \cong \triangle BXO$ by HL congruency for right triangles (since $XO = XO$). Thus $AX = XB$ and the radius bisects the chord if it is perpendicular to the chord.

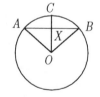

Second, to prove the "only if" part, we show that if the chord is bisected by the radius, it is perpendicular to the radius. If $AX = XB$, then by SSS congruency, $\triangle AXO \cong \triangle BXO$. Thus $\angle AXO = \angle BXO$. Since these two angles also form a line, their sum is 180°. Thus they are both 90° and the radius and chord are perpendicular.

11-12 Let O be the center of the circle. To show that $\overset{\frown}{AB} = \overset{\frown}{CD}$, we must show that $\angle AOB = \angle COD$. Since these central angles are equal to the arc measures, this will be sufficient to show the arcs are equal. Since OA, OB, OC, and OD are all radii of circle O, they are equal. Since we are also given $AB = CD$, we have $\triangle AOB \cong \triangle COD$ by SSS. Thus $\angle AOB = \angle COD$.

11-13 Since $\overset{\frown}{AB} = \overset{\frown}{CD}$, we know that $\angle AOB = \angle COD$. Thus by SAS we have $\triangle AOB \cong \triangle COD$ (remember that sides of these triangles are radii of the circle). Thus $AB = CD$.

11-14 Since $AB = AC$ and $AX = AX$, by HL for right triangles we have $\triangle AXB \cong \triangle AXC$. Thus $\angle B = \angle C$.

11-15 In an isosceles triangle, the altitude from the vertex is also a median, an angle bisector, and the perpendicular bisector of the base. This is all a result of the triangle congruency $\triangle AXC \cong \triangle AXB$ proven in the previous exercise (for example, since $\angle CAX = \angle BAX$, AX is an angle bisector). Thus the points described in the problem all lie on this segment.

For the equilateral triangle, the altitude from each vertex is also a median, a perpendicular bisector, and an angle bisector, because each vertex of an equilateral triangle can be thought of as the "vertex" of an isosceles triangle. Thus if we draw all the medians, angle bisectors, etc. of an equilateral triangle, we will actually only draw one line from each vertex, and the intersection of these lines is the orthocenter, the centroid, the incenter, and the circumcenter of the triangle.

11-16 First, $\triangle EUM$ is a right triangle, so we can eliminate all triangles which are not necessarily right. This eliminates triangles ABM and ABU. Second, we eliminate all right triangles whose acute angles do not necessarily equal those of $\triangle EUM$. This eliminates triangles EFC and FMC, leaving $\triangle \boldsymbol{EFA}$. To see that $\triangle EFA$ is right, note that $\angle EAF$ is inscribed in a semicircle and is therefore right. Since $\angle AEF = \angle UEM$, the two triangles are similar by AA.

11-17 Since $AM/AB = AN/AC = 1/2$ and $\angle MAN = \angle BAC$, we have $\triangle MAN \sim \triangle BAC$ by SAS similarity. Thus $MN/BC = 1/2$, and $MN = \boldsymbol{3}$.

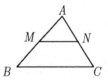

11-18 We are given three parallel lines, so we know there are equal angles, and hence similar triangles, all over the place. We will use these similarities to determine OZ, then IZ, and then take $OI = IZ - OZ$. First, by AA Similarity, $\triangle OID \sim \triangle OAP \sim \triangle OZT$. Angles of these triangles are equal due to vertical, corresponding, and alternate interior angles. Thus $OA/OZ = AP/TZ = 16/7$, and $OA = (16/7)(OZ)$. Since $OZ + AO = AZ = 46$, we have $OA = 32$ and $OZ = 14$. Also, from AA similarity we have $\triangle ZIE \sim \triangle ZAP$. Since $ZE/ZP = 1/2$, we find $ZI/ZA = 1/2$ and $ZI = ZA/2 = 23$. Thus $OI = ZI - OZ = \boldsymbol{9}$.

11-19 From the parallel lines, we look for similar triangles involving the side lengths x, y, and z. Since $\triangle AFB \sim \triangle CFD$, we have $z/x = DF/BF$. Since $\triangle CBD \sim \triangle EBF$, we have $z/y = BD/BF$. Since $BD + DF = BF$, we can combine these equalities as $z/x + z/y = DF/BF + BD/BF = BF/BF = 1$. Dividing by z gives $1/x + 1/y = 1/z$.

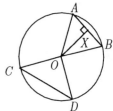

11-20 Since $\angle COD = 90°$ and $OC = OD$, $\triangle COD$ is an isosceles right triangle with hypotenuse CD. Thus $CD = OC\sqrt{2} = 6\sqrt{2}$. To determine AB in isosceles triangle AOB, we draw altitude OX, dividing the triangle into two 30°-60°-90° triangles as shown. Thus $AX = AO/2 = 3 = BX$, so $AB = 6$ and $\triangle AOB$ is equilateral. Thus $CD - AB = \mathbf{6\sqrt{2} - 6}$.

11-21 Since $\sin\theta = \cos(90° - \theta)$, we have $\sin 3x = \cos(90° - 3x) = \cos 7x$. Thus $90° - 3x = 7x$ and $x = \mathbf{9°}$.

11-22 Since $\sec B = 4$, we have $BC/AB = 4$. Thus $BC = 4(AB) = 24$. From the Pythagorean Theorem we find $AC = \sqrt{BC^2 - AB^2} = \mathbf{6\sqrt{15}}$.

11-23 Drawing the altitude of an equilateral triangle forms a 30°-60°-90° triangle, such that the altitude is opposite the 60° angle and a side of the equilateral triangle is the hypotenuse. Letting the side length of the equilateral be x, we have $x/12 = 2/\sqrt{3}$, so $x = 8\sqrt{3}$. Thus the area is $(8\sqrt{3})(12)/2 = \mathbf{48\sqrt{3}}$.

11-24 The proof for the case where the altitude is drawn from the vertex of the obtuse angle is the same as that for the acute triangle. For an altitude from the vertex of an acute angle, consider the diagram. The area of $\triangle ABC$ is the difference between the areas of $\triangle ACX$ and $\triangle ABX$. Hence,

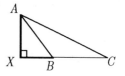

$$[ABC] = [ACX] - [ABX] = (CX)(AX)/2 - (BX)(AX)/2$$
$$= (CX - BX)(AX)/2 = (BC)(AX)/2.$$

11-25 The circle is the incircle of $\triangle ABC$ because it is tangent to all three sides of the triangle. Since the semiperimeter of the triangle is 25 and the area is 100, we have $25r = 100$, so the radius of the circle is 4. Thus the area of the circle is $(4^2)\pi = \mathbf{16\pi}$.

11-26 Drawing the radii to each of the vertices, we form 8 congruent triangles. The angle of each at the center of the circle is $360°/8 = 45°$. The sides of each of these angles have length 1, as they are radii of the circle. Hence the area of each small triangle is $[1(1)(\sin 45°)]/2 = \sqrt{2}/4$, and the area covered by all eight triangles is $8(\sqrt{2}/4) = \mathbf{2\sqrt{2}}$.

Solutions to Problems

167. Since $\angle ADM = \angle DCA$ and $\angle DAC = \angle DAM$, we have $\triangle ADM \sim \triangle ACD$ by AA similarity. Thus $AD/AM = AC/AD$, or $AD^2 = (AC)(AM)$.

168. In order for three numbers to be side lengths of a scalene triangle with perimeter less than thirteen, the three numbers must be distinct (scalene), the sum of the smallest two must be greater than the third (Triangle Inequality), and their sum must be less than 13. The only triples which satisfy these restrictions are $(2, 4, 5)$; $(3, 4, 5)$; and $(2, 3, 4)$. Thus there are **3** such triangles.

169. From the Angle Bisector Theorem, BD divides AC in the ratio BA/BC. We are given in the problem that AC is the shortest side in a triangle whose sides have ratio $2:3:4$. Thus the remaining two sides have ratio $3/4$. If we let the longer segment of AC have length x and the shorter y, we have $y/x = 3/4$. Thus $y = 3x/4$. Since AC has length 10, $x + 3x/4 = 10$, so $x = 40/7$. Thus the length of the longer segment of AC is **40/7**.

170. As discussed earlier in the chapter, the altitude, median, and angle bisector drawn from the vertex of an isosceles triangle are all the same line. When these lines are drawn from the base angles, however, they are all different lines unless the triangle is equilateral. Since we are given that the triangle is not equilateral, we have 3 lines from each base angle and just one from the vertex angle, for a total of **7** lines.

171. Since BC is the median to the hypotenuse of a right triangle, it is equal to half the hypotenuse as shown in the diagram. Since we are also given $AB = BC$, we have $AB = BC = AC = CD$, so $\triangle ABC$ is equilateral and $\angle DAB = \mathbf{60°}$.

172. The two given sides of the right triangle are in the ratio $6:7$. If they are the legs of the triangle, then the sides together are in the ratio $6:7:\sqrt{6^2+7^2} = 6:7:\sqrt{85}$. If one of the given sides is a leg and the other the hypotenuse, the sides have ratio $\sqrt{7^2-6^2}:6:7 = \sqrt{13}:6:7$. If the former is true, the third side has length $11\sqrt{85}$ since the first two sides have lengths $11(6)$ and $11(7)$. If the latter is true, the third side has length $11\sqrt{13}$. Since $\sqrt{13} < 4$, $11\sqrt{13} < 44$. Thus, since the third side is greater than 50, it must be $11\sqrt{85}$ and the desired answer is $11 + 85 = \mathbf{96}$.

173. Since the area of the triangle is half the product of an altitude and the side to which it is drawn, the product of the altitude and the side to which it is drawn is the same for all three sides. Thus the shortest altitude is drawn to the longest side and the longest altitude to the shortest side. Letting x be the longest and y the shortest altitude, we have $40x = 80y$, so $y = x/2$ and the shortest altitude is half the longest. Thus $K = \mathbf{1/2}$.

174. Let $DC = x$. Thus $BC = x$ and $AC = 3 - \sqrt{3} + x$. Since $\triangle ADC$ is a $30°$-$60°$-$90°$ triangle, we have $DC/AC = 1/\sqrt{3}$. Thus $x/(3 - \sqrt{3} + x) = 1/\sqrt{3}$, so $x\sqrt{3} = 3 - \sqrt{3} + x$. Therefore $x = (3 - \sqrt{3})/(\sqrt{3} - 1) = \sqrt{3}$. Thus $[BCD] = (BC)(CD)/2 = \mathbf{3/2}$.

175. The intersection of the perpendicular bisectors of the sides of a triangle is the circumcenter of the triangle. Since two of the perpendicular bisectors (shown in the diagram) intersect at O, a point on the third side of the triangle, O must be the circumcenter of the triangle. Since the center of the triangle is on AC, AC is a diameter of the circle. Angle B is then an angle inscribed in a semicircle and hence $\angle B = 90°$.

176. Since the problem involves an inequality, we think of the triangle inequality, $a < b+c$, where a, b, and c are the sides of the triangle. Since the inequality in the problem involves altitudes, we must relate the sides in the triangle inequality to altitudes. This can best be done through area since $ah_a = bh_b = ch_c = 2K$, where K is the area of the triangle. Hence, $a < b + c$ becomes $2K/h_a < 2K/h_b + 2K/h_c$. Dividing this by $2K$ gives the desired

$1/h_a < 1/h_b + 1/h_c$.

177. Since $\sin A = 7/25$, we have $BC/AB = 7/25$. Thus if $AB = x$, then $BC = 7x/25$. From the Pythagorean Theorem (or if you remember the Pythagorean triple 7-24-25), we find $AC = 24x/25$. Thus $\sin B = AC/AB = \mathbf{24/25}$, $\cos A = AC/AB = \mathbf{24/25}$, $\cot A = AC/BC = \mathbf{24/7}$, and $\csc B = AB/AC = \mathbf{25/24}$.

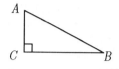

178. Since we are given the altitude to the hypotenuse, we can find the area of the triangle if we can determine AB. Since $\angle CMH = 30°$ in right triangle CHM, we have $CM = 2(CH) = 8$. Since the median to the hypotenuse of a right triangle equals half the hypotenuse, the hypotenuse has length $2(CM) = 16$. Thus $[ABC] = (AB)(CH)/2 = \mathbf{32}$.

179. Since $\triangle ABC$ is divided into three regions of equal area by WX and YZ, we have $[AYZ] = 2[ABC]/3$. Since $WX \parallel YZ \parallel BC$, $\triangle AYZ \sim \triangle ABC$. Thus $[AYZ]/[ABC] = (YZ/BC)^2$. Since this ratio of areas is 2/3, we find $YZ = BC\sqrt{2/3} = \mathbf{5\sqrt{6}}$.

180. Let the centers of the circles be W and Z and the common external tangent meet the circles at X and Y. Since the radius of a circle is perpendicular to a tangent at the point of tangency, we have $WX \perp XY$ and $YZ \perp XY$. Since $\angle WXY = \angle ZYD$, we find $WX \parallel YZ$

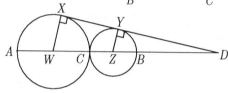

and $\triangle WXD \sim \triangle ZYD$. Let the radius of the smaller circle be x, so the radius of the larger is $3x$. Since $DZ/ZY = DW/WX$, we have $(DB + x)/x = (DB + 5x)/3x$. Thus $(DB + x)/(DB + 5x) = 1/3$. Rearranging, we find that $DB = x$, so DB equals the radius of the smaller circle.

181. Since $CD = BC/2$, we have $AD^2 = AC^2 + CD^2 = AC^2 + BC^2/4$ from the Pythagorean Theorem. Similarly, $BE^2 = BC^2 + AC^2/4$. Also, from applying the Pythagorean Theorem to $\triangle ABC$ we have $AC^2 + BC^2 = AB^2$. If a right triangle is made with leg lengths AD and BE, the hypotenuse will have length $\sqrt{AD^2 + BE^2} = \sqrt{(5/4)(AC^2 + BC^2)} = \mathbf{AB\sqrt{5}/2}$.

182. Since $\triangle ABC$ is equilateral, median CM is also an altitude. Since $\angle CBM = 60°$, we know that $\triangle NMB$ is a $30°$-$60°$-$90°$ triangle. Thus $BN = BM/2$. Since BM is half side AB, we have $BN = (AB/2)/2 = AB/4 = BC/4$. Thus $4BN = BC$.

183. Since $AB = 1$, $AD - BD = 1$. Dividing by CD gives $AD/CD - BD/CD = 1/CD$. The two ratios on the left of this equation can be expressed as trigonometric functions of α and β. Since $AD/CD = \cot\alpha$ and $BD/CD = \cot\beta$, we have $\cot\alpha - \cot\beta = 1/CD$. Thus $CD = 1/(\cot\alpha - \cot\beta)$.

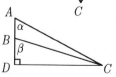

184. Segments BD and BE are angle bisectors of $\triangle ABE$ and $\triangle BCD$, respectively. Thus applying the Angle Bisector Theorem to these yields $AD/DE = AB/BE$ and

$DE/EC = BD/BC$. Multiplying these two equations gives the desired $AD/EC = (AB)(BD)/(BE)(BC)$.

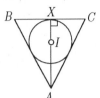

185. Angle bisector AX, which passes through the incenter I, is also an altitude and a median. Thus $CX = BC/2 = 4$ and from applying the Pythagorean Theorem to $\triangle AXC$ we find $AX = 3$. Thus $[ABC] = (BC)(AX)/2 = 12$. Since the perimeter of ABC is 18, we can determine the inradius IX from $[ABC] = rs = 9r$. Thus $r = 4/3$. Thus $AI = AX - IX = 3 - 4/3 = \mathbf{5/3}$.

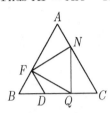

186. First, we draw FD, where D is the midpoint of BQ. Thus $BD = BQ/2 = (2BC/3)/2 = BC/3$. Hence, $BD = BF = BC/3$. Thus from SAS similarity, we have $\triangle BDF \sim \triangle BCA$ and $\triangle BDF$ is equilateral. Since BDF is equilateral, we find $FD = BD = BQ/2$. Since the median from F to BQ is half the side to which it is drawn, $\angle BFQ$ must be a right angle, as must $\angle NQC$ and $\angle FNA$. Since $\angle B = 60°$, $\angle BQF = 30°$. Similarly, $\angle AFN = \angle QNC = 30°$. Thus $\angle NFQ = 180° - \angle AFN - \angle QFB = 60°$. Similarly, $\angle FNQ = \angle NQF = 60°$. Thus $\triangle FQN$ is equilateral.

187. Let the median and altitude of $\triangle ABC$ be AM and AH, respectively. Thus the area of the triangle can be given in two ways: $[ABC] = (AH)(AM) = (AH)(BC)/2$. Thus $AM = BC/2$ and the median is half the side to which it is drawn, so the triangle is right.

188. Since HM is a median to the hypotenuse of right triangle AHC, we have $MH = AM = MC$. Thus $\triangle MHC$ is isosceles and $\angle MHC = \angle C = \mathbf{30°}$.

189. As we showed in a previous problem, $1/h_a < 1/h_b + 1/h_c$. Thus if we let the third altitude be x, we must have $1/x < 1/4 + 1/12$, so $1/x < 1/3$ and $x > 3$. Also, x must satisfy both $1/4 < 1/x + 1/12$ and $1/12 < 1/x + 1/4$. The first yields $x < 6$ and the second $x > -6$ or $x > 0$. Thus we must have $3 < x < 6$, so the largest possible integer value of x is **5**. Note that we must examine all three inequalities to determine the maximum value of x because x must satisfy all three of them.

190. Let the legs of the right triangle be a and b. Thus median AD is the hypotenuse of a right triangle with legs b and $a/2$ and has length $\sqrt{b^2 + a^2/4}$. Similarly, the second median has length $\sqrt{a^2 + b^2/4}$. Since we are given these two median lengths, we have

$$\sqrt{a^2/4 + b^2} = 5$$
$$\sqrt{a^2 + b^2/4} = \sqrt{40}.$$

We seek $\sqrt{a^2 + b^2}$, the length of the hypotenuse of the original triangle. If we square each of the above equations and add the results, we have $(5/4)(a^2 + b^2) = 65$. Thus $\sqrt{a^2 + b^2} = \sqrt{52} = \mathbf{2\sqrt{13}}$.

191. If we interpret $\angle x$ as $\angle A$ of right triangle ABC, with right angle at C, and $2ab$ and $a^2 - b^2$ as the sides BC and AC, respectively, we have $\sin x = \sin A = BC/AB$. From the Pythagorean Theorem we find $AB = \sqrt{(2ab)^2 + (a^2 - b^2)^2} = \sqrt{a^4 + 2a^2b^2 + b^4} = a^2 + b^2$. Thus $\sin x = \boldsymbol{2ab/(a^2 + b^2)}$.

192. Draw $FX \perp BC$. By AA similarity, $\triangle FXB \sim$ $\triangle ACB$. Since $BF/BA = 1/2$, we have $BX/BC =$ $FX/AC = 1/2$. Thus if $AC = x$, then $FX = x/2$, $BC = 3x$, and $BX = 3x/2$. Thus $EX = BX - BE =$ $3x/2 - x = x/2 = FX$. Also, $XD = BD - BX = x/2 = FX$, so FX is a median of $\triangle DEF$ and has length half the side to which it is drawn. This implies that $\angle F = 90°$. From SAS, $\triangle FXD \cong \triangle FXE$, so $FD = FE$ and DEF is an isosceles right triangle.

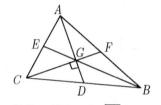

193. As the centroid, G divides each median in the ratio $2 : 1$, so $CG/GF = BG/GE = AG/GD = 2/1$. Since $AD = 9$, we have $AG = 6$ and $GD = 3$. Since D is the midpoint of BC, $CD = BC/2 = 5$. From right triangle CGD, we have $CG = 4$. From right triangle AGC, we have $AC = \sqrt{4^2 + 6^2} = 2\sqrt{13}$. Since EG is a median to the hypotenuse of $\triangle AGC$, its measure is $AC/2 = \sqrt{13}$. Since $BG/GE = 2/1$, $BG = 2\sqrt{13}$. Then $BE = EG + GB = \boldsymbol{3\sqrt{13}}$.

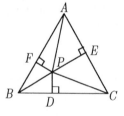

194. If we connect the chosen point P to the vertices as shown, we form 3 triangles. The perpendicular segments from P to the sides are altitudes of these three triangles. We then find $[ABC]$ as the sum of the areas of the three smaller triangles: $[ABC] = (AB)(FP)/2 + (BC)(PD)/2 + (AC)(EP)/2 = (AB)(PD + PE + PF)/2$. Since the area of $\triangle ABC$ also equals $(AB)h_c/2$, where h_c is the altitude of $\triangle ABC$, we have $(AB)h_c/2 = (AB)(PD + PE + PF)/2$, so $h_c = PD + PE + PF$.

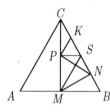

195. Draw segments SP and SM. Since $BS/BC = 1/2 = BM/BA$, by SAS similarity we have $\triangle MSB \sim \triangle ACB$. Hence $\triangle MSB$ is an equilateral triangle. Since MN is a median of an equilateral triangle, it is also an altitude; thus $\angle MNB = 90°$. Now, since $CP/CM = CS/CB$, we have $\triangle PCS \sim \triangle MCB$ by SAS similarity. Thus $SP = BM/2 = AB/4 = SK = SN$. Hence, SP is a median of $\triangle KPN$ which is half KN, so $\angle KPN = 90°$.

196. If $\angle A$ is obtuse, we have $b^2 = h^2 + x^2$ and $a^2 = h^2 + (c+x)^2$ (first diagram). Since $(c + x)^2 > c^2$, we find $a^2 > b^2$. If $\angle A$ is acute we draw altitude CX. Since $\angle A > \angle B$, we have $\sin A > \sin B$. (Why?) Thus $h/b > h/a$, so $a > b$, or $BC > AC$, as desired. The converse of this relation is also true; that is, if $BC > AC$, then $\angle A > \angle B$.

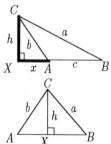

Chapter 12

Quadrilaterals

Solutions to Exercises

12-1 The median has length equal to the average of the bases. Since the area of the trapezoid is the product of the altitude and the median, the area is $3(6) = \mathbf{18}$.

12-2 In trapezoid $ABCD$ with $AB \parallel CD$, we always have $\angle A + \angle D = 180°$ and $\angle B + \angle C = 180°$. Thus, if one angle of the trapezoid is $20°$, no matter which angle it is there must be another with measure $180° - 20° = \mathbf{160°}$.

12-3 Since opposite angles of a parallelogram are equal, the angle included between the given sides is $30°$. Thus, the area of the parallelogram is $3(6)\sin 30° = \mathbf{9}$.

12-4 Since $EFGH$ is a parallelogram, we can draw YZ through X so that it is perpendicular to both EF and HG. Since $EX = GX$, $\angle YFX = \angle XHZ$, and $\angle XZH = \angle XYF$, we have $\triangle XYF \cong \triangle XZH$. Thus, $XZ = YX$. Since $[EFGH] = (YZ)(EF)$, we have $8(YZ) = 56$. Thus, $YZ = 7$ and $XY = YZ/2 = \mathbf{7/2}$.

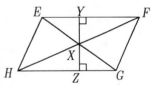

12-5 Since all the sides of a rhombus are equal, we have $3x + 2 = x + 7$, so $x = 5/2$ and each side has length $19/2$. Thus the perimeter is $4(19/2) = \mathbf{38}$.

12-6 Since $ABCD$ is a rhombus, $AC \perp BD$. Since it is also a parallelogram, the diagonals bisect each other. Thus, since $BD = 10$, $BE = 5$. Since $AB = 17$ the Pythagorean Theorem gives $AE = \sqrt{289 - 25} = 2\sqrt{66}$. Since AE is half the diagonal AC, $AC = \mathbf{4\sqrt{66}}$.

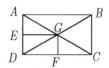

12-7 Drawing GE and GF perpendicular to sides AD and CD, respectively, we see that $\triangle ADC \sim \triangle GFC$ from AA similarity ($\angle ACD = \angle GCF$ and $\angle ADC = \angle GFC$). Since G is the midpoint of AC, we have $GC = AC/2$, so $GF = AD/2$. Similarly, $CD = 2(GE)$. Thus, the dimensions of rectangle $ABCD$ are double the distances from the center, G, of the rectangle to the sides. The dimensions are then 10 and 6. Thus, the area of the rectangle is **60**.

12-8 Since $\angle ACD = 30°$ in right triangle ACD, we find $AD = AC/2 = 4$ and $CD = AD\sqrt{3} = 4\sqrt{3}$. Thus, the perimeter of the rectangle is $2(4 + 4\sqrt{3}) = \mathbf{8 + 8\sqrt{3}}$.

12-9 Since a square is also a rectangle, the diagonals are equal. Since a square is also a rhombus, the area of a square is half the product of the diagonals. Hence, the area of the square is $(8)(8)/2 = \mathbf{32}$.

12-10 Since $AE = 2(EB)$ and $AB = AE + EB = 6$, we have $EB = 2$. Similarly, $FD = 2$. If we draw $FG \perp AB$, we form rectangle $AGFD$. Thus, $AG = FD = 2$ and $GF = AD = 6$. Hence $EG = AB - EB - AG = 2$. Applying the Pythagorean Theorem to $\triangle EGF$ yields $EF = \sqrt{4 + 36} = \mathbf{2\sqrt{10}}$.

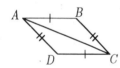

12-11 From SAS, $\triangle ABC \cong \triangle CDA$. Thus $\angle BCA = \angle CAD$, so $BC \parallel AD$. Since $\angle BAC = \angle DCA$, we have $AB \parallel CD$. Thus $ABCD$ is a parallelogram.

12-12 We wish to show that $AD = CB$. We start by drawing altitudes DF and CE, which are equal because $CD \parallel AB$. Thus $\triangle FAD \cong \triangle EBC$ by SA for right triangles, so $AD = CB$.

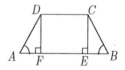

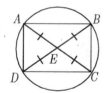

12-13 Since the diagonals are equal and bisect each other, $EA = EB = EC = ED$ as shown in the diagram. Thus, the circle with center E and radius EA passes through A, B, C, and D. Since AE and EC are radii of the circle, AC is a diameter. Similarly, BD is also a diameter. Because they are all inscribed in semicircles, the interior angles of quadrilateral $ABCD$ are all right angles. Hence $ABCD$ is a rectangle.

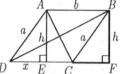

12-14 Seeing sums of squares, we think of the Pythagorean Theorem. Thus, we draw altitudes AE and BF to form right triangles to which we can apply the Pythagorean Theorem. Applying the Pythagorean Theorem to $\triangle AED$ yields $a^2 = h^2 + x^2$. Since $AD \parallel BC$, we have $\angle ADC = \angle BCF$, and since $AB \parallel CD$, we find $AE = BF$. Thus, SA for right triangles gives us $\triangle BFC \cong \triangle AED$. Applying the Pythagorean Theorem to triangles AEC and BDF yields $AC^2 = h^2 + (b - x)^2$ and $BD^2 = h^2 + (b + x)^2$. Thus, the sum of the squares of the sides is $2(a^2 + b^2) = 2h^2 + 2x^2 + 2b^2$

and the sum of the squares of the diagonals is $AC^2 + BD^2 = 2h^2 + 2b^2 + 2x^2 - 2bx + 2bx = 2h^2 + 2b^2 + 2x^2$. Hence the sum of the squares of the sides of a parallelogram equals the sum of the squares of the diagonals.

12-15 Extend median BM past M to D such that $MD = MB$. Since AC and BD bisect each other, $ABCD$ is a parallelogram. Thus, the sum of the squares of its sides equal the sum of the squares of the diagonals, or $2(AB^2 + CB^2) = AC^2 + BD^2$. Thus, $BD^2 = 73$ and $BM = BD/2 = \sqrt{73}/2$.

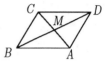

Solutions to Problems

197. We find the area of $ABCD$ by adding the areas of $\triangle ACD$ and $\triangle ABC$. Thus,

$$\begin{aligned}[ABCD] &= [ACD] + [ABC] = (AC)(ED)/2 + (AC)(BE)/2 \\ &= (AC)(ED + BE)/2 = (AC)(BD)/2.\end{aligned}$$

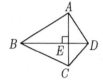

Thus, the area of $ABCD$ is half the product of its diagonals.

198. Rhombus $ABCD$ is inscribed in circle O. Segments BD and AC are diameters of circle O (since they bisect each other and are perpendicular) and hence are equal. Thus, the second diameter has length $8x$. The rhombus in question is a square.

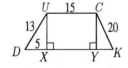

199. From right triangle DUX we have $UX = 12$. Since CY is also an altitude of the trapezoid, it has length 12. Thus, from $\triangle CYK$ we find $YK = 16$. Hence,

$$\begin{aligned}[DUCK] &= [DUX] + [CYK] + [UCYX] = (5)(12)/2 + (15)(12) + (12)(16)/2 \\ &= 30 + 180 + 96 = \mathbf{306}.\end{aligned}$$

200. The diagonals of rhombus $ABCD$ bisect each other, so $BE = 12$. Applying the Pythagorean Theorem to $\triangle ABE$ gives $AE = 5$ since $AB = 13$. Thus, the diagonals are 24 and 10, and the area of $ABCD$ is **120**.

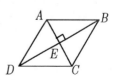

201. Let the width be w. The length is then $3w - 1$. Applying the Pythagorean Theorem yields $w^2 + (3w - 1)^2 = 37^2$, so $(w - 12)(5w + 57) = 0$. Thus, $w = 12$ and the length is 35, so the perimeter is $2(47) = \mathbf{94}$.

202. We first draw altitudes AY and BZ. Since $ABZY$ is a rectangle, we have $YZ = AB = 5$. From isosceles right triangle BZC, we find $BZ = ZC = BC/\sqrt{2} = 3$. Thus $AY = 3$. Since AYD is a 30°-60°-90° triangle, we have $DY = AY/\sqrt{3} = \sqrt{3}$; thus $DC = DY + YZ + ZC = \mathbf{8 + \sqrt{3}}$.

203. Since E and H are midpoints of the sides of $\triangle ABD$, we have $EH \parallel BD$. Similarly, $FG \parallel BD$. Since $BD \perp AC$, AC is perpendicular to both EH and FG. In a similar manner, EF and HG are parallel to AC and hence perpendicular to BD, EH, and FG. Thus, $EFGH$ is a rectangle.

204. Let the width of the picture be w, so that the length of the picture is $3w$. The width of the picture with frame is $w + 8$, since 4 inches are added to each side of the picture. The length with frame is similarly $3w + 8$. Thus the perimeter with frame is $2(4w + 16) = 8w + 32 = 96$. Hence, $w = 8$ and the length of the picture is **24**.

205. We find the areas of $AMED$ and $MBCE$ as trapezoids: $[AMED] = (18)(12+x)/2$ and $[BMEC] = (18)(12+24-x)/2$. Since $[AMED] = 2[BMEC]$, we have $12+x = 72-2x$, so $x = \mathbf{20}$.

206. Since the shown radii are perpendicular to CD, when we draw AE parallel to CD we form a rectangle. We can determine the length of AE from applying the Pythagorean Theorem to $\triangle AEB$. Hypotenuse AB is the sum of the radii of the two circles, or 19. Since $AECD$ is a rectangle, we have $EC = AD = 8$, so $EB = BC - EC = 3$. Thus $AE = \sqrt{361 - 9} = \mathbf{4\sqrt{22}} = CD$, the length of the common external tangent.

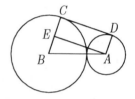

207. We find the length of AB by finding the length of median GH in two ways, as the average of the bases and the sum of segments GE, EF, and FH. Letting $AB = x$, we find $GH = (97 + x)/2$. Also, since $CF/CA = CH/CB = 1/2$, by SAS similarity we have $\triangle ABC \sim \triangle FHC$. Thus $FH = x/2$; similarly, $EG = x/2$, so $GH = x/2 + 3 + x/2 = x + 3$. Setting our expressions for GH equal, we have $3 + x = (97 + x)/2$, so $x = \mathbf{91}$.

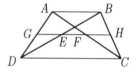

208. By AA similarity, we have $\triangle AEB \sim \triangle CED$, since $\angle EAB = \angle ECD$ and $\angle EBA = \angle EDC$ as these are pairs of alternate interior angles. Thus $EA/EC = AB/CD = 2$. Hence, $AC = EC + EA = 3EC = 11$, so $EC = \mathbf{11/3}$.

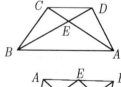

209. Since E and H are midpoints of sides AB and AD of $\triangle ABD$, we have $AE/AB = AH/AD = 1/2$. By SAS similarity, we find $\triangle AEH \sim \triangle ABD$; thus $\angle AEH = \angle ABD$ and $EH \parallel BD$. Similarly, we can show $FG \parallel BD$. Thus, $FG \parallel EH$. In the same manner, we can show $EF \parallel HG$. Since the opposite sides of quadrilateral $EFGH$ are parallel, $EFGH$ is a parallelogram.

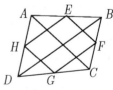

210. Let the side length of $EFGH$ be x. Since $\triangle BHE$ and $\triangle GDF$ are isosceles right triangles, we have $GD = GF = EH = BH = x$. Thus, $BD = BH + HG + GD = 3x$. Since

BD is a diagonal of a square of side length 1, $BD = \sqrt{2}$. Thus, $3x = \sqrt{2}$ and $x = \sqrt{2}/3$. The area of $[EFGH]$ is then $x^2 = \mathbf{2/9}$.

211. The squares of sides suggest the Pythagorean Theorem. Using the Pythagorean Theorem to express the squares of the sides of $ABCD$ in terms of the distances from E to the vertices, we have $AB^2 + CD^2 = (AE^2 + EB^2) + (EC^2 + ED^2) = (AE^2 + ED^2) + (BE^2 + EC^2) = AD^2 + BC^2$.

212. Seeing the squares, we think of the Pythagorean Theorem. In fact, if we could find a right triangle with legs AC and BD and hypotenuse $(AB + CD)$, we would have the desired relation. To form a triangle with sides AC and BD, we draw BE such that $BE \parallel AC$. Thus, $ABEC$ is a parallelogram, and since $AC \perp BD$,

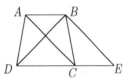

we have $BE \perp BD$. Thus, $\triangle BDE$ is a right triangle. Since $ABEC$ is a parallelogram, $BE = AC$ and $CE = AB$. Thus, the hypotenuse of $\triangle BDE$, DE, equals $CD + AB$. Finally, applying the Pythagorean Theorem, we have $BD^2 + BE^2 = BD^2 + AC^2 = (AB + CD)^2$.

213. Draw BE such that $BE \parallel AD$. Since $AB \parallel ED$, $ABED$ is a parallelogram, so $\angle ABE = \angle D$ and $DE = AB = b$. Since $\angle ABC = 2\angle D$, we have $\angle EBC = \angle ABC - \angle ABE = \angle D$. Since $AD \parallel BE$, we know $\angle D = \angle BEC$, so $\angle EBC = \angle BEC$. Thus, $EC = BC = a$. Finally, $DC = DE + EC = \mathbf{a + b}$.

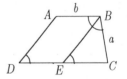

214. Since PQ and BF are perpendicular to AF, we have $PQ \parallel BD$. Thus, $\angle APT = \angle ABD = \angle BAC$, and $\triangle APT$ is isosceles with $AT = TP$. Since $\angle ATQ = \angle PTR$, we find $\triangle PTR \cong \triangle ATQ$ by SA for right triangles. Thus, $AQ = PR$. Since the interior angles of $PQFS$ are all right angles, $PQFS$ is a rectangle, so $PS = QF$. Combining these results, we have $PS + PR = AQ + QF = \mathbf{AF}$.

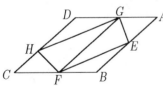

215. $EFHG$ is *not* a parallelogram! Drawing diagonal FG, we divide $EFHG$ into two triangles. Since $AG = FB$ and $AG \parallel FB$, we have $FG \parallel AB$ (try to prove this rigorously). Thus, $AGFB$ and $DGFC$ are parallelograms. Let the distance between AB and GF be x. Then $[ABFG] = x(FG)$ and $[EGF] = x(FG)/2$, so $[EGF] = [AGFB]/2$. Similarly, $[HGF] = [DGFC]/2$. Thus, $[EFHG] = [EFG] + [HFG] = ([DGFC] + [AGFB])/2 = [ABCD]/2 = \mathbf{5}$.

216. Since $AD = BC$, $\angle ADC = \angle BCD$, and $DC = DC$, we have $\triangle ACD \cong \triangle BDC$ by SAS congruency. Thus $\triangle EDC$ is an isosceles right triangle, so $\triangle ABE$ is also an isosceles right triangle. We draw altitude XY through E. Since $EY = EY$ and $\angle EDY = \angle YCE$, we find $\triangle EDY \cong \triangle ECY$, so $DY = YC$ and EY is the median to the

hypotenuse of $\triangle EDC$. Thus, $EY = CD/2$. Similarly, $EX = AB/2$, and $XY = EX + EY = (AB + CD)/2$.

217. Since the circumcenter of a triangle lies on each of the perpendicular bisectors of the sides of the triangle, P and S both lie on the perpendicular bisector of AE. Thus, $PS \perp AC$. Similarly, $QR \perp AC$. Since PS and QR are perpendicular to the same line, they are parallel. Similarly, we can show $PQ \perp BD$ and $SR \perp BD$, so $PQ \parallel SR$. The opposite sides of $PQRS$ are parallel, so $PQRS$ is a parallelogram.

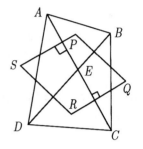

Chapter 13

Polygons

Solutions to Exercises

13-1 A regular polygon with interior angle measure $162°$ has exterior angle measure $18°$. Thus $360°/n = 18°$, so $n = \mathbf{20}$ sides.

13-2 To show that $ACEG$ is a square we must show that all its sides are equal and all its angles are equal. Since the octagon is regular, all its sides are equal, as are all its angles. Thus by SAS congruency we have $\triangle ABC \cong \triangle CDE \cong \triangle EFG \cong \triangle GHA$. Hence, the sides of $ACEG$ are all equal. Since ABC is isosceles and $\angle B = 135°$, we find $\angle BCA = 45/2 = 22.5°$; similarly, $\angle DCE = 22.5°$. Since $\angle BCD = 135°$, we have $\angle ACE = 135° - 2(22.5°) = 90°$. Similarly, all the angles of $ACEG$ are right. Thus $ACEG$ is a square.

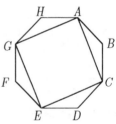

13-3 Since $\triangle ABF$ is isosceles and $\angle FAB = 120°$, we know $\angle ABF = 30°$. Since $\angle ABY = 120°$, we find $\angle FBY = 90°$. Similarly, $\angle BFX = 90°$. Since XY is a diameter of the circle, it is perpendicular to BC and EF at Y and X. Thus $FBYX$ is a rectangle and $XY = FB = 8\sqrt{3}$. The radius of the circle is $\mathbf{4\sqrt{3}}$.

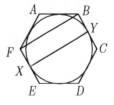

Solutions to Problems

218. The number of diagonals in a polygon with 100 sides is $100(100 - 3)/2 = \mathbf{4850}$.

219. Since $\triangle CDE$ is isosceles, we have $\angle DCE = 30°$, so $\angle ECB = 90°$. Segment BE bisects $\angle B$ because the hexagon is regular, so $\angle CBE = 60°$. Since $BC = 6$, we have $CE = 6\sqrt{3}$. Thus $[BCE] = (6)(6\sqrt{3})/2 = \mathbf{18\sqrt{3}}$.

220. Let the two smaller angles have measure x, so the larger angles have measure $3x$. Thus, the sum of the measures of the angles is $2(x) + 6(3x) = 20x$. The sum of the interior angles of any octagon is $180(8 - 2) = 1080$. Thus $20x = 1080$, so $x = 54$. Hence the larger angles each have measure $3(54) = \mathbf{162°}$.

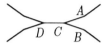

221. Since the polygon is 20-sided, we have $\angle ACD = \angle DCB = 180° - 360°/20 = 162°$. Since $\angle ACD + \angle DCB + \angle ACB = 360°$, we find $\angle ACB = \mathbf{36°}$.

222. Since the area of an equilateral triangle with side length s is $s^2\sqrt{3}/4$, we have $s^2\sqrt{3}/4 = 2$, so $s^2 = 8/\sqrt{3}$. Since the perimeters of the two figures are equal and the hexagon has twice as many sides, the side length of the hexagon is half that of the triangle, or $s/2$. Since the hexagon is made up of 6 equilateral triangles with side length $s/2$, it has area $6[(s/2)^2\sqrt{3}/4] = 3s^2\sqrt{3}/8 = (3\sqrt{3}/8)(8/\sqrt{3}) = \mathbf{3}$.

223. Since $\triangle FBC$ is isosceles and $\angle BFC = 360° - \angle DCF - \angle BFE - \angle EFC = 120°$, we find $\angle FCB = \angle FBC = 30°$. Since $\angle ABF = \angle CDF = 60°$, we have $\angle ABC = \angle DCB = 90°$. Similarly, the other two angles of $ABCD$ are also right; thus $ABCD$ is a rectangle. Let $EF = x$. Since the longest diagonal of a regular hexagon is twice the length of a side, we have $AB = CD = 2x$. Drawing EX and FY as shown, we find $\triangle EXA \cong \triangle EXD$. Thus $\angle XEA = \angle XED = 60°$, so $EX = EA/2 = x/2$ and $AX = x\sqrt{3}/2$. Hence $AD = BC = x\sqrt{3}$. Finally, the perimeter of $ABCD$ in terms of x is $x(4 + 2\sqrt{3}) = 44 + 22\sqrt{3} = 11(4 + 2\sqrt{3})$, so $x = \mathbf{11}$.

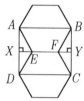

224. In the diagram, AB is a side of the dodecagon and O is the center of the dodecagon. Since a dodecagon has 12 sides, 12 such triangles comprise the polygon. Thus AO and OB are radii of the circumscribed circle. Since this circle has circumference 12π, it has radius 6. We can now find the area of $\triangle ABO$ as $[(AO)(BO)\sin\angle AOB]/2$. Since there are 12 such triangles about O, we have $\angle AOB = 360/12 = 30°$, and $[AOB] = 9$. Thus the area of the dodecagon is $(9)(12) = \mathbf{108}$.

225. In the diagram, OB is a radius of the circumcircle and OX is a radius of the incircle. Since $\triangle OXB$ is a 30°-60°-90° triangle, we have $OX/OB = \sqrt{3}/2$. Since all circles are similar to each other, the ratio of the area of the incircle to the area of the circumcircle equals the square of the ratio of the radii of the two circles. Thus the desired ratio is $(\sqrt{3}/2)^2 = \mathbf{3/4}$.

226. Let x be the exterior angle measure. Thus the interior angle measure is $7.5x$ and $x + 7.5x = 180$, so $x = 360/17$. Thus there are $360/(360/17) = 17$ sides and the sum of the interior angles is $180(17 - 2) = \mathbf{2700°}$. The polygon is not necessarily regular because the sides are not necessarily all equal.

227. First, we find the number of sides the polygon has. A polygon with n sides has $n(n - 3)/2$ diagonals. Setting this equal to 20, we find that the polygon has 8 sides. In the diagram, AB is a side of the octagon and O is the center of the circumscribed circle. Thus OA and OB are radii; let their length be r. Since there are 8 such triangles about O, we have $\angle AOB = 360°/8 = 45°$ and the area of the octagon is $8[(r^2)\sin 45°]/2 = 2r^2\sqrt{2}$. Thus $2r^2\sqrt{2} = 144\sqrt{2}$ and $r = 6\sqrt{2}$. Hence the area of the circle is $\mathbf{72\pi}$.

228. We must first determine which diagonals are greater than the 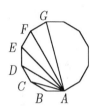 radius of the circle and less than the diameter. Diagonals such as AC are equal in length to the radius. This can be seen by noting that $ACEG\cdots$ is a regular hexagon, and the sides of a regular hexagon are equal in length to the radius of the circumscribed circle. (Why?) Diagonals such as AG are diameters of the the circle. This leaves us with diagonals like AD, AE, and AF, which are longer than AC and shorter than AG. From each vertex there are 6 such diagonals, for a total of $6(12) = 72$. However, we have counted each diagonal twice, once for each endpoint of the diagonal. Hence, there are actually $72/2 = \mathbf{36}$ diagonals longer than the radius of the circle and less than the diameter.

229. Since the polygon is regular, we have $AB = BC$ and 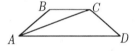 $\angle ABC = \angle BCD = x$. Thus, $\triangle ABC$ is isosceles and $\angle BCA = (180° - x)/2$. Since $\angle BCD = \angle BCA + \angle ACD = x$, we find $(180° - x)/2 + 120° = x$, so $x = 140°$. Thus, the exterior angles of the polygon each have measure $180° - 140° = 40°$ and the polygon has $360°/40° = \mathbf{9}$ sides.

230. Since 15 and 49 are opposite each other, there are $49 - 15 - 1 = 33$ vertices of the polygon on either side of the diameter drawn connecting vertices 15 and 49. For example, on one side, we have vertices 16 through 48, a total of 33 vertices. Thus, there are the vertices on either side of the diameter plus those on the diameter for a total of $2(33) + 2 = \mathbf{68}$ vertices on the circle.

 231. The grazing region is the area enclosed by the arc and the sides of the polygon AB and BC. We determine the area of this region by subtracting the proportion of the circle which is inside the polygon from 1, leaving the proportion of the circle which is outside the polygon. The ratio of the region of the circle inside the polygon to the whole circle is the ratio $\angle ABC : 360°$. Since $\angle ABC = 180(n-2)/n$, the grazing region is $1 - [(180(n-2)/n)/360] = (n+2)/2n$ of the entire circle. Hence, the area of the grazing region is $\boldsymbol{\pi r^2(n+2)/2n}$.

232. Let there be n sides in the polygon. The obtuse angles must be less than 180° and the $n - 3$ acute angles must each be less than 90°. Hence, the sum of the angles, $180(n-2)$, is less than $3(180) + 90(n-3)$. Thus we have $180(n-2) < 540 + 90n - 270$, or $n < 7$. Hence, the maximum number of sides is **6**.

233. If Alice starts at A and heads toward B, after 5 kilometers she'll be at X. As we have shown in several problems, $\angle ACD = 90°$ since the hexagon is regular. Since in going from A to C, Alice has traveled 4 km, we have $CX = 1$. We determine AC by drawing BI, separating $\triangle ABC$ into two 30°-60°-90° triangles, so $IC = AI = \sqrt{3}$. Thus, $AC = 2\sqrt{3}$ and $AX = \sqrt{1^2 + (2\sqrt{3})^2} = \sqrt{13}$.

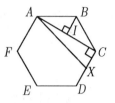

234. Since the last angle is between 0° and 180°, the sum of the angles, $180(n-2)$, is between 2190 and 2370. Thus, $2190 < 180(n-2) < 2370$. Treating these inequalities separately gives $85 < 6n$ and $6n < 91$. The only integer satisfying these is **15**.

235. Let the desired sum be x. We look for polygons containing the numbered angles. By adding the angles in triangles AWC, EVB, DZA, CYE, and BXD, we add each of the numbered angles twice and also the angles of pentagon $VWXYZ$ once. A pentagon contains $3(180) = 540°$, and 5 triangles contain $5(180) = 900°$. Thus, we have $2x + 540° = 900°$, so $x = \mathbf{180°}$. We could also have determined the desired sum by adding the external angles of $VWXYZ$ and using the Exterior Angle Theorem on the aforementioned triangles.

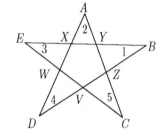

Chapter 14

Angle Chasing

Solutions to Problems

236. Since $\triangle ABC$ is isosceles, we have $\angle A = \angle ABC = 57°$. Thus, $\angle ACB = 180° - 2(57°) = 66°$. Thus, in right triangle BEC we have $\angle EBC = 90° - 66° = 24°$. Since $\triangle BDC$ is isosceles, we find $\angle D = \angle DCB$. Thus $\angle D + \angle DCB + \angle DBC = 2\angle D + 24° = 180°$, and $\angle D = \mathbf{78°}$.

237. Even though it is a concave quadrilateral, the sum of the angles of $ADBC$ is $360°$. Reflex angle BDA of $ADBC$ has measure $360° - w$. Thus $x + y + z + (360° - w) = 360°$, so $\boldsymbol{x = w - y - z}$.

238. In $\triangle AFD$, $\angle AFD + \angle FDA + \angle FAD = \angle AFD + 2x + 2y = 180°$. Thus $\angle AFD = 180° - 2(x+y)$, so we must determine $(x+y)$. From quadrilateral $ABCD$ we have $\angle B + \angle C + 3x + 3y = 360°$, so $x + y = (360° - 110° - 100°)/3 = 50°$. Thus $\angle AFD = 180° - 2(50°) = \mathbf{80°}$.

239. Since $AD = AB = AE$, $\triangle ADE$ is isosceles. Since $\angle DAE = \angle DAB + \angle BAE = 90° + 60° = 150°$, we find $\angle ADE = \angle AED = \mathbf{15°}$.

240. Since $\angle R = 36°$ and it is an inscribed angle, we have $\overset{\frown}{SV} = 2(36°) = 72°$. As an angle between two secants, $\angle T = (\overset{\frown}{RU} - \overset{\frown}{VS})/2$. Thus, $2\angle T = \overset{\frown}{RU} - 72°$ and $\overset{\frown}{RU} = 156°$. Finally, we have $\angle RQV = (\overset{\frown}{RV} + \overset{\frown}{US})/2 = (360° - 156° - 72°)/2 = \mathbf{66°}$.

241. Since $\angle CFB + \angle CFD = 180°$, we have $\angle CFB = 70°$. From right triangle CBF, $\angle FCB = 20°$. Since CE is an angle bisector, we know $\angle FCD = \angle FCB = 20°$. Thus, from $\triangle FCD$, we get $\angle FDC = 180° - 110° - 20° = \mathbf{50°}$.

242. Let $\angle B = x$. Since $\triangle BQP$ is isosceles, we find $\angle QPB = \angle QBP = x$ and by the Exterior Angle Theorem, we have $\angle AQP = 2x$. Since $\triangle QAP$ is isosceles, we find $\angle QAP = 2x$ and $\angle QPA = 180° - 4x$. Thus, $\angle CPA = 180° - \angle QPA - \angle QPB = 3x$. Since $\triangle PAC$ is isosceles, we have $\angle PCA = 3x$. Since $\triangle ABC$ is isosceles, we find $\angle BAC = \angle PCA = 3x$. Thus, summing the angles of $\triangle ABC$ gives us $x + 3x + 3x = 180°$, so $x = \angle B = \mathbf{25\frac{5}{7}}°$

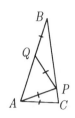

243. Draw segment OC. Since $\overarc{CD} = 60°$, we have $\angle COD = 60°$ and $\angle CAD = 60°/2 = 30°$. The Exterior Angle Theorem gives $\angle ACO + \angle CAO = \angle COD$, so $\angle ACO = 30°$. Since $\angle CBO + \angle ABO = 180°$, we have $\angle OBC = 120°$. Thus, $\angle BOC = 180° - 30° - 120° = 30°$, so $\triangle OBC$ is isosceles and $BC = OB = \mathbf{5}$.

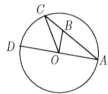

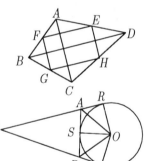

244. As shown in a prior problem, $\angle AEB = 15°$. Similarly, $\angle CED = 15°$, so $\angle BED = \angle BEC - \angle DEC = \mathbf{45°}$.

245. From the Exterior Angle Theorem we get $m = x + y$ and $n = a + b$. Adding these yields the desired $a + b + m = x + y + n$.

246. Since $AF/AB = AE/AD = 1/2$ and $\angle FAE = \angle BAD$, we have $\triangle ABD \sim \triangle AFE$. Thus, $\angle AEF = \angle ADB$, so $EF \parallel BD$. Similarly, $AC \parallel FG$. Since $EFGH$ is a rectangle, we have $EF \perp FG$. Since $AC \parallel FG$ we find $AC \perp EF$, and since $BD \parallel EF$ we find $BD \perp AC$, so $ABCD$ is orthodiagonal.

247. Since $\angle APB$ is formed by two tangents, its measure is half the difference of major arc RT and minor arc RST.

Letting $\overarc{RST} = x$, we have $(360 - x - x)/2 = 40$, so $x = 140$. Now, we prove that AO and OB are bisectors of angles ROS and SOT, respectively. We draw radii OR and OT. Since $AR = AS$, $AO = AO$, and $OR = OS$, we have $\triangle RAO \cong \triangle SAO$ by SSS congruency. Thus, $\angle ROA = \angle SOA$ and AO is an angle bisector. Similarly, $\angle BOS = \angle BOT$. Thus, $\angle AOB = \angle AOS + \angle SOB$ is half of $\angle ROT$. Since $\angle ROT = \overarc{RST} = 140°$, we find $\angle AOB = \mathbf{70°}$.

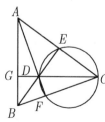

248. Since angles DEC and DFC are inscribed in semicircles, they are both right angles. Since two of the three lines from the vertices of $\triangle ABC$ through D are altitudes ($BE \perp AC$ and $AF \perp BC$), the third, CG, must also be an altitude. Thus, $\angle DGA = 90°$.

Since $\angle EAD = 40°$ and is half the difference between arcs $\overarc{ED}$ and $\overarc{FC}$, we have $\overarc{FC} - \overarc{ED} = 2\angle EAD$, so $\overarc{FC} = 120°$. As an inscribed angle, we know $\angle CDF = \overarc{FC}/2 = 60°$, so $\angle ADG = 60°$

and $\angle DAB = 90 - \angle ADG = \mathbf{30°}$.

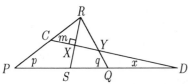

249. Since RS is an angle bisector, we have $\angle XRC = \angle XRY$. Thus, by SA for right triangles, we find $\triangle RXC \cong \triangle RXY$. Hence $\angle DYQ = \angle RYX = \angle RCX = m$. Applying the Exterior Angle Theorem to $\triangle CDP$ and $\triangle YQD$, we get $m = p + x$ and $q = m + x$. Eliminating x from these by subtracting the two equations, we find $m - q = p - m$, so $m = (p + q)/2$.

250. We wish to relate the small arcs to each other by relating them to equal angles in the diagram. Thus we draw AC, CE, and AE, forming many inscribed angles. Since $BC \parallel AD$, we have $\angle CAD = \angle ACB$. Since $\angle CAD = \overset{\frown}{CD}/2$ and $\angle ACB = \overset{\frown}{AB}/2$ and these two angles are equal, the arcs must also be equal. Similarly, we can show $\overset{\frown}{AB} = \overset{\frown}{CD} = \overset{\frown}{EF} = y$ and $\overset{\frown}{AF} = \overset{\frown}{BC} = \overset{\frown}{DE} = x$ as shown. Since the sum of the arcs is a circle, $3x + 3y = 360°$, so $x + y = \overset{\frown}{AB} + \overset{\frown}{DE} = \mathbf{120°}$.

251. Connect the points of tangency to the centers of the circles, points C and D, as shown. Since $\angle PAC = \angle PBD = 90°$, $\angle BDR = b$, and $\angle ACR = a$, we have $\angle APB = 540° - 180° - a - b$ from pentagon $APBDC$. Thus, $\angle APB = 360° - a - b$. Since a and c together make a semi-circle, as do b and d, we have $a + b + c + d = 360°$. Hence $a + b = 360° - c - d$ and $\angle APB = c + d$. [Special thanks to Lauren Williams for this clever solution.]

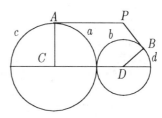

Chapter 15

Areas

Solutions to Problems

252. Since ABC is a right triangle, we draw hypotenuse AC, which has length 5. Since $AC^2 + CD^2 = AD^2$, we know $\triangle ACD$ is a right triangle. Hence, $[ABCD] = [ABC] + [ACD] = (3)(4)/2 + (5)(12)/2 = \mathbf{36}$.

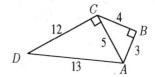

253. The quadrilateral is described as a rhombus with one right angle; hence it is a square. We find the area of the figure by summing the areas of the square and the two right triangles. The square has area 625. The right triangle which shares a side with the square has legs 15 and $\sqrt{25^2 - 15^2} = 20$, so it has area 150. Finally, the last right triangle has legs 15 and 8 (you should be familiar with the Pythagorean triple 8-15-17), and thus has area 60. The total area of the figure is $625 + 150 + 60 = \mathbf{835}$.

254. Let the radius of the circle be r. Since a side of the square equals AE, the square has side length $2r$ and hence area $4r^2$. To find the area of the triangle, we must find a side of the triangle. Thus we draw radius OC to a vertex of the triangle. Triangle OCD is a 30°-60°-90° triangle because OC is an angle bisector of $\angle ACB$ (any line through a vertex and the center of an equilateral triangle is an angle bisector). Thus $\angle OCD = 30°$, $OD = r/2$, and $CD = r\sqrt{3}/2$. Thus $CB = 2CD = r\sqrt{3}$ and $[ABC] = (r\sqrt{3})^2\sqrt{3}/4 = 3r^2\sqrt{3}/4$. Hence the ratio of the area of the triangle to that of the square is $(3r^2\sqrt{3}/4)/4r^2 = \mathbf{3\sqrt{3}/16}$.

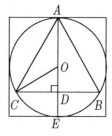

255. Let the radius of the circle be r and a side of the square be
$2s$. Thus $OC = s$ and $CB = 2s$. From right triangle OCB we have
$r^2 = 5s^2$. Since the area of the small square is 8, we find $(2s)^2 = 8$, so
$s^2 = 2$. Thus $r^2 = 10$. We see in the diagram that the diagonal of the
square inscribed in the circle is a diameter of the circle. Since a square
is a rhombus, its area can be found as half the product of its diagonals.
The square in question has diagonals of length $2r = 2\sqrt{10}$, so the area is $(2\sqrt{10})^2/2 = \mathbf{20}$.

256. Triangle AEF is similar to $\triangle ABC$ and its sides are half those of ABC. Thus
$[AEF] = [ABC]/4$. Similarly, $[DEF] = [BDF] = [DEC] = [ABC]/4$. Since the inner
shaded triangle is formed by connecting the midpoints of equilateral triangle DEF, it is
similar to $\triangle DEF$ and has sides $1/2$ the length of the sides of $\triangle DEF$. Thus its area is
$[DEF]/4$, or $([ABC]/4)/4 = [ABC]/16$. Thus the sum of the shaded areas, S, is the sum
$[ABC]/4 + [ABC]/4 + [ABC]/4 + [ABC]/16 = 13[ABC]/16$. Thus the ratio of the shaded
area to $[ABC]$ is $\mathbf{13/16}$.

257. The rectangle in the figure is the shed. The potential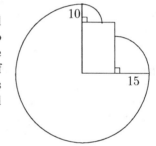
grazing area is given by the $3/4$ circle of radius 30 and the two
quarter circles of radius 10 and 15. These quarter circles are
part of the grazing area because when the cow rounds a corner of
the shed, she has the remaining length of her leash which allows
her to graze the additional quarter circular areas. Thus her total
grazing area is $(3/4)(30^2\pi) + (15^2\pi + 10^2\pi)/4 = \mathbf{3025\pi/4}$.

258. Let side CD of the rectangle be x. Thus the rectangle has area $3ax$. The triangle has
base $AE = 2a$ and altitude to that base $CD = x$. Thus the triangle has area $(2a)(x)/2 = ax$,
so the ratio of the area of the triangle to that of the rectangle is $ax/3ax = \mathbf{1/3}$.

259. One side of the triangle must be the diameter of the semicircle. Why? Given any
triangle ABC with vertex A furthest from the diameter, compare the area of ABC to that
formed by A and the endpoints of the diameter. Thus we have one side of the triangle and
we must now maximize the altitude to that side. The furthest a point on the semicircle can
be from the diameter is the radius of the semicircle, so r is the maximum altitude. Thus
the largest possible area is $r(2r)/2 = \mathbf{r^2}$.

260. Since the two hexagons are regular, they are similar. Thus we need only to find the
ratio of sides to determine the ratio of areas. We note that a side of the smaller hexagon is the
difference of a hypotenuse and the smaller leg of one of the right triangles. Since the longer
leg of the triangle has length 6, the shorter has length $6/\sqrt{3} = 2\sqrt{3}$, and the hypotenuse
has length $4\sqrt{3}$. Thus the sides of the smaller hexagon have length $2\sqrt{3}$. The ratio of the
sides of the two hexagons is $2\sqrt{3}/6 = \sqrt{3}/3$, so the ratio of areas is $(\sqrt{3}/3)^2 = \mathbf{1/3}$.

261. First, we split the region into congruent right triangles XAY and ZAY. These are congruent by HL, where $AY = AY$ and $AX = AZ$ because these are both altitudes of congruent equilateral triangles ABC and ADE. Thus we just find the area of $\triangle AXY$. From $\triangle AXB$ (a 30°-60°-90° triangle), we have $AX = 2\sqrt{3}$. Thus $XD = 4 - 2\sqrt{3}$, and we can determine XY from 30°-60°-90° triangle DXY. Hence $XY = \sqrt{3}(4 - 2\sqrt{3}) = 4\sqrt{3} - 6$. Thus $[AXYZ] = 2[AXY] = 2(2\sqrt{3})(4\sqrt{3} - 6)/2 = \mathbf{24 - 12\sqrt{3}}$.

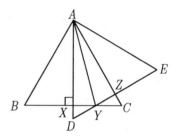

262. If we draw the diagonal of the rhombus which is also a radius of the circle, we form two equilateral triangles (because the sides of the rhombus also equal the radius of the circle). Thus the area of the rhombus is the sum of the areas of the two triangles, or $2(16^2\sqrt{3}/4) = \mathbf{128\sqrt{3}}$.

263. By drawing the two shown radii of the circle, we divide the unshaded area into a 3/4 circle of radius 2 and a square of side length 2. The shaded area is then the difference of the area of the large square and the total unshaded area, or $9^2 - [(3/4)(2^2\pi) + 2^2] = \mathbf{77 - 3\pi}$.

264. If we just add the areas of the squares, we count the region $EHCD$ twice. Thus we must subtract the area of $EHCD$ from the sum of the areas of the squares to get the area of region $ABHFGD$. To determine $[EHCD]$, we split the quadrilateral into two right triangles by drawing DH. The legs of these triangles have lengths 2 and 4 as one leg is the side of a square and the other is half the side of a square. Thus $[EHCD] = [EHD] + [CHD] = 2[(2)(4)/2] = 8$. Since the squares each have area 16, the total area of the figure is $2(16) - 8 = \mathbf{24}$.

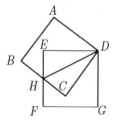

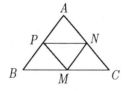

265. Since $AP/AB = AN/AC$ and $\angle PAN = \angle BAC$, we have $\triangle PAN \sim \triangle BAC$ by SAS Similarity. Since the ratio of sides in these triangles is 1/2, the ratio of areas is 1/4. Thus $[APN] = [ABC]/4$. Similarly, we can show $[BPM] = [CNM] = [ABC]/4$. To find the area of $\triangle PNM$, we must subtract the areas of the other three small triangles from that of $\triangle ABC$. Thus $[PNM] = [ABC] - 3([ABC]/4) = [ABC]/4$. Thus the four triangles formed by drawing NP, MN, and MP have equal area.

266. Let $AB = CD = l$, $BC = AD = w$, and altitude EX of $\triangle EDC$ be x. Thus EY, an altitude of $\triangle AEB$ is $w - x$. Hence $[AEB] + [CED] = l(w - x)/2 + lx/2 = lw/2$. Thus the sum of the areas of triangles AEB and EDC depends only on the length and width of the rectangle and hence is independent of where E is chosen within the rectangle.

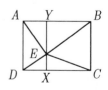

267. First we draw the hypotenuse of the right triangle with legs 12 and 16. This hypotenuse has length 20 and is a diameter of the circle (because a right angle subtends it). Drawing the radii to the other two vertices of the pentagon, we form 3 equilateral triangles of side length 10. These each have area $10^2\sqrt{3}/4 = 25\sqrt{3}$. Thus the total area of the pentagon is $12(16)/2 + 3(25\sqrt{3}) = \mathbf{96 + 75\sqrt{3}}$.

268. Since CM is a median, $AM = BM$. Since these bases are on the same line, the distance from N to each of these is the same. Hence, triangles ANM and BMN have equal bases and equal altitudes and hence have equal area. To show that $[ACN] = [BNC]$, we note that $[AMC] = [BMC]$ because $AM = MB$ and the triangles have the same altitude from C. Since $[AMN] = [BMN]$, we can subtract this from $[AMC] = [BMC]$, yielding $[AMC] - [AMN] = [BMC] - [BMN]$. These differences are equal to $[CAN]$ and $[CBN]$, respectively, so $[CAN] = [CBN]$.

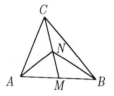

269. We will show that the area of $DEFG$ equals the area of the square formed by drawing perpendicular segments from D to the sides of the smaller square as shown. Since $\angle GDY = 90° - \angle YDE = \angle XDE$ and $DX = DY$, we have $\triangle DXE \cong \triangle DYG$ by SA congruence for right triangles. Thus $[DXE] = [DYG]$ and $[DEFG] = [DEFY] + [DGY] = [DEFY] + [DXE] = [DXFY] = (3/2)^2 = \mathbf{2.25}$.

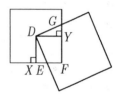

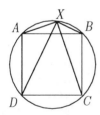

270. Let a side of the square have length $2x$ and the distance from X to AD be y. Thus the distance from X to BC is $2x - y$, as AD and BC are $2x$ apart. Hence $[XAD] + [XBC] = 2x(2x - y)/2 + 2xy/2 = 2x^2$. Hence, if we determine $2x^2$ we can solve the problem. If we let z be the distance from X to AB, we have $[XAB] = (2x)(z)/2 = xz = 1$ and $[XCD] = (2x)(z + 2x)/2 = 2x^2 + xz = 993$. Since $xz = 1$, we have $2x^2 + 1 = 993$, and $2x^2 = 992$. Thus the desired sum of areas is **992**.

271. As shown in the diagram, we could draw EC and divide $ABCDE$ into a trapezoid and a triangle, but there is a more clever approach. Whenever you see 120° or 60° angles, look for equilateral triangles. Here, we extend sides DE, AB, and DC so that they meet at X and Y. We notice that $ABCDE$ is the result of removing equilateral triangles AXE and CBY from $\triangle DEC$. Since $DC = 4$ and $CY = CB = 2$, $DY = 6$. Thus $[ABCDE] = [DXY] - [AXE] - [CBY] = (6^2\sqrt{3}/4) - 2(2^2\sqrt{3}/4) = \mathbf{7\sqrt{3}}$.

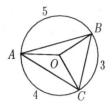

272.   Since none of the three arcs are more than half the circle, we know the triangle is acute. Thus divide the triangle into 3 pieces by drawing radii as shown. Since the circumference of the circle is 12, the radius is $6/\pi$. First, since $\overset{\frown}{BC}= 3$, we have $\angle BOC = (3/12)(360°) = 90°$. Thus $[OBC] = \frac{1}{2}(OB)(OC)\sin BOC = (6/\pi)^2/2 = 18/\pi^2$. Similarly, $[AOC] = \frac{1}{2}(OA)(OC)\sin AOC = (18/\pi^2)\sin[(4/12)(360°)] = 9\sqrt{3}/\pi^2$. Finally, $[AOB] = (18/\pi^2)\sin[(5/12)(360°)] = 9/\pi^2$. Thus the area of $\triangle ABC$ is the sum of these three, or $(27 + 9\sqrt{3})/\pi^2$.

273.   We draw AC to divide $ABCE$ into two triangles of which we can easily find the areas. In $\triangle ABC$, base $CB = 17$, and the altitude from A has length 50 since A is the center of the square. In $\triangle ACE$, $CE = 100 - x$ and the altitude from A once again has length 50. Since we are told the area of $ABCE$ is 1/5 that of the large square, we have $[ABCE] = 2000 = [ABC] + [ACE] = 425 + 25(100 - x)$. Thus $x = \mathbf{37}$.

274.   Triangles ABM and ADM have the same base, so by showing their altitudes are equal, we show their areas are equal. We draw altitudes DY and BX. Since $ABCD$ is a rectangle, we have $AD = BC$ and $\angle CAD = \angle ACB$ as alternate interior angles. Thus $\triangle BXC \cong \triangle DYA$ by SA for right triangles. From this congruence, we find $BX = DY$, so $[AMB] = [AMD]$.

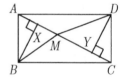

275.   Let $AF = x$. We find the area of the shaded region in terms of x by subtracting the areas of triangles BEH and FDG from square $ABCD$. Since $AF = x$, we have $EB = BH = FD = DG = 5 - x$. Thus $[FDG] = [EBH] = (5 - x)^2/2$. Since the shaded region is 5/9 that of $ABCD$, it has area 125/9. Thus $[AEHCGF] = [ABCD] - [EBH] - [FDG] = 25 - (5 - x)^2 = 125/9$. Hence, $(5 - x)^2 = 100/9$ and $x = \mathbf{5/3}$.

276.   Recall that as an example in this chapter we showed that the medians of a triangle divide a triangle into 6 triangles of equal area. Triangle ABG contains two of these triangles (if we draw the third median, it divides ABG into two triangles). Thus $\triangle ABG$ has 1/3 the area of the entire triangle. Since ABG is an isosceles right triangle (why?), we have $AG = BG = 2\sqrt{2}$, and $[ABG] = (2\sqrt{2})^2/2 = 4$. Thus the area of the whole triangle is $4(3) = \mathbf{12}$.

277.   We can find the desired area by subtracting sector DAB from the region bounded by $\overset{\frown}{AE}$, $\overset{\frown}{EB}$, and side AB. To find the latter region, we draw EA and EB. The desired region is then the sum of the areas of circular segments AE and EB and the area of $\triangle ABE$. Since the sides of ABE are radii of length 6, the triangle is equilateral, and the two circular segments span $60°/360° = 1/6$ of the circle. Since the circular segment AE has area equal to sector EBA minus the area of $\triangle EAB$, its area is $6^2\pi/6 - (6^2\sqrt{3})/4 = 6\pi - 9\sqrt{3}$. Thus the region enclosed by the two arcs and AB has area $2(6\pi - 9\sqrt{3}) + (6^2\sqrt{3}/4) =$

$12\pi - 9\sqrt{3}$. Since AD is part of the diagonal of the square, we find $\angle DAB = 45°$ and sector DAB is 1/8 of the circle. Thus the area of the sector is $6^2\pi/8 = 9\pi/2$. Finally, the desired shaded area is $12\pi - 9\sqrt{3} - 9\pi/2 = \mathbf{15\pi/2 - 9\sqrt{3}}$.

Chapter 16

The Power of Coordinates

Solutions to Exercises

16-1   We just plot the points one by one, as in the two figures.

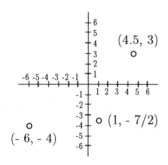

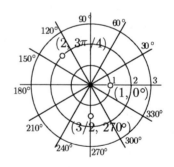

16-2   Since the quadrants go counterclockwise starting in the upper right, the lower right is quadrant **IV**.

16-3   The equation stands for all points with $\theta = 47°$; r can be anything. All the points must form the same angle with the x-axis, so they form a line as shown. You may have only drawn the half of this line which is in the first quadrant, since that is the range of possibilities with positive r. However, it turns out that negative values of r are also allowed, so we get the entire line.

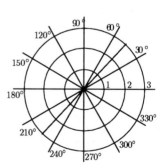

16-4   Under a reflection across the x-axis, the x-coordinate will stay the same and the y-coordinate will reverse to $-y$, as in the left-hand figure below. Similarly, r will stay the same but θ will go to $-\theta$. Under the reflection through the y-axis, the Cartesian coordinates will simply go to $(-x, y)$, but the polar coordinates do something slightly more complicated, going to $(r, \pi - \theta)$ (switching to radians to keep you on your toes), as in the right figure.

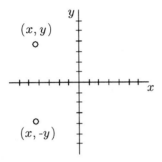 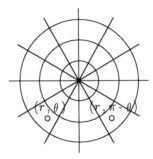

16-5   The triangle will have a right angle at the origin (do you see why?), so all we need to do is to find the lengths of the legs. The leg which lies along the x-axis starts at $(0,0)$ and ends at the x-intercept of the line, or $(4,0)$. Thus the leg has length 4. The leg which lies along the y-axis starts at $(0,0)$ and ends at the y-intercept of the line, or $(0,3)$; thus this leg has length 3. The area of the triangle is half the product of the legs, or $(3)(4)/2 = \mathbf{6}$.

16-6   You'll have to do this one on your own.

16-7   Since a horizontal line is not steep at all, we would expect it to have steepness 0. Since the line doesn't go up (or down) at all (rise = 0) when it goes over by any amount k (run = k), we have $m = 0/k = 0$, as hoped for. We might expect a vertical line to have "infinite steepness," since it goes straight up. Computing m, we find the line doesn't go over at all (run = 0) when it goes up by any amount k (rise = k), so $m = k/0$. The slope is not defined. Very loosely speaking, then, we could say that m is "infinite." (Mathematically dealing with infinity is pretty complicated, so don't take this too seriously.)

16-8   We start with the slope-intercept form $y = mx + b$. We immediately have $y = mx + 3$, by substituting in the y-intercept. We can then find m by substituting in the other point we have, $(-4, 0)$. Putting -4 for x and 0 for y yields $0 = -4m + 3$; solving yields $m = \frac{3}{4}$. Putting this back in the equation leaves us with the line equation $y = \frac{3}{4}x + 3$. (Do you see why the line could also be written $3x - 4y = -12$?)

16-9   This is just like the last one. Substituting in the y-intercept yields $y = mx - 6$. Substituting the x-intercept $(2, 0)$ into this and solving gives $m = 3$. The line is thus $y = 3x - 6$.

16-10   This is just a matter of substituting back in. The point (p_1, q_1) yields

$$(q_1 - q_2)p_1 - (p_1 - p_2)q_1 = p_2q_1 - p_1q_2,$$

which is $0 = 0$ after expanding and canceling. Isn't that nice? The second point, (p_2, q_2), yields $0 = 0$ in exactly the same way. Thus our original points are in fact on the line.

16-11 We'll start with slope-intercept form $y = mx + b$ and get rid of b. (We can leave m in the equation, since it is assumed to be given.) Substituting in the known solution (p, q) yields $q = mp + b$, so $b = q - mp$ and the equation is $y = mx + q - mp$. More revealing forms can be found by rearranging:

$$y = m(x - p) + q \qquad \text{or} \qquad m = \frac{y - q}{x - p}.$$

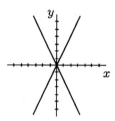

16-12 Let's take simple lines through the origin with slopes of 2 and -2: $y = 2x$ and $y = -2x$. Plotting the lines, as at right, shows that they are certainly not perpendicular.

16-13 Looks good:

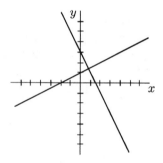

16-14 We plot these two by the methods stated in the text. The first is already in slope-intercept form, so we can use this to immediately plot the y-intercept $(0, 2)$ and the point $(1/2, -4)$. (The second point was found by following the slope, -12, over $1/2$ and down 6.) For the second, we have used the slope to follow the line. Either of these lines could just as well have been plotted by straight plug-ins; we have used slightly different methods to show that there are such shortcuts.

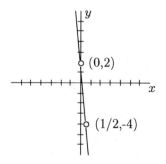

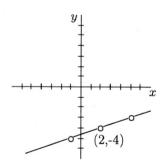

16-15 If the number had been negative, we would have the sum of two squares equaling a negative number, which never happens for real numbers. Thus there would be no circle. If the number had been zero, the circle would have had radius zero, so would be a single point at the center.

16-16 We solve the linear equations by adding twice the first equation to the second, getting

$$(2x + 2y) + (-2x + 3y) = -6 + 2.$$

Then simplifying yields $5y = -4$, or $y = -4/5$. Substituting this into the first equation yields $x = -3 + \frac{4}{5} = -\frac{11}{5}$; the solution is at $(-\mathbf{11/5}, -\mathbf{4/5})$.

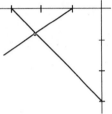

It will take a pretty careful graph to get something as precise as $(-11/5, -4/5)$, but we have tried at right. You can see that our analytic solution is correct, but it's hard to get a precise answer from the graph by itself. (On nicer systems, though, a quick graph might be much simpler than grinding through the equations.)

16-17 It is evident that two lines can intersect in either 0 points, 1 point, or (if they coincide) infinitely many points. This corresponds to the fact that a linear equation can have either 0, 1, or (if the two equations coincide) infinitely many solutions.

A line and a circle can intersect in 0, 1, or 2 points, just as a quadratic equation can have 0, 1, or 2 roots.

Two different circles can intersect in 0, 1, or 2 points. There is no correspondence to equations we have yet studied.

16-18 Since this problem asks us to prove a geometric relationship and not something about coordinates, we can choose our coordinates as we please. We thus let the vertices be $A(a, 0)$, $B(b, 0)$, and $C(0, c)$ as before. Then we know that the centroid G is given in coordinates by $((a+b)/3, c/3)$. Moreover, we have M; it is the midpoint of $\overline{BC}$, so is given by $(b/2, c/2)$. By the distance formula,

$$AG = \sqrt{[a - (a+b)/3]^2 + (c/3)^2} \quad = \quad \sqrt{[(2a-b)/3]^2 + (c/3)^2}$$
$$= \quad \sqrt{4a^2 - 4ab + b^2 + c^2}/3.$$

Using the distance formula again, we have

$$GM = \sqrt{[(a+b)/3 - b/2]^2 + [c/3 - c/2]^2} \quad = \quad \sqrt{[(2a-b)/6]^2 + (-c/6)^2}$$
$$= \quad \sqrt{4a^2 - 4ab + b^2 + c^2}/6,$$

which is half of the value we obtained for AG above.

16-19 Since we are trying to prove something about the coordinates themselves, we are not allowed to choose our coordinates as we please. We must take completely general coordinates, like (a_1, b_1), (a_2, b_2), and (a_3, b_3), and find the centroid here. Just push the equations through, finding the intersection of any two medians, and you should find that the centroid is $((a_1 + a_2 + a_3)/3, (b_1 + b_2 + b_3)/3)$.

That solution, though perfectly rigorous, is pretty tedious. After you read the chapter on transformations, you will have access to the following, more elegant proof.

Any triangle can be suitably translated such that the average of the vertices is $(0, 0)$. (Make sure that you see this.) We prove that the point we seek is the average of the coordinates in the new position, and then show that this property is *preserved* by the translation.

If the average of the vertices is at the origin, then we will let the vertices be $(2a, 2b)$, $(2c, 2d)$, and $(-2a - 2c, -2b - 2d)$, where the 2's are added just to simplify the calculation. One median goes from $(-c, -d)$ to $(2c, 2d)$, and is thus given by $y = dx/c$. Another goes from $(-a, -b)$ to $(2a, 2b)$; this one is given by $y = bx/a$. The intersection of the two medians is clearly at $(0, 0)$. Thus *after* the translation the average of the vertices coincides with the centroid; now what about *before*?

Let the vertices before the translation be (x_1, y_1), (x_2, y_2), and (x_3, y_3), with average $((x_1 + x_2 + x_3)/3, (y_1 + y_2 + y_3)/3)$. Then after a translation by (p, q), the vertices are $(x_1 + p, y_1 + q)$ etc., with average $((x_1 + x_2 + x_3)/3 + p, (y_1 + y_2 + y_3)/3 + q)$. The average of the translated vertices is the translation of the average of the untranslated vertices, or in the language of transformations, the average is **preserved** by translations. We have shown that if the centroid and average coincide after the translation (which we proved they do), then they must have coincided before the translation, and we are done. (Try hard to follow the logic here; ideas of this type are important again and again.)

As a final note, don't think it's easy to choose the translation which makes everything come out nicely. In writing this solution, I first tried translating a vertex to $(0, 0)$, which left horrible calculations to do; then I tried translating the midpoint of a side to $(0, 0)$, which was not much better. Only on the third try did I hit upon translating the average of the coordinates to $(0, 0)$, which finally did the trick. The almost calculation-free argument above is proof that thought will beat equation-pushing any day.

Solutions to Problems

278. We just plug the numbers into the distance formula to get

$$\sqrt{(2 - (-4))^2 + (12 - 10)^2} = \sqrt{6^2 + 2^2} = \sqrt{40} = \mathbf{2\sqrt{10}}.$$

279. The endpoints of the hypotenuse are $(3, 0)$ and $(0, 4)$, so its midpoint is given by $(3/2, 4/2) = (\mathbf{3/2, 2})$.

280. By the distance formula, a point (m, n) is 5 units away from $(0, 0)$ if and only if $\sqrt{m^2 + n^2} = 5$, or $m^2 + n^2 = 25$. The problem is thus one of breaking 25 down into squares of integers. Experimentation will reveal that $25 = 4^2 + 3^2$ and $25 = 5^2 + 0^2$ are the only two ways to break 25 down into two squares of nonnegative integers. These two solutions yield many more points, though: $(5, 0)$, $(0, 5)$, $(-5, 0)$, $(0, -5)$, $(3, 4)$, $(-3, 4)$, $(3, -4)$, $(-3, -4)$, and four more from the pair $(4, 3)$ with different signs. The total is **12** points.

281. A line cuts the area of a circle in half if and only if it goes through the center. (Do you see why?) The center of our circle is given by $(-12, -3)$, so we seek a line passing through $(5, 7)$ and $(-12, -3)$. The line has slope $(7 + 3)/(5 + 12) = 10/17$, so has the form $y = 10x/17 + b$. Plugging in $(5, 7)$, we can solve for b to find $b = 69/17$, so the equation of the line is

$$y = \frac{10}{17}x + \frac{69}{17}.$$

We check this answer by substituting in the other point, $(-12, -3)$, and find that it is correct. Can you put the line in standard form?

282. The centroid is the average of the vertices, or $((10 + 19 + 17)/3, (66 + 72 + 56)/3) = $ $(\mathbf{46/3}, \mathbf{194/3})$.

283. We move the constant to the other side of the circle equation and divide the entire equation by the common factor of 4, to get

$$(x^2 + 2x) + (y^2 - 4y) = 4.$$

Completing the square separately on x and y, we then have

$$(x^2 + 2x + 1) + (y^2 - 4y + 4) = 4 + 1 + 4 = 9,$$

or

$$(x + 1)^2 + (y - 2)^2 = 9,$$

so the center of the circle is $(-1, 2)$. By the distance formula, the distance from this point to $(5, 7)$ is $\sqrt{6^2 + 5^2} = \sqrt{\mathbf{61}}$.

284. The line intersects the y- and x- axes at $y = 6/b$ and $x = 6/a$ respectively, just by substituting 0 in for first x, then y. The right triangle thus has area $18/ab$, since the segments along the two axes form its legs. Setting this equal to 6, we find that $ab = \mathbf{3}$.

285. Since AB and DC are parallel, of equal length, and oriented the same way, going from D to C should be the same as going from A to B. The latter is achieved by translating by 2 in the x direction and 4 in the y. Thus the coordinates of C are $(5 + 2, 1 + 4)$, or $(\mathbf{7}, \mathbf{5})$.

286. The slope of the first line is $-\frac{1}{3}$, as can be seen from putting it in slope-intercept form. The slope of the second line is $-\frac{k}{2}$. The product of the two slopes must equal -1, so we have $\frac{k}{6} = -1$, and k is $\mathbf{-6}$.

287. To go *all* the way from the first point to the second, we must translate by $(-3, -3)$, meaning we change x by -3 and y by -3. To go two-thirds of the way, the translation is two-thirds as much, or $(-2, -2)$. The point two-thirds of the way along is thus $(2-2, 4-2)$, or $(\mathbf{0, 2})$.

288. The distance from a point to a line is always the perpendicular distance. Thus if a point is equidistant from two lines, it must lie on one of the bisectors of the angles formed by the lines. (You should be able to show that a point on an angle bisector is equidistant from the sides of the angle. You should also be able to show, for fun, that the angle bisectors of a pair of lines are perpendicular.) Thus if a point is equidistant from the axes, it must lie on one of the lines $x = y$ or $x = -y$, which bisect the right angles formed by the axes. We can easily find that $3x + 5y = 15$ intersects those two lines at $(15/8, 15/8)$ and $(-15/2, 15/2)$, points which are in quadrants I and II.

289. Since the result we are asked to prove says nothing about coordinates, we can choose our coordinates at will. We thus make our Cartesian axes be such that the vertices of the rectangle are $(a, 0)$, $(0, b)$, $(0, 0)$, and (a, b). The midpoints of both diagonals are $(a/2, b/2)$, so these diagonals must bisect each other, since they share a midpoint.

290. First we find that the line in question is given by $4x + 6y = 9$. Plugging in $(3, y)$ we have $12 + 6y = 9$, so that $y = \mathbf{-1/2}$.

291. A line bisects the area of a square if and only if it passes through the center of the square, as at right. (Why?) Thus, placing the vertices of the square at $(0, 0)$, $(s, 0)$, (s, s), and $(0, s)$, where s is the side length of the square, the lines are all those which pass through $(s/2, s/2)$. The family of lines is thus given by $(y - s/2) = m(x - s/2)$ for all m, using the point-slope form of a line which we derived earlier.

292. Since the diagonals are parallel to the coordinate axes, the vertices lie directly above and below the center of the square. The distance the vertices are from the center is half the length of a diagonal, or $\frac{1}{2}(4\sqrt{2}) = 2\sqrt{2}$. Thus the vertices are at the four points $(\mathbf{-17 \pm 2\sqrt{2}, 23 \pm 2\sqrt{2}})$, where all combinations of the signs are taken.

293. The circle is given by the equation $x^2 + y^2 = 9$. The sides of the square are given by the equations $x = 2$, $x = -2$, $y = 2$, and $y = -2$. Substituting the x-value given by the first side equation into the circle equation, we have $4 + y^2 = 9$, or $y = \pm\sqrt{5}$. Thus the $x = 2$ side of the square intersects the circle at $(2, \sqrt{5})$ and $(2, -\sqrt{5})$. By using the other three sides of the square we similarly find the points $(\mathbf{-2, \pm\sqrt{5}})$ and $(\mathbf{\pm\sqrt{5}, \pm2})$, where all combinations of the signs are taken.

Chapter 17

Power of a Point

Solutions to Exercises

17-1   We have shown in an earlier example that $CY = s - c = (a + b - c)/2$. Since IX is a radius, we have $IX \perp AC$. Similarly, $IY \perp BC$. Since $XC \perp CY$, $IXCY$ is a rectangle. Since $IX = IY$ as radii of the same circle, $IXCY$ is a square. Thus, the radius of the circle is equal to CY, or $(a + b - c)/2$.

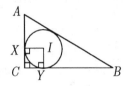

17-2   From power of point X we have $(AX)(XB) = (CX)(DX)$. Since diameter AB is perpendicular to chord CD, it bisects the chord. Thus, $DX = CX$ and $(AX)(XB) = CX^2$. Often in problems you will just be given a semicircle with a segment, like CX, perpendicular to the diameter.

Solutions to Problems

294.   Let the radius of the circle be r. Thus, $PT = 13 + r$ and $PS = 13 - r$. From power of a point, we have $(PT)(PS) = (PQ)(PR)$, so $(13 + r)(13 - r) = 9(16)$ and $r = \mathbf{5}$.

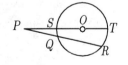

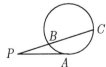

295.   Let $PB = x$. Thus, $(PB)(PC) = PA^2$ and $x(x + 20) = (10\sqrt{3})^2$, so $x^2 + 20x - 300 = 0$. Solving for x we find $x = 10$ or $x = -30$. Since x must be positive, $x = \mathbf{10}$.

296.   Since $CF = FD$, we can use power of a point to determine CD because $(CF)(FD) = CF^2 = (EF)(FB) = 6$. Thus, $CF^2 = 6$ and $CD = 2\sqrt{6}$. Since C is the midpoint of AD, we have $AD = 4\sqrt{6}$ and $AC = 2\sqrt{6}$. Letting GB be x, since $(AB)(AG) = (AC)(AD)$, we find $16(16 - x) = 48$. Thus, $x = GB = \mathbf{13}$.

297.   Since PQ and PB are tangents from a point to the same circle, we have $PQ = PB$. Similarly, $RQ = RC$ and $AB = AC$. The perimeter of $\triangle APR$ is then $AP + PR + AR = AP + PQ + QR + AR = AP + PB + RC + AR = AB + AC = 2(AB) = \mathbf{40}$.

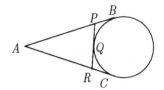

298.   As discussed in the chapter, the lengths r and s are $(8 + 13 - 17)/2 = 2$ and $(8 + 17 - 13)/2 = 6$. Thus, the desired ratio is $2 : 6 = \mathbf{1 : 3}$.

299.   Let the radius of the circle be r and $AD = x$. Since $AB = 2r$ and $AP = AD = x$, we have $PB = 2r - x$. Thus, we are asked to show $x^2 = (2r - x)(2r)$, or $4r^2 - 2xr - x^2 = 0$. Since AB is perpendicular to a diameter of the circle, it is tangent to the circle. Thus, $AB^2 = AD(AE)$. Since $AB = 2r$, $AD = x$, and $AE = x + 2r$, we have $(2r)^2 = x(x + 2r)$, so $4r^2 - 2xr - x^2 = 0$ as desired.

300.   When given the side lengths of the triangle as in this problem, you should check if the triangle is right. In this case, since $20^2 + 21^2 = 29^2$, the triangle is right. As discussed in the chapter, the radius of the incircle is $(20 + 21 - 29)/2 = 6$. Thus, it has area $\mathbf{36\pi}$.

301.   Since the problem involves tangents and secants of a circle, we think of power of a point; however, as drawn, the diagram reveals little. Thus, we 'complete' secant BE and chord FG by extending BD to E and OD to F and G. Letting $DE = x$, we determine x from $AB^2 = (BC)(BE)$, so $36 = 3(6 + x)$ and $x = 6$. Letting the radius of the circle be r, we find the radius from the power of point D: $(DF)(DG) = (DE)(DC)$. Thus, $(r - 2)(r + 2) = 18$. Thus, $r = \sqrt{\mathbf{22}}$.

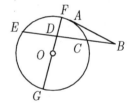

302.   As a problem at the end of the chapter on quadrilaterals, we showed that if a quadrilateral is orthodiagonal, then $AB^2 + CD^2 = BC^2 + AD^2$. In this chapter, we showed that if $ABCD$ can be circumscribed about a circle, then $AB + CD = BC + AD$. We can get the desired relation using manipulations like those we learned in our discussion of factorizations and manipulations. Squaring the second relation above gives $AB^2 + 2(AB)(CD) + CD^2 = BC^2 + 2(BC)(AD) + AD^2$. Since $AB^2 + CD^2 = BC^2 + AD^2$, we have $2(AB)(CD) = 2(BC)(AD)$, so $(AB)(CD) = (BC)(AD)$.

Chapter 18

Three Dimensional Geometry

Solutions to Exercises

18-1 Segment AC is a radius of circle C and is equal to half the width of the hole. Thus $AC = 12$. Since the hole is 8 cm deep, we know $BC = 8$. Letting the radius of the ball be x, from $\triangle OCA$ we have $x^2 = 12^2 + (x-8)^2$, so $x = \mathbf{13}$.

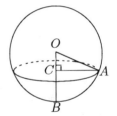

18-2 Solving $4\pi r^2 = 100$, we find that the radius of the sphere is $5/\sqrt{\pi}$. Thus the sphere has volume $4\pi(5/\sqrt{\pi})^3/3 = \mathbf{500\sqrt{\pi}/3\pi}$.

18-3 Since the diagonal has length 6, each edge has length $6/\sqrt{3} = 2\sqrt{3}$. Thus the cube has volume $(2\sqrt{3})^3 = \mathbf{24\sqrt{3}}$.

18-4 Triangles ALM, AMN, and ANL are all congruent isosceles right triangles. Since $LM = MN = NL$ as the hypotenuses of these triangles, $\triangle LMN$ is equilateral. Thus $\angle LMN = \mathbf{60°}$.

18-5 Since the dimensions of the box are even, the cubes will fit snugly in the box. Since the box has volume $4(8)(10) = 320$ and each cube has volume $2^3 = 8$, $320/8 = \mathbf{40}$ cubes are required. Note that this approach wouldn't work if one of the dimensions were odd, as the cubes would not perfectly fit the box and hence would not fill the box.

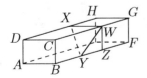

18-6 Since we are dealing with a box, we use right triangles. We draw WX parallel to HG and draw WZ parallel to CB. Thus $XH = WG = ZF = 9 - DX = 4$. Hence, $YZ = YF - ZF = 6 - 4 = 2$. Since $WZ = CB = 3$, from right triangle WZY we have $WY = \sqrt{4+9} = \sqrt{13}$. Since planes $CGFB$ and $CDHG$ are perpendicular, we find $WY \perp WX$. Since $WX = CD = AB = 4$, from right triangle XWY we have $XY = \sqrt{13 + 16} = \mathbf{\sqrt{29}}$.

18-7 Since the volume is given by $\pi r^2 h$ and $h = 5$, we have $5\pi r^2 = 45\pi$, so $r = 3$. Thus the circular faces each have area 9π and the curved surface has area $(2\pi r)h = 30\pi$. Thus the total surface area is **48π**.

18-8 In the figure, the point on the cylinder furthest from B is point C. We find BC by considering right triangle ABC. Since AB is a diameter and AC is the height, $AB = 8$ and $AC = 6$. Thus $BC = 10$.

18-9 "Unrolled", the curved surface of the cone is sector OAB, where O was the vertex of the cone and $\overset{\frown}{AB}$ was the circumference of the base. To determine the portion of entire circle O which sector OAB comprises, we recall that the length of $\overset{\frown}{AB}$ is $2\pi r$ since this arc was the circumference of the base of radius r. The circumference of the complete circle O is $2\pi l$, where l is the slant height of the cone and hence the radius of the sector. Thus the sector is $2\pi r/2\pi l = r/l$ of the entire circle. Since the circle has area πl^2, the sector has area $(\pi l^2)(r/l) = \pi r l$, so the lateral surface area of a cone with slant height l and radius r is $\pi r l$.

18-10 Let O be the center of the sphere, I the center of the base of the cone and A a point on the circumference of the cone's base. Since $OI = 3$ and $OA = 5$ (as a radius of the sphere), we have $AI = 4$. Thus the radius of the cone is 4 and the height is 3. Hence, the volume is $(16)(3)\pi/3 = \mathbf{16\pi}$.

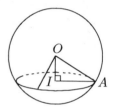

Solutions to Problems

303. Since the cube has 12 edges, each edge has length $144/12 = 12$. Thus the diagonal has length $\mathbf{12\sqrt{3}}$.

304. The cylinder with height 5 has circumference 8 and hence radius $8/2\pi = 4/\pi$. Thus it has volume $5(4/\pi)^2\pi = 80/\pi$. Similarly, the cylinder with height 8 has radius $5/2\pi$ and volume $8(5/2\pi)^2\pi = 50/\pi$. Thus the desired ratio is $(50/\pi)/(80/\pi) = \mathbf{5/8}$.

305. Let the base of the pyramid have x sides. Thus there are x base edges, x base vertices, and x edges connecting these vertices to the vertex of the pyramid, for a total of $2x$ edges. Since our pyramid has 10 edges, there are $x = 10/2 = 5$ sides in the base of the pyramid, so there are **5** triangular faces.

306. Let the cube have edge length x. Since the sides of the hexagon are the hypotenuses of isosceles right triangles whose legs are half the length of an edge of the cube, the sides have length $x\sqrt{2}/2$. Thus the area of the hexagon is $3(x\sqrt{2}/2)^2\sqrt{3}/2 = 3x^2\sqrt{3}/4$. The surface area of the cube is $6x^2$. Thus the ratio of the area of the hexagon to the area of the cube is $\mathbf{\sqrt{3}/8}$.

307. Let the edge length of the cube be x. From the given information we have $6x^2 = 2x^3$, so $x = 3$ and the diagonals of the cube have length $\mathbf{3\sqrt{3}}$.

308. Let the radius be r, the height h and the slant height l. Since the volume is 1.5 times the lateral area, we have $\pi r^2 h/3 = 1.5\pi rl$. Since the radius is half the slant height we know $l = 2r$, so $h = \sqrt{l^2 - r^2} = r\sqrt{3}$. Thus the original equation is $\pi r^3 \sqrt{3}/3 = 3\pi r^2$, so $r = \mathbf{3\sqrt{3}}$.

309. A diagonal of the cube is a diameter of the sphere. Thus if the cube has side length x, the diameter of the sphere is $x\sqrt{3}$. Thus the surface area of the sphere is $4\pi(x\sqrt{3}/2)^2 = 3\pi x^2$ and the surface area of the cube is $6x^2$. Finally, the ratio of the area of the sphere to the area of the cube is $\boldsymbol{\pi/2}$.

310. Let the dimensions of the floor be x and y. Thus for the areas of the walls we have $xh = a$ and $yh = b$. We seek the product xy. Multiplying the above equalities, we have $xyh^2 = ab$, so $xy = \mathbf{ab/h^2}$.

311. The volume of the the fluid in the box is $3(6)(12) = 216$. We seek the radius of a cylinder with height 0.1 such that the volume is 216. Hence, we have $\pi r^2(0.1) = 216$, so $r = \sqrt{2160/\pi} = \mathbf{12\sqrt{15\pi}/\pi}$.

312. Let the amount added be x. Thus $\pi(8+x)^2(3) = \pi(8^2)(3+x)$, so $192 + 48x + 3x^2 = 192 + 64x$ and $x = \mathbf{16/3}$.

313. The radius of the 'unrolled' curved surface is the slant height of the original cone, so the cone's slant height is 10. The arc of the 'unrolled' surface is the circumference of the base of the cone. Thus the circumference of the base is $2(10)\pi/2 = 10\pi$, so the radius of the cone is 5. Since the height, slant height, and radius of a cone are related by the Pythagorean Theorem, the cone has height $\sqrt{100 - 25} = \mathbf{5\sqrt{3}}$.

314. As we can see in the diagram, the sides of the tetrahedron are diagonals of the faces of the cube. Let the side length of the cube be x, so the surface area of the cube is $6x^2$ and the edge length of the tetrahedron is $x\sqrt{2}$. Since the tetrahedron has four equilateral triangle faces, the surface area of the tetrahedron is $4[(x\sqrt{2})^2\sqrt{3}/4] = 2x^2\sqrt{3}$. Thus the desired ratio is $6x^2/(2x^2\sqrt{3}) = \mathbf{\sqrt{3}}$.

315. Draw $\triangle FXB$. As half diagonal BD, we have $BX = \sqrt{2}/2$. Since $FB = 1$, from right triangle FXB we find $FX = \sqrt{1 + 1/2} = \mathbf{\sqrt{6}/2}$.

316. The cubes with no faces painted form an $(n-2)$ by $(n-2)$ by $(n-2)$ cube in the interior of each cube. Hence, there are $(n-2)^3$ cubes with no faces painted. The cubes with only one face painted form an $(n-2)$ by $(n-2)$ square in the center of each face. Since there are 6 faces, there are $6(n-2)^2$ cubes with only one face painted. Thus $(n-2)^3 = 6(n-2)^2$, so $n - 2 = 6$ and $n = \mathbf{8}$.

317. The surface area of the outside of the cube is 6 faces which are 3 by 3 squares with one 1 by 1 square omitted, for a total area of $6(9 - 1) = 48$. Inside each hole in each face are four 1 by 1 squares, for a total of $6(4) = 24$. Thus the total surface area of the figure is $48 + 24 = \mathbf{72}$.

318. First, we consider the area contributed by the eight cubes which are placed in the corners of the original cube. For these cubes, three of the faces are complete squares with area 4, while the other three faces are 2 by 2 squares with 1 by 1 squares cut out, corresponding to where these cubes are placed in the original cube. These faces have area $4 - 1 = 3$. Thus the surface area of each of these is $3(4) + 3(3) = 21$. There are eight of these, for a total area of $8(21) = 168$. The exposed area of the original cube now consists of six 3 by 3 faces with 1 by 1 squares omitted from the corners (where the unit cubes have been cut from the original cube). Thus these faces have area $9 - 4(1) = 5$. Hence, the total area is $168 + 6(5) = \mathbf{198}$.

319. Let $CH = x$. Since $\triangle DCH$ is an isosceles right triangle, we have $DC = CH = x$ and $DH = CH\sqrt{2} = x\sqrt{2}$. From $\triangle BCH$, since $\angle CHB = 30°$, we have $CB = x/\sqrt{3} = x\sqrt{3}/3$ and $BH = 2x\sqrt{3}/3$. By LL congruency for right triangles we find $\triangle BCD \cong \triangle BCH$, so $BD = BH = 2x\sqrt{3}/3$. Thus $\triangle BHD$ is isosceles. Since we seek the cosine of $\angle BHD$, we draw an altitude from B to DH. Since $\triangle BHD$ is isosceles, BX is also a median. Thus $\cos BHD = HX/BH = HD/2BH = \sqrt{2}/[2(2\sqrt{3}/3)] = \mathbf{\sqrt{6}/4}$.

320. The six squares contribute $6(4) = 24$ vertices and the 8 hexagons contribute $8(6) = 48$ vertices. Since two hexagons and one square meet at each vertex, we have counted each vertex three times among the above $24 + 48 = 72$ vertices, once for the square and once for each hexagon. Thus there are a total of $72/3 = \mathbf{24}$ distinct vertices. (Notice that our final answer matches the number of square vertices. Is this a coincidence?)

321. As we did earlier in the chapter, we find the volume of the octahedron as the volume of two pyramids with square bases. To find the length of the edges of the octahedron, we note that they are the hypotenuses of isosceles right triangles in which the legs are segments from the midpoints of the edges of the cubes to the centers of the cubes. These legs have half the length of the cube edges, or 3. Thus, the edges of the octahedron have length $3\sqrt{2}$.

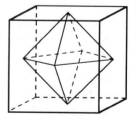

Hence, the square base has area $(3\sqrt{2})^2 = 18$ and the altitude of each pyramid, as half the diagonal of a square with side $3\sqrt{2}$, has length 3. Thus the volume of the octahedron, as two such pyramids, is $2[3(18)/3] = \mathbf{36}$. If you did not follow our method of finding the volume of the octahedron, return to the example in the chapter.

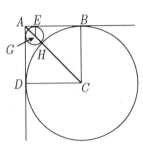

322. To solve this, we consider the cross-section perpendicular to the wall and the floor and passing through the centers of both spheres when the smaller sphere is directly "under" the larger ball. Clearly, the largest such ball will be tangent to the larger ball, so in the diagram the two circles are tangent at H. We find the radius, r, of the smaller circle by finding AC in two different ways, first as a diagonal of square $ABCD$ and second as the sum $AG + GH + HC$:

$$AC = AG + GH + HC$$
$$R\sqrt{2} = r\sqrt{2} + r + R$$

Solving for r in terms of R yields $r = R(\sqrt{2} - 1)/(\sqrt{2} + 1) = \mathbf{R(3 - 2\sqrt{2})}$.

323. We consider a cross-section of the tank passing through the vertex of the tank and the center of the base. In the diagram, G is the center of the base and F is the center of the water level. The volume of the tank is $\pi(96)(16^2)/3$. Thus the volume of the water is $\pi(96)(256)/12 = 2048\pi$. In the diagram, we see that $\triangle CFE \sim \triangle CGB$. Thus if we let r be the radius of the top level of the water and h be the height of the water, we get $r/h = 16/96 = 1/6$, so $r = h/6$. Since the

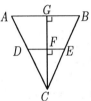

volume of the water is $2048\pi = \pi r^2 h/3 = \pi h^3/108$, we have $h^3 = 108(2048)$ and $h = \mathbf{48\sqrt[3]{2}}$.

324. Let x of the faces be hexagons. Thus $32 - x$ of the faces are pentagons. We determine x by counting the edges in the solid. The x hexagons have $6x$ edges and the pentagons have $5(32 - x) = 160 - 5x$ edges. Since each edge is shared by 2 polygons, we have counted each one twice in our above total of $6x + 160 - 5x = 160 + x$ edges. Thus there are $(160 + x)/2$ edges in the solid. Since we are told there are 90 edges, we have $(160 + x)/2 = 90$, so $x = \mathbf{20}$.

325. We draw the perpendicular segment from B to plane ACD, meeting $\triangle ACD$ at O, the center of the triangle (since $\triangle ACD$ is equilateral). Continuing segment AO to M, we note that since O is the center of equilateral triangle ACD, AM is both an altitude and a median. Hence, $MD = 3$, so $AM = 3\sqrt{3}$. Since O is the centroid of $\triangle ACD$, we have $AO : AM = 2 : 3$, so $AO = 2\sqrt{3}$. Thus from right triangle AOB we find $BO = \sqrt{36 - 12} = \mathbf{2\sqrt{6}}$.

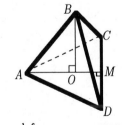

326. Consider a diagonal of the cube. It has length $\sqrt{3}$. As we travel from one corner of the cube to another along a diagonal, we go from the vertex of the cube to the center of a sphere, then to the center of the middle sphere, then to the center of a third sphere, then finally to the other vertex. The distance from the first sphere's center to the third sphere's center is four radii, or $4r$. The distance from the vertex of the cube to the first sphere's center (and from the third sphere's center to the final vertex) is $r\sqrt{3}$ because this is a diagonal of a cube with side length r (draw the radii of the sphere to the points where the sphere touches the cube). Thus in terms of r, the diagonal of the cube is $4r + 2r\sqrt{3}$, so

$4r + 2r\sqrt{3} = \sqrt{3}$ and $r = (2\sqrt{3} - 3)/2$.

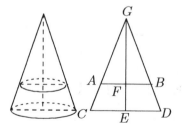

327. Shown in the figure is the cone and the plane intersecting the cone to form the desired region (called a frustum). We will find the volume of this region as the difference in the volumes of the large cone and the smaller
one formed by the new plane. The shown cross-section is
one passing through the vertex of the cone and the centers of the two circles which are the bases of the frustum.
Since $CE = EG = 6$ and $\triangle AFG \sim \triangle CEG$, we have
$AF/FG = 6/6 = 1$. Thus since $FE = 2$, we find $GF = 4 = AF$. Hence, the desired volume
is $\pi[6^2(6) - 4^2(4)]/3 = \mathbf{152\pi/3}$.

Try using this approach to develop a formula for the volume of a frustum with general height
h and base radii r_1 and r_2.

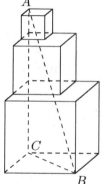

328. We find the length of AB as the hypotenuse of $\triangle ACB$. Since
$AC = 1 + 2 + 3 = 6$ and $BC = 3\sqrt{2}$, we have $AB = \sqrt{36 + 18} = 3\sqrt{6}$.
Just as $2/(1+2+3) = 1/3$ of segment AC is in the cube of edge length
2, 1/3 of AB is in the middle cube. (Make sure you see why.) Thus the
desired length is $(1/3)(3\sqrt{6}) = \mathbf{\sqrt{6}}$.

Chapter 19

Shifts, Turns, Flips, Stretches, and Squeezes

Solutions to Exercises

19-1 To get from the point $(3,4)$ to the point $(5,-3)$, we need to increase x by 2 and decrease y by 7. Thus the translation is $x \to x + 2$, $y \to y - 7$.

19-2 Every point in the plane moves the same distance under a translation. If there is a fixed point, that point moves distance 0, so all points move distance 0. Thus the only translation which has a fixed point is the trivial translation $(x', y') = (x, y)$.

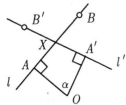

19-3 Consider the figure at left. We have drawn the perpendiculars from the center of rotation, O, to the line l and its rotation l'; the perpendiculars intersect the lines at A and A' respectively. The sum of the angles of quadrilateral $OAXA'$ is $\alpha + \angle OAX + \angle OA'X + \angle AXA' = 180° + \alpha + \angle AXA'$. Setting this equal to $360°$, the sum of the angles of any quadrilateral, we find that $\angle AXA' = 180° - \alpha$. Since angles AXB' and AXA' together make a straight line, we have $\angle AXB' + \angle AXA' = 180°$, so $\angle AXB' = 180° - \angle AXA' = 180° - (180° - \alpha) = \alpha$, as desired.

19-4 To specify a rotation, you just specify the center and angle. Here we know that the center is D, so we just need to find the angle of rotation, $\angle BDF$ at right. We can find this angle by evaluating angles CDB and EDF and subtracting them from $\angle CDE$. (Do you see why?) Since $\triangle BCD$ is isosceles, angle $CDB = (180° - \angle BCD)/2$. But $ABCDEF$ is a regular hexagon, so $\angle BCD = 120°$ as an interior angle. Thus $\angle CDB = (180° - 120°)/2 = 30°$. In exactly the same way, we can show that $\angle EDF = 30°$. All that remains is to find $\angle CDE$; but as an interior angle, $\angle CDE = 120°$.

Thus we have $\angle BDF = 120° - 30° - 30° = \mathbf{60°}$.

19-5   Let the simultaneous center of rotation and point symmetry be O. Given any point A, let A' and A'' be the images of A under the reflection and the rotation, respectively. We will show that A' and A'' are necessarily the same point. From the definition of reflection through a point, O is the midpoint of the segment connecting A to its reflected image A'. From the definition of a 180° rotation about O, the angle AOA'' is 180°, so AOA'' is a straight line. Moreover, $OA = OA''$, so that O is also the midpoint of AA''.

Thus, for any A, the image A' under reflection is the same point as the image A'' under rotation by 180°, so the transformations are the same.

 19-6   The 7-gon at left has the vertical line of symmetry shown, but no point of symmetry. Why? A point reflection would have to take each vertex A to another vertex B, while simultaneously taking B to A. Since there are seven vertices, pairing them up this way will leave one out. The only way to avoid this dilemma is if the point through which we are reflecting is one of the vertices; but it is clear that none of the vertices can be a point of symmetry. Hence there can be no point symmetry.

At right is a figure with point symmetry but no line symmetry, answering the last two questions. The point symmetry is clear, but how can we be sure that there is no line symmetry? A simple criterion can establish this. A segment AB is always parallel to its image $A'B'$ under a point symmetry, but is never parallel to its image under a line symmetry unless it is parallel or perpendicular to the line of reflection. (You should be able to prove these assertions.) In our figure, imagine we were trying to find a line of symmetry. Since a segment and its reflection are of equal length, the shortest two segments must reflect to one another. But they are parallel because they are related by a point symmetry! Thus any line of symmetry must be parallel or perpendicular to these smallest segments. We can make the same argument for each pair of segments which are related by the point symmetry: any line of symmetry has to be parallel or perpendicular to every pair. Obviously such a line cannot exist for arbitrarily oriented segments like ours.

A hexagon possesses point symmetry, but also line symmetry. Carefully figure out why the above argument doesn't make this an impossibility.

19-7   Examine the diagram at right, where we have drawn six lines of symmetry. (Make sure you see that all these lines are lines of symmetry.) We will now prove that these are *all* the lines of symmetry the hexagon possesses. Consider a fixed vertex A. Clearly a reflection across any line of symmetry must take A to some vertex of the hexagon (either to a different vertex or to itself). There must be exactly one line of symmetry which reflects A into each other vertex X. The line in question is the perpendicular bisector of $\overleftrightarrow{AX}$. (Do you see why?) That gives five lines of symmetry. What about lines of symmetry which reflect A to itself, and hence pass through A? We prove there is exactly one such line of symmetry.

Such a line must group the other five vertices into pairs (P, Q) such that P reflects to Q and Q to P. Since there are five vertices which need to be paired this way, one vertex R will be left over. Thus the reflection has to take R to itself, and thus the line of symmetry in question passes through R. The candidates for the line we are seeking are thus all the lines passing through A and another vertex R. But it is easy to see that unless R is directly opposite A, the line $\overleftrightarrow{AR}$ is not a line of symmetry of the hexagon. Thus there are exactly five lines of symmetry which reflect A into a different vertex X, and exactly one which reflects A to itself, for a total of **six** lines of symmetry.

19-8 We will prove the desired result in two steps. First, we will show that the result holds for triangles with one side parallel to the direction of distortion. This is easy: consider the two triangles at left, one a distortion of the other parallel to a side. The triangles share the same height, and the bases are in the ratio $k : 1$, so the areas are in the ratio $k : 1$ as well.

It won't always be the case that the triangle we are distorting has a side parallel to the distortion. Thus, to prove the result for a general triangle, we will show that it can be broken up into triangles which *do* have a side parallel to the distortion. A line can always be drawn through one of the vertices which is parallel to the distortion direction and crosses the interior of the triangle, as shown. Then each of the two smaller triangles into which the larger triangle is broken have a side parallel to the direction of distortion. Thus the area of each smaller triangle will change in area by a factor of k under distortion, so the larger triangle will scale in area by k as well.

Rectangles follow easily from triangles, as any rectangle can be simply broken into two triangles.

19-9 All we need to prove is that the length of a segment AB equals the length of its image segment $A'B'$. (Note that even the fact that the image of a segment is another segment, rather than some crazy curve, has to be proven at some point; this proof rests on the proof of that more fundamental fact.) We can prove this by proving that two triangles containing the desired segments are congruent.

Drawing the lines AA' and BB', we know that both are perpendicular to the reflecting line, so they are parallel. Drawing perpendiculars AX and $A'X'$ to BB', we have $AX = A'X'$ since $AA'X'X$ is a rectangle. Moreover, since A' is the image of A, the two points are equidistant from the reflecting line; since AX and $A'X'$ are parallel to the reflecting line (do you see why?), we thus have $XO = X'O$. But since B and B' are images of one another, we also have $BO = B'O$, so $BX = B'X'$. Since $\triangle ABX$ and $\triangle A'B'X'$ are right triangles, we can apply Leg-Leg congruence with $BX = B'X'$ and $AX = A'X'$. Thus $\triangle ABX \cong \triangle A'B'X'$, and consequently $AB = A'B'$, as desired.

Solutions to Problems

329. Just let O be the midpoint of AA', which always exists. Recall that a 180° rotation is the same as a reflection. Then a 180° rotation about O brings A to A' as desired.

330. We have seen in the chapter on analytic geometry that reflection across the x-axis leaves x alone and takes y to $-y$. Thus the equation becomes $x - 3y + 11 = 0$. Converting this into slope-intercept form gives $y = \frac{1}{3}x + \frac{11}{3}$. We can read off the slope and y-intercept as $\frac{1}{3}$ and $\frac{11}{3}$ respectively, and their sum is **4**.

331. The image of P_1 under a reflection through P_0 is the point P_2 such that P_0 is the midpoint of P_1P_2. Since the coordinates of the midpoint of a segment are the averages of the coordinates of the endpoints, we thus have $(0,0) = ((3 + x_2)/2, (4 + y_2)/2)$, where (x_2, y_2) are the coordinates of P_2. Solving, we find that P_2 has coordinates $(-3, -4)$.

The image of P_2 under reflection through P_1 is obtained similarly: we write $(3, 4) = ((-3 + x_3)/2, (-4 + y_3)/2)$ and solve to find $P_3 = (9, 12)$. In the same way we find that the image of P_3 under a reflection through P_2 is $P_4 = (-15, -20)$. The sum of the x- and y-coordinates of P_4 is $-15 - 20 = -\mathbf{35}$.

332. The two successive rotations by $x°$ and $y°$ are equivalent to a single rotation by $(x+y)°$. We have established that a reflection through the origin is equivalent to a rotation by 180° about the origin, so we have $x + y = \mathbf{180°}$.

333. The hard part here is figuring out how to put the question in terms that make a proof possible. In this case, the question is more approachable if we phrase it as: "Prove that each point X on AB has an image Y on CD, and that every point Y on CD is the image of some point X on AB." Do you see why this is equivalent to the original statement? To prove that segment AB rotates onto segment CD, we must show that every point lands on CD, and that we get every point on CD from some point on AB.

So consider the diagram. We first assume that X is on AB and prove that Y, the image of X, is on CD. How can we prove that Y is on the segment? The easiest way is to show that the sum of angles CYO and DYO is 180°, a straight line. Since $\angle AOC = \angle XOY$, we have $\angle AOX = \angle COY$. Since $AO = CO$ and $XO = OY$, we 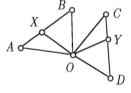 have $\triangle AOX \cong \triangle COY$. Thus, $\angle AXO = \angle CYO$ and similarly $\angle BXO = \angle DYO$. Finally, $\angle CYO + \angle DYO = \angle AXO + \angle BXO = 180°$.

But how do we know that every point Y on CD comes from some point X on AB? Just take the point X to be such that $AX/BX = CY/DY$. Since rotations preserve distances, this makes $AX = CY$. Similar triangles show us that $OX = OY$, and it is easy then to show that $\angle XOY = \angle AOC$, so that X and Y are equidistant from the center of rotation and separated by the angle of rotation. Thus the point X we have defined must have image Y, as desired.

Make sure you understand the interesting logical subtleties of this proof.

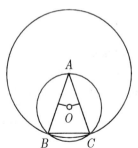

334. If you did the previous problem, you know that all you need to do to show that one segment rotates onto another is to show that the endpoints rotate onto one another. Thus, for the first rotation all we need is to rotate B about A onto C, since A stays fixed. Rotating about A, B travels along the larger circle. Since $AB = AC$, C is also on the circle, so B will come to the original position of C after some rotation around the circle. (Can you figure out what the angle of rotation is?)

For the second rotation, none of the vertices stays fixed. Thus rather than take $A \to A$, $B \to C$, we have to take $A \to C$, $B \to A$. All three vertices are the same distance from O, since O is the circumcenter. Thus, under rotations about O the vertices traverse the smaller circle above. Consider the motion of $\angle BOA$ as this rotation occurs. The angle stays fixed, but moves around the circle. Since $\angle BOA = \angle AOC$, $\angle BOA$ will at some point lie right on top of where $\angle AOC$ was before the rotation. Thus, some rotation about O maps AB to AC.

335. Remember that the angle of rotation is equal to the angle between any point, the center, and the image of the point. Since A goes to C under our rotation about O, the angle of rotation is equal to $\angle AOC$. This angle is the vertex angle of isosceles $\triangle AOC$; the base angle of the triangle is half of $\angle BAC$, or $\alpha/2$. Thus the angle of rotation is $\angle AOC = 180° - \alpha$. Since M clearly rotates to N (the image of M must be on AC and must be a distance BM from A), the angle MON is also the angle from a point to the center to the image of the point, so this also equals the rotation angle $180° - \alpha$.

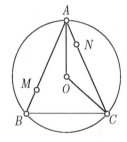

336. In reflection through a line l, the image of a point lies along a line m which passes through the point and is perpendicular to l. In our case, l is $x + 2y = 4$, so the slope of l is $-1/2$ and the slope of m, as a perpendicular, must be 2. Thus m has the form $y = 2x + b$; substituting in $(2, 2)$ yields $b = -2$, so m is $y = 2x - 2$.

The midpoint of the segment connecting $(2, 2)$ and its image is the intersection of l and m. This intersection can be found by simultaneously solving $x + 2y = 4$ and $y = 2x - 2$, to get $(8/5, 6/5)$. Since this is the midpoint of $(2, 2)$ and its image (p, q), we have $(8/5, 6/5) = ((2 + p)/2, (2 + q)/2)$, or $(p, q) = (\mathbf{6/5, 2/5})$.

337. Reflection across the line $y = x$ takes every point (p, q) to the point (q, p) with the coordinates reversed. (Can you prove this using the techniques of the previous problem?) Thus the old center, $(6, -5)$, goes to the new center $(\mathbf{-5, 6})$.

338. The equilateral triangle does not have point symmetry. Such a symmetry, if it existed, would pair two points up (reflecting one to the other and vice versa) and leave the other out. The remaining point would have to be the center of reflection. But clearly a vertex of an equilateral triangle is not the midpoint of the segment connecting the other two vertices, so the left-out vertex can't be the center.

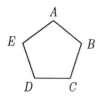

339. The angle of rotation is the smallest angle connecting a point, the center, and the image of the point. Thus our angle of rotation is $\angle AED$, which as an interior angle of a pentagon is equal to $108°$.

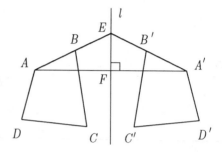

340. Since line AB is the image of line $A'B'$, the intersection point E of the lines must map to itself. Hence, point E must be on l. Since A' is the image of A, AA' is perpendicular to l. Thus, the area of $\triangle AEA'$ is equal to $(AA')(EF)/2$, where F is the intersection of AA' with l. We are given that $AA' = 10$. We can find EF from the Pythagorean Theorem on $\triangle A'EF$: $(A'E)^2 = (AF)^2 + (EF)^2$, so $(EF)^2 = 13^2 - 5^2 = 144$ and $EF = 12$. Thus $[AEA'] = (10)(12)/2 = \mathbf{60}$.

341. As was discussed in the chapter on analytic geometry, reflection across the y-axis leaves the y-coordinate alone but takes the x-coordinate to $-x$. Thus the line $y = 3x + 2$ becomes $y = 3(-x) + 2 = -3x + 2$.

342. The point $(5, 3)$ must be the midpoint of the segment from $(9, 14)$ to (a, b). Thus we have $(5, 3) = ((9 + a)/2, (14 + b)/2)$, and solving yields $(a, b) = (\mathbf{1, -8})$.

Chapter 20

A Potpourri of Geometry

Solutions to Problems

343. Since $OA \perp AP$ and $OA/OP = 1/2$, $\triangle OAP$ is a 30°-60°-90° triangle with $\angle APO = 30°$. Thus $OA/AP = 1/\sqrt{3}$, so $OA = \mathbf{5\sqrt{3}}$.

344. From the Pythagorean Theorem we have $AC = \sqrt{16 + 36} = 2\sqrt{13}$. Thus the area of the square is $AC^2 = \mathbf{52}$.

345. The sum of these arcs must be 360°. Thus $x + 40 + 2x + 20 + 2x - 20 = 360$, so $x = \mathbf{64°}$.

346. Since $\angle BAC = 90°$, BC is a diameter of the circle. Thus $BC = 8$. Since $\angle ABC = 30°$, we have $AC = BC/2 = 4$ and $AB = AC\sqrt{3} = 4\sqrt{3}$. Thus $[ABC] = (4)(4\sqrt{3})/2 = \mathbf{8\sqrt{3}}$.

347. Since triangles ABD and DBC have the same altitude (the altitude from B to AC), the areas of the triangles are equal if $AD = DC$. Hence, D is the midpoint of AC, or $([0 + 10]/2, [15 + 0]/2) = (\mathbf{5, 7.5})$.

348. By AA similarity we have $\triangle BAE \sim \triangle CAD$. Since $BE/CD = 1/4$, we find $AB/AC = 1/4$. Thus $AB = 5$. From the Pythagorean Theorem applied to triangles ABE and ACD we find $AE = 4$ and $AD = 16$. Thus $[BCDE] = [ACD] - [ABE] = (12)(16)/2 - (3)(4)/2 = \mathbf{90}$.

349. If the two circles intersect in two points, there are 2 tangents. If they are tangent, there are three tangents, and if the two circles do not intersect, there are four common tangents. Thus the possible numbers are $\mathbf{2, 3, 4}$.

350. Let the side length of the rhombus be x. Since $FEDB$ is a rhombus, we have $FE \parallel BD$. Thus $FE \parallel BC$, so $\triangle ABC \sim \triangle AFE$. Thus $FE/BC = AF/AB$, so $x/15 = (10 - x)/10$. Solving for x, we find $x = DE = \mathbf{6}$.

351. Since the trapezoid is isosceles, we have $AD = BC$ and $\angle C = \angle D$. Thus $\triangle ADC \cong \triangle BDC$ by SAS congruency. Since DE and EC are corresponding altitudes of these triangles, we have $DE = EC$, so $\triangle DEC$ is an isosceles right triangle. Since $DB = AC$ and $DE = EC$, we have $AE = EB$ and $\triangle AEB$ is also isosceles. Thus $ED = EC = 4/\sqrt{2} = 2\sqrt{2}$ and $AE = EB = 4\sqrt{2}$. Finally, $[ABCD] = [EDC] + [ECB] + [EAB] + [EAD] = 4 + 8 + 16 + 8 = \mathbf{36}$.

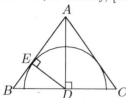

352. Since $\triangle ABC$ is isosceles, altitude AD is also a median. Thus $BD = 20$ and applying the Pythagorean Theorem to $\triangle ADB$ yields $AD = 15$. We draw radius DE of the semicircle, where E is on AB. Thus $DE \perp AB$ and $\triangle DEB \sim \triangle ADB$. Hence, $ED/DB = AD/AB$ and $ED = 12$. The semicircle is half a circle of radius 12, so it has area $(12^2)\pi/2 = \mathbf{72\pi}$.

353. We must find the length of the band between the two pulleys, AB and FG in the figure, and the length of the band on the pulleys. Since AB is tangent to the two circles, it is perpendicular to radii AD and BE. Thus we draw $CD \parallel AB$, forming rectangle $ABCD$. Hence, $BC = AD = 1$ and $CE = 4 - 1 = 3$. Since $DE = 6$, right triangle 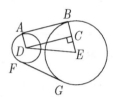 CDE is a $30°$-$60°$-$90°$ triangle. Thus $CD = AB = FG = 3\sqrt{3}$, $\angle BEG = 2\angle CED = 120°$, and $\angle ADF = 360° - 2(90° + \angle CDE) = 120°$. The portion of the band on pulley D has length $(2\pi)(120/360) = 2\pi/3$ and the portion on pulley E has length $(8\pi)(240/360) = 16\pi/3$. Thus the total length of the pulley is $2\pi/3 + 2(3\sqrt{3}) + 16\pi/3 = \mathbf{6(\pi + \sqrt{3})}$.

354. Let x be the common altitude and m be the median length. The area of the triangle is $18x/2 = 9x$ and that of the trapezoid is mx. Since these are equal, $mx = 9x$ and $m = \mathbf{9}$.

355. Since $\overset{\frown}{AY} = \overset{\frown}{YC}$ and $\angle ABY$ and $\angle YBC$ are inscribed angles which subtend these arcs, we know that $\angle ABY = \angle YBC$. Thus BY is an angle bisector. Applying the Angle Bisector Theorem to $\triangle ABC$, we find $AB/AD = BC/DC$. Letting $DC = x$, we have $4/(9 - x) = 8/x$, and $x = \mathbf{6}$.

356. Since $BC \parallel AE$, $\angle EAB + \angle CBA = 180°$. Since the pentagon is symmetric with respect to DP, these two angles are equal. Thus $\angle EAB = \angle CBA = 90°$ and $ECBA$ is a rectangle, so $EC = AB = 16$. Since $BC = 4$ and $FP \parallel CB$, we have $DF = DP - FP = 7 - 4 = 3$. Thus $[ABCDE] = [ABCE] + [DEC] = (4)(16) + (16)(3)/2 = \mathbf{88}$.

357. Drawing segments TR and PU such that $PU \perp RQ$, we see that $PURT$ is a rectangle. Also, any line perpendicular to a tangent to a circle which passes through the point of tangency must also pass through the center of the circle. Hence, TR is a diameter of the circle and has length $2r$. Thus $PU = 2r$. Since $PS = PT = RU$ and $RQ = QS$, we have $QU = RQ - TP = 5$ and $PQ = PS + SQ = 13$. Applying the Pythagorean Theorem to $\triangle PUQ$, we find $PU = 12$ and the radius of the circle is $\mathbf{6}$.

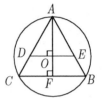

358. Let the square have side length x. Thus the perimeter of the square is $4x$. Since M and N are midpoints of AD and DC, we have $MD = DN = x/2$ and from the Pythagorean Theorem applied to $\triangle AMB$ and $\triangle BCN$ we find $BM = BN = x\sqrt{5}/2$. Thus the perimeter of $BMDN$ is $x\sqrt{5} + x$ and the desired ratio is $(\sqrt{5} + 1)/4$.

359. Let $DC = DE = x$. Since $ABCD$ is a rectangle, we have $AB = x$ and $AE = x - 3$. Applying the Pythagorean Theorem to $\triangle ADE$ we find $25 + (x - 3)^2 = x^2$. Thus $6x = 34$, so $DE = x = \mathbf{17/3}$.

360. We could let the radius of the circle be x and find the sides of each triangle in terms of x, but there is a much faster solution in which we use the similarity of the two triangles. In the diagram, since O is the circumcenter of $\triangle ABC$, it is also the orthocenter as well as the centroid. Thus continuing AO to meet CB at F, we have $AF \perp CB$. Since O is the centroid, we know that $AO/AF = 2/3$. Since AO and AF are corresponding altitudes of similar triangles ADE and ABC, the ratio of the sides of the triangles, and hence the ratio of the perimeters, is $\mathbf{2/3}$.

361. Since $DE \parallel BC$, by AA similarity we have $\triangle ABC \sim \triangle AED$. Thus $[AED]/[ABC] = (AE/AB)^2 = (3/10)^2 = 9/100$ and $[ABC] = 100[AED]/9$. Hence,

$$[AED]/[BCDE] = [AED]/([ABC] - [AED]) = [AED]/(91[AED]/9)$$
$$= \mathbf{9/91}.$$

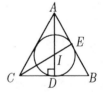

362. As the incenter of equilateral triangle ABC, I is also the centroid. Thus $ID/AD = 1/3$, so $AD = 3ID = 27$. From 30°-60°-90° triangle ACD we have $CD = AD/\sqrt{3} = 9\sqrt{3}$. Thus $BC = 2CD = 18\sqrt{3}$, so $[ABC] = (BC)(AD)/2 = \mathbf{243\sqrt{3}}$.

363. We draw the piece of paper before it is folded and after, where F is where the corner was before the fold and C where the corner is after. Thus $BF = CB = 5$ and $FE = CE$. Since $AF = 8$, we have $AB = 8 - 5 = 3$. From right triangle ABC we find $AC = 4$. Let $FE = x$. Thus $CD = x - 4$ and $CE = x$. Since $ED = AF = 8$, we have $(x-4)^2 + 8^2 = x^2$ from triangle CDE. Hence $x = 10$ and from right triangle BCE we find $l = \sqrt{25 + 100} = 5\sqrt{5}$.

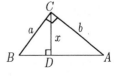

364. Since $\angle CAD = \angle CAB = \angle BCD$, from AA similarity we have $\triangle CDB \sim \triangle ADC \sim \triangle ACB$. Since $CD/CB = AC/AB$, we find $x/a = b/c$. Thus $x = ab/c$. Squaring this and applying the Pythagorean Theorem gives $x^2 = a^2b^2/(a^2 + b^2)$. Taking the reciprocal of both sides of this equation yields the desired $1/x^2 = 1/a^2 + 1/b^2$.

365. Continue CP to meet AB at F. Since $CP \perp ED$, we have $CF \perp$ AB. Since $\triangle APF \cong \triangle BPF$ by HL for right triangles, we have $AF = FB = 3$. If we let $PA = PB = PC = x$, we get $PF = 6 - x$. Thus right triangle PAF gives us $9 + (6 - x)^2 = x^2$, so $x = 15/4$. Hence, $PF = 6 - x = 9/4$ and $[ABP] = (PF)(AB)/2 = \mathbf{27/4}$.

366. We draw the radii to the points of tangency, so $OA \perp$ AP and $OB \perp BP$. Since $OP = OP$ and $OA = OB$, we have $\triangle APO \cong \triangle BPO$ by HL congruency for right triangles. Thus $\angle APO = \angle OPB$ and OP bisects angle APB. Note also that OP bisects $\angle AOB$.

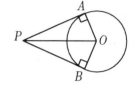

367. Continue FE to meet CD at G. Since $FE \parallel AD$, we have $FG \perp DC$. Letting $GD = x$, from 30°-60°-90° triangle DEG we find $EG/DG = \sqrt{3}$. Thus $EG = x\sqrt{3}$ and $FG = x\sqrt{3} + 1$. Since $FG = AD = DC = 2DG = 2x$, we have $2x = x\sqrt{3}+1$, so $x = 2+\sqrt{3}$ and $DC = 2x = \mathbf{4 + 2\sqrt{3}}$.

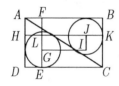

368. Let G and J be the centers of the incircles. Since $AC = 13$ (from the Pythagorean Theorem), the circles have radius $(5 + 12 - 13)/2 = 2$ since the triangles are right. We draw rectangle $GIJL$. Since $FL = GE = 2$ (they are equal to the radii of the circles), we find $LG = FE - 2(2) = 5 - 4 = 1$. Similarly, $LJ = HK - 2(2) = 12 - 4 = 8$. The desired distance, GJ, is a diagonal of rectangle $LGIJ$, so $GJ = \sqrt{1 + 64} = \mathbf{\sqrt{65}}$.

369. Since $DE \parallel BC$, we have $\triangle ADE \sim \triangle ABC$. Since $\triangle AGB$ is a 30°-60°-90° triangle, we find $BG = AB/2 = 5$ and $AG = BG\sqrt{3} = 5\sqrt{3}$. Similarly, $AF = 3\sqrt{3}$. Since $\triangle AFE$ and $\triangle AGC$ are isosceles right triangles, we find $FE = AF = 3\sqrt{3}$ and $GC = AG = 5\sqrt{3}$. Thus $[FECG] = [AGC] - [AFE] = (5\sqrt{3})^2/2 - (3\sqrt{3})^2/2 = \mathbf{24}$.

370. In the diagram is half the dodecagon. Diagonal AB is the desired length. Since the polygon has 12 sides, the interior angles each have measure 150°. Draw AC and CB, then FD and GE such that FD and GE are perpendicular to AC. Thus $EDFG$ is a rectangle and $\angle AFD = \angle EGC = 150° - 90° = 60°$. Hence,

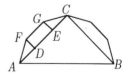

$AC = AD + DE + EC = AF\sqrt{3}/2 + FG + CG\sqrt{3}/2 = 1 + \sqrt{3}$. Since $\angle GCE = 30°$, we have $\angle ACB = 150° - 2(30°) = 90°$. Thus $\triangle ABC$ is an isosceles right triangle and $AB = AC\sqrt{2} = \mathbf{\sqrt{2} + \sqrt{6}}$.

371.   The perpendicular bisectors of the sides of a triangle meet at the center of the circumcircle as shown in the diagram. Thus $[AECDBF] = [AOBF] + [COBD] + [AOCE]$. Since the diagonals of these quadrilaterals are perpendicular, the area of each of these is half the product of its diagonals. Hence,

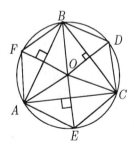

$$
\begin{aligned}
[AECDBF] &= (OF)(AB)/2 + (OD)(BC)/2 + (OE)(AC)/2 \\
&= r(AB + BC + AC)/2 = rp/2 \\
&= 8(35)/2 = \mathbf{140}.
\end{aligned}
$$

372.   For the same reason the Triangle Inequality holds, the sum of three sides of a quadrilateral must exceed the fourth side. Hence, $1 + 2 + 5 > x$ and $1 + 2 + x > 5$, so $2 < x < 8$. Thus the sum of the values x can have is $3 + 4 + 5 + 6 + 7 = \mathbf{25}$.

373.   Draw OT and OU. Since $\angle D = \angle OUD = \angle OTD = 90°$, $\angle UOT = 90°$. Hence, $\overarc{UR} = 360° - \overarc{RST} - \overarc{UT} = 60°$. Segment OA bisects $\angle UOR$, so $\angle AOR = 30°$. Thus $\triangle OAR$ is a 30°-60°-90° triangle. Since $AR = 3$, we find $OR = AR\sqrt{3} = 3\sqrt{3}$, so the area of the circle is $(3\sqrt{3})^2\pi = \mathbf{27\pi}$.

374.   Since they are radii of congruent circles, we know that $AC = CB = AB = AD = BD$. Hence, $\triangle ABC$ and $\triangle ABD$ are equilateral triangles. To find the desired area, we add 4 times the area of circular segment CB to twice the area of $\triangle ABC$. To find the area of segment CB we subtract the area of $\triangle ABC$ from the area of sector ABC. Since $\angle CAB = 60°$, the area of sector ABC is $6^2\pi/6 = 6\pi$. Since $[ABC] = 6^2\sqrt{3}/4 = 9\sqrt{3}$, the area of the segment is $6\pi - 9\sqrt{3}$, so the desired area is $4(6\pi - 9\sqrt{3}) + 2(9\sqrt{3}) = \mathbf{24\pi - 18\sqrt{3}}$.

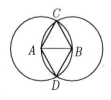

375.   Drawing radii IC and IB of the smaller circle, we see that since $OB \perp OC$ and $OB = OC$, we know $IBOC$ is a square (remember, $OB \perp IB$ and $OC \perp IC$). Letting $IC = r$, we have $IO = r\sqrt{2}$ and $AI = r$, so $AO = r(\sqrt{2} + 1)$. Since $OA = 12/2 = 6$, we have $r(\sqrt{2} + 1) = 6$, so $r = \mathbf{6\sqrt{2} - 6}$.

376.   Once the man, starting from point M, gets to the river at point B, the distance he must go to get home is the same whether his house is 8 miles north of the river at H or 8 miles south of the river at N (the reflection of H in R). Thus we find the shortest distance he must walk to get from M to N. Clearly, the shortest such distance is a straight line. Since M is 3 miles north of R and R is 8 miles north of N, M is 11 miles north of N. Since M is also 6 miles east of N, the man must travel $\sqrt{36 + 121} = \mathbf{\sqrt{157}}$ miles.

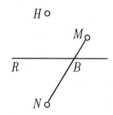

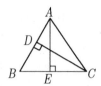

377.   In any of the cases described in the problem, we have $[ABC] = (AB)(CD)/2 = (CB)(AE)/2$, thus $CB = (AB)(CD)/AE$. Thus $DB = \sqrt{CB^2 - DC^2} = \sqrt{(AB^2)(CD^2)/AE^2 - CD^2} = CD\sqrt{AB^2/AE^2 - 1}$. If the triangle is acute or obtuse, this is as good as we can do. If $\angle A = 90°$, then D is A, and $DB = \mathbf{AB}$. If $\angle B$ is right, then D is B and $DB = \mathbf{0}$.

378.   Since $AB = 14$ and $AE = 8$, we find $EB = 6$. From the power of point E we have $(ED)(EC) = (EA)(EB)$, so $ED = 4$ and $CD = 12 + 4 = 16$. Since $\angle DAB$ and $\angle DCB$ subtend the same arc, we have $\angle DAB = \angle DCB$. Thus by AA similarity we have $\triangle ABX \sim \triangle CDX$ and $\triangle EDA \sim \triangle EBC$. From the latter similarity we find $BC/EC = DA/EA$, so $BC = 15$. From the former we get $DX/BX = DC/AB = 8/7$ so $BX = 7DX/8$. Since $AX/CX = AB/CD = 7/8$, we have $AX = 10 + DX = (7/8)(CX) = (7/8)(CB + BX) = (7/8)(15 + 7DX/8)$. Solving for DX gives $DX = 40/3$; therefore, $AX = DX + AD = \mathbf{70/3}$.

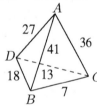

379.   Since the faces of the tetrahedron are triangles, they must satisfy the Triangle Inequality. Since AB is part of two triangles, one of them must contain the edge with length 36 and the other the side with length 27, because no triangle can be formed with 41 as one side and the other two sides chosen from the set $\{7, 13, 18\}$, for such a triangle would violate the Triangle Inequality. Hence, let $AD = 27$ and $AC = 36$. To satisfy the Triangle Inequality, we must have $DB = 18$ because $27 + 7 < 41$ and $27 + 13 < 41$. Finally, from $\triangle ACD$, CD must be **13** because $7 + 27 < 36$. Show that $AD = 27$ and $BC = 36$ is impossible.

380.   Since O is the incenter of equilateral $\triangle ABC$, it is also the centroid. Thus radius OY is $1/3$ of AY so $AY = 60$. Since $OX = OY = 20$, we have $AX = AY - XY = 20$. We draw DE through the point of tangency of the two circles such that $DE \parallel BC$. Since $DE \parallel BC$, we have $\triangle ADE \sim \triangle ABC$, so $\triangle ADE$ is equilateral. Circle P is the incircle of $\triangle ADE$. The center of this circle is also the centroid of $\triangle ADE$. The distance from the centroid to DE is $1/3$ of AX. This distance is the radius, so the radius of the smaller circle is $AX/3 = \mathbf{20/3}$.

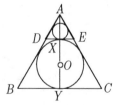

381.   Suppose the sides are ordered as shown in the left figure, where $AB = AF$ and $BC = CD = DE = EF$. Since $ABCD$ is symmetric with $AFED$, AD is a diameter. Thus we can 'flip' $AFED$ to form the figure on the right, where $AB = DF$ and $AE = EF = BC = CD$. To find the area of this hexagon, we draw DX and FY so that these are perpendicular to CE. Since $EABC$ is symmetric with $EFDC$, CE is a diameter. Since $\angle DCE = \angle FEC$ (because $\overset{\frown}{CF} = \overset{\frown}{DE}$), we have $\triangle CDX \cong \triangle EFY$

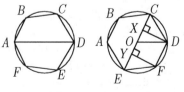

by SA for right triangles. Thus $FY = DX$ and $DF \parallel XY$. Hence, $DFYX$ is a rectangle and $XY = DF = 7$.

Let the radius of circle O be r and $FY = DX = x$. Draw radius OD. From right triangle OXD we have $x^2 + (7/2)^2 = r^2$, and from $\triangle CDX$ we find $(r - 7/2)^2 + x^2 = 400$. From the first equation we get $x^2 = r^2 - 49/4$. Substituting this in the second gives $r^2 - 7r + 49/4 + r^2 - 49/4 = 400$, so $2r^2 - 7r - 400 = (r - 16)(2r + 25) = 0$. Hence, $r = \mathbf{16}$.

382. Although this appears to be a power of a point question, looks are deceiving. Draw segment MB. Since $\angle AMB$ is inscribed in a semicircle, $\angle AMB = 90°$. Since $\angle MAB = \angle PAO$ and $\angle POA = \angle BMA$, we have $\triangle AMB \sim \triangle AOP$. Thus $AO/AP = AM/AB$ and $AP{\cdot}AM = \mathbf{AB \cdot AO}$.

383. As the intersection of two medians, G is the centroid. Since $AG/AD = 2/3$ and $GE/BE = 1/3$, we find $AG = 4$ and $GE = 3$. Since E is the midpoint of AC, we have $AE = 5$. Since its sides satisfy the Pythagorean Theorem, $\triangle AGE$ is a right triangle. Hence, it has area $(3)(4)/2 = 6$. Since it is formed by two medians of the triangle, the area of $\triangle AGE$ is $1/6$ that of $\triangle ABC$. Hence, $[ABC] = \mathbf{36}$.

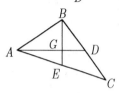

384. Since the lines are parallel, we have similar triangles, so $x/y = (x + c)/(y + d) = (x + c + a)/(y + d + b)$. Recalling our manipulations of proportions, we have

$$\frac{x}{y} = \frac{(x+c) - x}{(y+d) - y} = \frac{c}{d} = \frac{(x+c+a) - (x+c)}{(y+d+b) - (y+d)} = \frac{a}{b}.$$

For the second equality we know $f/y = g/(d+y) = h/(b+d+y)$ from our triangle similarity. Once again applying our proportion manipulations, we have

$$\frac{f}{y} = \frac{g - f}{(d+y) - y} = \frac{g - f}{d} = \frac{h - g}{(b+d+y) - (d+y)} = \frac{h - g}{b}.$$

385. Since $CD = CS$ and $BC = AB + CD$, we know that $BS = BA$. Since $BA = BS$ and $CD = CS$, we can write $\angle BSA = \angle BAS = x$ and $\angle CSD = \angle CDS = y$. Thus $\angle ASD = 180 - x - y$, $\angle SAD = 90 - x$, and $\angle SDA = 90 - y$. As the angles of a triangle, the sum of these 3 is $180°$. Thus $x + y = 90°$, so $\angle ASD = 180 - 90 = 90°$.

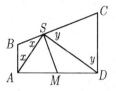

Since $\angle ASD$ is right and M is the midpoint of AD, SM is the median to the hypotenuse. Thus $SM = MD = AM$. Hence, $\triangle SMD$ is an isosceles triangle and $\angle MDS = \angle MSD$.

386. Draw CD. Since $\angle CDB$ is inscribed in a semicircle, it is a right angle. Letting $\angle CBD = x$ and $\angle BCD = y$, we have $x + y = 90°$. Since $\triangle ABC$ is a right triangle, we have $\angle A = 90 - \angle B = y$. Since DF and CF are tangents to a circle from a point, they are equal, so

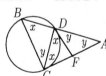

$\angle FCD = \angle FDC$. Because $\angle BCF = 90°$, we find $\angle FCD = 90° - y = x$. Since $\angle CDA = 90°$, we have $\angle FDA = 90° - \angle FDC = 90 - x = y$. This completes our proof that the angles are as labeled in the diagram.

Since $\triangle DFA$ is isosceles, $FA = FD = FC$ (part ii). Thus DF bisects CA (part i). We have above shown $\angle A = \angle BCD = y$ (part iii). The Exterior Angle Theorem then gives $\angle DFC = \angle A + \angle FDA = 2\angle A$ (part iv).

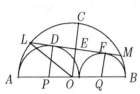

387. Let O be the center of the largest semicircle. Since the diameters of the smaller semicircles are 12 and 8, the diameter of the largest semicircle is 20. Thus $OL = 10$. Draw radius OC perpendicular to LM at E. Also, draw radii PD and FQ of the two small semicircles to the points of tangency, D and F, of LM. These radii are perpendicular to LM, so $PD \parallel EO \parallel FQ$. If we extend LM and AB to meet at N we find that the three aforementioned parallel segments are corresponding sides of similar triangles, so $(PD - EO)/OP = (EO - FQ)/OQ$ (recall the earlier problem in which we are asked to prove this). Since $OB = 10$ and $QB = 4$, we have $OQ = 6$. Similarly, $OP = 4$. Solving the above equation for EO, we find $EO = 26/5$. Finally, from right triangle EOL, we have $EL = 4\sqrt{114}/5$. Since radius OC is perpendicular to chord LM, it bisects the chord, so $LM = 2LE = \mathbf{8\sqrt{114}/5}$.

388. Extend wall BQ to C so that $RC \perp CB$. Since $\angle RPA = 75°$ and $\angle QPB = 45°$, we have $\angle RPQ = 180° - 75° - 45° = 60°$. Triangle PQR is isosceles, so $\angle PRQ = \angle PQR = (180° - 60°)/2 = 60°$. Hence, $\triangle PQR$ is equilateral and $RQ = a$. Finally, $\angle RQC = 180° - 60° - 45° = 75°$, so by SA for right triangles we find $\triangle RCQ \cong \triangle RAP$. Thus $RC = RA$ and $w = \mathbf{h}$.

389. Since $BF = 4$, the radius of the smaller circle is 4. Since $DB = 20$, the diameter of the larger circle is $20 - 4 = 16$, so its radius is 8. Since radii CE and BF are perpendicular to AE, they are parallel. Thus $\triangle ABF \sim \triangle ACE$. Since $BF/CE = 1/2$, we have $AF/AE = 1/2$. Thus $AF = EF$, so if we determine EF, we can find AE. Draw BQ such that $CE \perp BQ$.

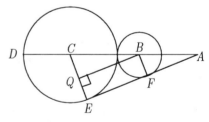

Hence, $BQEF$ is a rectangle, so $QE = BF = 4$ and $BQ = EF$. From right triangle BCQ we find $BQ = \sqrt{144 - 16} = 8\sqrt{2}$. Thus $AE = 2EF = 2BQ = \mathbf{16\sqrt{2}}$.

390. To prove that D is the circumcenter of $\triangle ICB$, we show that D is equidistant from the vertices of $\triangle ICB$; this will imply that there is a circle with center D and radius DC passing through the three vertices. Since I is the incenter of $\triangle ABC$, AD bisects angle CAB. Thus $\angle CAD = \angle DAB$. Since these angles are inscribed in arcs $\overset{\frown}{CD}$ and $\overset{\frown}{DB}$, these arcs are equal, so the chords subtending them are equal. Hence, $CD = BD$. Now, we show $ID = CD = DB$ by showing that

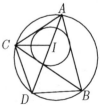

$\angle DCI = \angle DIC$. Let $\angle ACI = \theta$ and $\angle IAC = \phi$. By the Exterior Angle Theorem we have $\angle DIC = \theta + \phi$. Since IC bisects $\angle ACB$, we find $\angle ICB = \theta$. Since $\angle DCB = \overarc{BD}/2 = \angle DAB = \angle CAD$, we have $\angle DCB = \phi$. Thus $\angle DCI = \theta + \phi = \angle DIC$, so $ID = DC = BD$ and D is the circumcenter of $\triangle ICB$.

391. Draw RS through M parallel to DC. Thus $\triangle RMA \sim \triangle DEA$. Since $AM/AE = 1/2$, we have $RM = DE/2 = 5/2$. Since $RS = 12$, we find $MS = 19/2$. Since $AD \parallel BC$, we get $\triangle PMR \sim \triangle QMS$. Thus $PM/MQ = RM/MS = \mathbf{5/19}$.

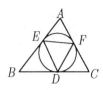

392. Since $\angle EDF$ is an inscribed angle, we have $\angle EDF = \overarc{EF}/2$. As an angle formed by two tangents we find $\angle A = (\overarc{EDF} - \overarc{EF})/2 = (360° - 2\overarc{EF})/2$. Thus $\angle A = 180° - \overarc{EF}$ and $\angle A = 180° - 2\angle EDF$. Solving for $\angle EDF$ yields $\angle EDF = 90° - (\angle A)/2$. Since $\angle A > 0$, we know that $\angle EDF < 90°$. Similarly, the other angles of $\triangle DEF$ are also acute.

393. For the first part, we let $ED = DG = DF = y$ and the other equal tangents be as indicated in the diagram. Thus $AB = w + x$, $BC = w + z + 2y$, $AC = x + z$, and $BD = w + y$. Thus $AB + BC - AC = 2w + 2y = 2(BD)$, so $BD = (a + c - b)/2$.

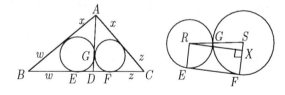

For the second part, consider the second diagram. This should be familiar by now. Radii RE and SF are perpendicular to the tangent. By drawing RX perpendicular to SF, we form rectangle $RXFE$. Hence, in right triangle RSX, we have $RS = r + s$, $SX = r - s$, and $RX = \sqrt{RS^2 - SX^2} = 2\sqrt{rs}$. Returning to the original diagram, since $DE = EF/2$, we find $DE = \sqrt{rs}$.

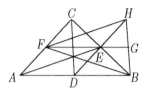

394. Since $AE \parallel FH$, we have $\angle AEF = \angle HFE$. Since $AE = FH$ (given) and $EF = EF$, we find $\triangle HFE \cong \triangle AEF$ from SAS congruence. Thus $\angle AFE = \angle FEH$ and $AF \parallel HE$. Hence, $AFHE$ is a parallelogram (part i).

The line through E parallel to AC must pass through D. (Why?) Since $ED = AC/2 = AF = HE$, we have $HD = 2EH = 2AF = AC$. Since $HD \parallel AC$, $\angle CAD = \angle HDB$. Finally, since D is the midpoint of AB, we have $AD = DB$ and we find $\triangle ACD \cong DHB$ by SAS congruence. Thus $CD = HB$ (part ii).

Since $EG \parallel DB$, we have $\triangle HDB \sim \triangle HEG$. Since $HE/HD = 1/2$, we get $HG/HB = 1/2$, so G is the midpoint of HB. Thus FG is a median of $\triangle BFH$ (part iii).

Since $\triangle CFE \sim \triangle CAB$ and $\triangle HEG \sim \triangle HDB$, we have $EF = AB/2$ and $EG = DB/2 = AB/4$. Thus $FG = FE + EG = 3AB/4$ (part iv).

395. Draw FE parallel to AD. We find the area of $BHGC$ as the sum of the areas of $\triangle BHG$ and $\triangle GBC$. Since $\cos\alpha = 4/5$ and $BH = 1$, we have $BF = 4/5$, so $FH = 3/5$. Thus $HE = 1 - 3/5 = 2/5$. Since $\angle EHG = 180° - 90° - \angle FHB = 90° - \angle FHB = \alpha$, we find $\cos\angle EHG = 4/5$. Thus $HG = 1/2$ and $EG = 3/10$. Since $DE = AF = AB - FB = 1/5$, we have $GC = DC - DG = 1 - 1/2 = 1/2$. Finally, $[BHGC] = (BH)(GH)/2 + (BC)(GC)/2 = \mathbf{1/2}$.

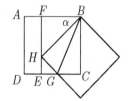

396. We show that $\triangle NMP$ is equal by showing that its sides are equal. Since the trapezoid is isosceles, we have $\angle CAB = \angle DBA$. Because $\angle AOB = 60°$ and $\angle OAB = \angle ABO$, triangle OAB is equilateral. Since BM is a median of equilateral triangle OAB, it is also an altitude. Thus $\triangle CMB$ is a right triangle and MP is a median to the hypotenuse of the triangle. Thus $MP = CB/2$. Similarly, $\triangle CNB$ is a right triangle and $NP = CB/2$. Since NM is a segment connecting midpoints of the sides of $\triangle ADO$, we have $MN = AD/2 = BC/2$ (since $ABCD$ is isosceles). Thus $MN = NP = MP$ and $\triangle MNP$ is equilateral.

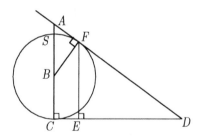

397. Let AD be the sun's ray, so CD is the shadow cast by the sphere. Point D is actually the shadow of point F on the sphere, so $FE/ED = 1/2$ (from the information that a shadow cast by a stick is twice the stick's length). Extend diameter CS of the sphere to point A on the sun's ray. Since AC and FE are perpendicular to CD, we have $AC \parallel FE$ and $\triangle ACD \sim \triangle FED$. Thus $AC = CD/2 = 5$. Since $\angle BAF = \angle DAC$ and $\angle BFA = \angle DCA$, we find $\triangle BAF \sim \triangle DAC \sim \triangle DFE$. Thus $AF/BF = EF/ED = 1/2$. Since $BF = r$, we get $AF = r/2$, so $AB = r\sqrt{5}/2$. Since $AC = AB + BC = r(1 + \sqrt{5}/2) = 5$, we find $r = \mathbf{10\sqrt{5} - 20}$.

398. Let $AB = y$ and $BF = x$ as shown. Since $\angle ABF = \angle ADP$ and $\angle DAP = \angle FAB$ (because AF is an angle bisector), we have $\triangle FAB \sim \triangle PAD$. Since $AP/AF = 12/20 = 3/5$, we have $PD = 3x/5$ and $AD = 3y/5$. From right triangle ADB, since $AB = y$ and $AD = 3y/5$, we have $BD = 4y/5$. The Angle Bisector Theorem applied to $\triangle ADB$ gives $BP/PD = AB/AD$, so $BP = x$. Thus $BD = 8x/5 = 4y/5$ and $x/y = 1/2$. Thus $\tan\angle BAF = x/y = \mathbf{1/2}$. From triangle ABF we get $x^2 + 4x^2 = 400$, so $x = 4\sqrt{5}$. Thus $PD = 3x/5 = \mathbf{12\sqrt{5}/5}$.

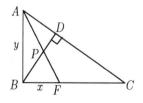

399. The median of trapezoid $ABCD$ has length $(AB + CD)/2$. If we draw $BF \parallel AC$, $BF \perp BD$ since $AC \perp BD$. Also, $FC = AB$ and $BF = AC$ because $ABFC$ is a parallelogram. Thus from right triangle DBF we have $BF^2 + BD^2 = DF^2$, so $AC^2 + BD^2 = (AB + CD)^2$. Since AC and BD are 7 and 9, we find $(AB + CD)/2 = \sqrt{49 + 81}/2 = \sqrt{130}/2$.

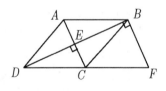

400. Since $[AEB] = [AED] + [EDB]$, $[BDFE] = [BDE] + [DEF]$, and $[BDFE] = [AEB]$, we have $[DEF] = [AED]$. Since $\triangle DEF$ and $\triangle DEA$ share base DE and have the same area, the altitudes from A and F must be equal. Since two points on AC are equidistant from DE, we know that $AC \parallel DE$. Thus $\triangle ACB \sim \triangle DEB$. Since

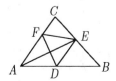

$DB/AB = 3/5$, we have $[DEB]/[ACB] = (3/5)^2 = 9/25$, so $[DEB] = 18/5$. Since triangles AEB and DEB have the same altitude from E, the ratio of their areas is $AB/DB = 5/3$. Hence, $[AEB] = (5/3)[DEB] = \mathbf{6}$.

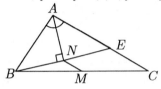

401. Extend BN to meet AC at E. Since AN bisects angle BAE, we have $\triangle ANB \cong \triangle ANE$ by SA congruence for right triangles. Thus $AE = AB = 14$ and N is the midpoint of BE. Hence, segment MN connects midpoints of the sides of $\triangle BEC$, so $MN = EC/2 = (AC - AE)/2 = \mathbf{5/2}$.

Chapter 21

Functions

Solutions to Exercises

21-1　No. For instance, $x = 2$, a vertical line, allows the choice of any y; only x is restricted. However, any nonvertical line does choose exactly one y for each x, since we can always put such a line in slope-intercept form. (We can't put a vertical line in slope-intercept form because the slope is undefined.)

21-2　The cube root of x is a function, since there is only one real x which cubes to any value. For example, $\sqrt[3]{8} = 2$; -2 is not a possibility, as its cube is -8, not 8. The fourth root, however, is not a function for the same reason the square root isn't: $\sqrt[4]{16}$ could equal 2 or -2. For the third expression, does each x give one and only one output? Yes. If you plug in x, there is only one result you can get.

21-3　For the first, we have $f(64) = \sqrt[3]{64} = 4$; for the third, $f(64) = \mathbf{64/65}$. The second is not a function.

21-4　We have $f(4) = 2^4 = 16$ and $f(3) = 2^3 = 8$, so the quotient is $16/8 = \mathbf{2}$.

21-5　Since we have $f(x+1)$ rather than $f(x)$, we need to substitute in $x = 3$, not $x = 4$, to find $f(3+1) = f(4)$. Thus $f(4) = (3^3) + 6(3^2) + (3) + 3 = 27 + 54 + 3 + 3 = \mathbf{87}$.

21-6　We graph these functions by the simple plug-in method. For example, for x^3, we can plug in $x = -2, -1, 0, 1,$ and 2 to get the points $(-2, -8)$, $(-1, -1)$, $(0, 0)$, $(1, 1)$, $(2, 8)$.

The results are as shown. Getting the values for $x^3 + 3$ is fairly simple once we have x^3, and the graph again comes out of our plotted points.

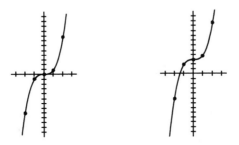

21-7 Although the function is complicated, the plug-in method works fine. Starting at 0 at working outward with integer values, we find the points $(0, 1)$, $(1, 1/2)$, $(-1, 1/2)$, $(2, 1/5)$, $(-2, 1/5)$, ... Evidently the function is tending to 0 as we move outward. To get an idea of the shape of the graph near $x = 0$, we supplement our integer values of x with $x = \pm 1/2$ and $x = \pm 1/4$, to get the points $(\pm 1/2, 4/5)$ and $(\pm 1/4, 16/17)$. Drawing all our points in the plane and connecting with a reasonable looking curve, we get the bell-shaped graph below.

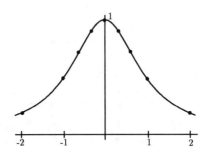

21-8 Remember that the domain of $\log x$ is $x > 0$; thus we do not plug in any numbers less than or equal to 0. Plugging in $x = 1/2$, we get -1; $x = 1$ gives 0; and $x = 2$ yields 1. These three points alone don't seem to tell us very well where the curve is going, so we add a couple more: $x = 1/4$ yields -2; $x = 4$ yields 2, and $x = 8$ yields 3. Plotting all the points we now have and thinking about what the logarithm does, it is evident what is happening: for larger and larger x, the function is flattening out, and for x closer to 0, the function is falling to negative infinity. (For extreme examples, consider that $\log_2(1/1024) = -10$ and $\log_2 1024$ is only 10.) Connecting the dots with a curve that behaves correctly, we get the graph on the following page.

The graph of $\log_2 x$ is:

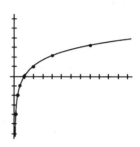

21-9

    i. This function is perfectly fine unless the bottom equals zero. The zeroes of the bottom can be found by factoring it into $(x - 2)(x - 1)$; they are 1 and 2. Thus the domain is all real numbers except 1 and 2. This can be written in interval notation as $(-\infty, 1) \cup (1, 2) \cup (2, \infty)$. Do you see why?

    ii. We can exponentiate any real number, so the domain is all real numbers.

    iii. We can take the square root of any positive number or zero, so this is the domain: $x \geq 0$. (The square root cannot be taken of negatives, unless we allow complex answers, which were specified as undesirable here.) What is the interval notation for this domain?

21-10 We have established that $\log x$ is only defined over the positive reals. By considering various positive reals, then, we can figure out the range. Since we have a base-10 logarithm, it is easiest to use powers of 10. For example, $\log 10 = 1$, since $10^1 = 10$. Similarly, $\log 100 = 2$, $\log 1000 = 3$, and so on. Clearly we can get anything greater than 1 by finding appropriate intermediate values. (So to find something whose log is 2.3, we just take $10^{2.3}$, for example.) Can we get things less than 1? Sure! We have $\log 1 = 0$, $\log 0.1 = -1$, $\log 0.01 = -2$, and so on. We can get as small as we want. We thus can see that the range is **all reals**.

    For the second one, we realize that the term x^2 takes all values ≥ 0, so that $x^2 + 1$ takes all values ≥ 1. The range can be written in interval notation as $[1, \infty)$.

    For the third, we can get any number which has a reciprocal r by plugging in $r + 1$, for then the value of the function is $1/r$, which is the original number. The only number we can't get is 0, which has no reciprocal.

21-11 This is a nice one. We immediately see that the domain is everything except -1, but we expect to find a value everywhere else. Plugging in x's, we find $f(0) = 0$, $f(1) = \frac{1}{2}$, $f(2) = \frac{2}{3}$, $f(3) = \frac{3}{4}$. As x gets larger, the fraction will approach 1, but not reach it.

    What happens to the function as it approaches the forbidden value of -1? This can be seen by trying some values which get closer to that black hole. We find $f\left(-\frac{1}{2}\right) = -1$, $f\left(-\frac{1}{3}\right) = -2$, $f\left(-\frac{1}{4}\right) = -3$. We see that the function goes off to $-\infty$ as we approach -1.

    The points *below* -1 act much like those above. Here we find that the curve approaches $+\infty$ as we approach -1, and approaches 1 as we go off to $-\infty$. It is clear that every real number is in the range, *except* 1, which is approached but never reached.

21-12   For each one, we just substitute the output of the function into the function again. Thus if $f(x) = x/(x+1)$, then

$$f(f(x)) = f\left(\frac{x}{x+1}\right) = \frac{\frac{x}{x+1}}{\frac{x}{x+1}+1} = \frac{\left(\frac{x}{x+1}\right)}{\left(\frac{2x+1}{x+1}\right)} = \frac{x}{2x+1}.$$

Similarly, if $f(x) = 1/x$, then $f(f(x)) = f(1/x) = 1/(1/x) = x$. Also, if $f(x) = x$, then $f(f(x)) = f(x) = x$.

21-13   A simple counterexample is $f(x) = x + 1$, $g(x) = 1/x$. Then $(f \circ g)(x) = \dfrac{1}{x} + 1$, but $(g \circ f)(x) = \dfrac{1}{x+1}$. Make sure you see why the two are different (try some values of x in both).

21-14   A function is symmetric across the y-axis if and only if the value of the function at the reflection of x equals the value at x. But the reflection of x is $-x$, so this means we have $f(x) = f(-x)$.

21-15   Such a function changes sign when we reflect across the y-axis. The function thus flips over on reflection. Such a function has *point symmetry* with respect to the origin, since the origin is the midpoint of any segment connecting $(x, f(x))$ to $(-x, f(-x))$.

21-16   Let your creative juices flow—you don't have to be able to express the function you draw as a simple formula, as long as it has the right symmetry.

21-17   An example of an even function might be x^2, since $(-x)^2 = x^2$. Similarly, an example of an odd function might be x. One example of a function which is neither is one we've seen before, $x/(x+1)$; substituting in $-x$ for x yields $-x/(-x+1)$, which is not related to $x/(x+1)$ in any simple way.

21-18   We can test all these by simply substituting $-x$ for x. We find that $(-x) = -(x)$, so x is odd; $(-x)^2 = x^2$, so x^2 is even; $(-x)^3 = -(x^3)$, so x^3 is odd; $(-x)^4 = x^4$, so x^4 is even. In the same way, $x^6 + 27x^4 + x^2$ is even. The last one is neither, since $(-x)^6 + (-x)^5 = x^6 - x^5$, which is not simply related to $x^6 + x^5$. Similarly, $x^5 + 1$ is neither, since $(-x)^5 + 1 = -x^5 + 1$.

21-19   The generalization is fairly clear from the previous example. Any term which is an even power of x is even; any term which is an odd power of x is odd. By adding up such terms, we can also see that any polynomial all of whose terms are even powers of x is even, and any with only odd powers of x is odd. (This is where the terms "even" and "odd" for the two types of functions come in.)

21-20   What if we didn't have the absolute value? Clearly if $x > y$, then $x - y < 2$ means that x and y are less than 2 apart. However, if y is greater than x, then $x - y < 2$ doesn't mean anything; x could be -100 while y was 0. In this case, we need to consider $y - x$ rather than $x - y$. The absolute value takes both cases into account at once.

21-21   This is pretty easy. For positive x, we have $f(x) = x$; for negative x, $f(x) = -x$. Putting these two sections together, we get the graph at right. (If you don't follow this semi-clever method, draw the graph by plugging in points instead.) From the graph we can easily see that the domain and range of the absolute value are {all reals} and {nonnegative reals}, respectively.

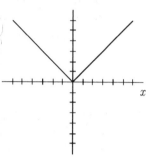

21-22   As in the text example, this is equivalent to either $(x + 2)/(3x - 1) = 5$ or $(x+2)/(3x - 1) = -5$. Solving the first yields $x = \mathbf{1/2}$; solving the second yields $x = \mathbf{3/16}$. These are the two solutions.

21-23   The square root of 17 is between 4 and 5, since $4^2 = 16 < 17 < 25 = 5^2$. Thus $-5 < -\sqrt{17} < -4$, so $\lfloor -\sqrt{17} \rfloor = \mathbf{-5}$.

The cube root of 17 is between 2 and 3, since $2^3 = 8 < 17 < 27 = 3^3$. Thus $2 < \sqrt[3]{17} < 3$, and $\lfloor \sqrt[3]{17} \rfloor = \mathbf{2}$.

Again: $-3 < -\sqrt[4]{17} < -2$, so $\lfloor -\sqrt[4]{17} \rfloor = \mathbf{-3}$.

Lastly, $1 < \sqrt[5]{17} < 2$, since $1^5 = 1 < 17 < 32 = 2^5$, so $\lfloor \sqrt[5]{17} \rfloor = \mathbf{1}$.

21-24 $\{17\} = 17 - \lfloor 17 \rfloor = 17 - 17 = \mathbf{0}$.

$\{-17/2\} = -17/2 - \lfloor -17/2 \rfloor = -17/2 - (-9) = \mathbf{1/2}$.

$\{17/3\} = 17/3 - \lfloor 17/3 \rfloor = 17/3 - 5 = \mathbf{2/3}$.

$\{-17/4\} = -17/4 - \lfloor -17/4 \rfloor = -17/4 - (-5) = \mathbf{3/4}$.

$\{17/5\} = 17/5 - \lfloor 17/5 \rfloor = 17/5 - 3 = \mathbf{2/5}$.

Enough said.

To plot the function, let's examine the behavior for $0 \le x < 1$. In this entire range, $\lfloor x \rfloor = 0$, so the function is equivalent to the function x. In the range $1 \le x < 2$, though, we always have $\lfloor x \rfloor = 1$, so the function is equivalent to $x - 1$, rising from 0 at 1 to approach 1 as 2 is approached. But when x reaches 2, $\lfloor x \rfloor$ increases to 2, so the function drops to 0 again. The behavior becomes a sawtooth pattern, as shown.

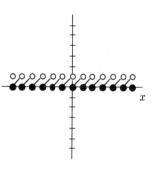

21-25   The two graphs coincide only when x is an integer.

21-26   If x is an integer, then $\lfloor x \rfloor = \lceil x \rceil = x$; if x is not an integer, then $\lfloor x \rfloor = \lceil x \rceil - 1$. Thus the difference $\lceil x \rceil - \lfloor x \rfloor$ is 0 if x is an integer, 1 otherwise. We seek an expression $a(x)$ which does this.

So how can we find some appropriate $a(x)$? If we could find some other expression $b(x)$ which is 1 when x is an integer and between 0 and 1 otherwise, then $a(x) = 1 - \lfloor b(x) \rfloor$ would do the trick. Make sure you see why before you proceed.

So now the problem is finding some $b(x)$ which is 1 when x is an integer and between 0 and 1 otherwise. Some trial and error leads to $b(x) = 1 - \{x\}$. Again, make sure you see why this has the property we seek. Writing $a(x) = 1 - \lfloor b(x) \rfloor = 1 - \lfloor 1 - \{x\} \rfloor$, we are done... almost. We still have a fractional part floating around, and we were asked to solve in terms of $\lfloor x \rfloor$ and x only. No problem: using the definition of the fractional part, we have $\{x\} = x - \lfloor x \rfloor$, so finally $a(x) = 1 - \lfloor 1 - x + \lfloor x \rfloor \rfloor$. Thus $\lceil x \rceil - \lfloor x \rfloor = 1 - \lfloor 1 - x + \lfloor x \rfloor \rfloor$, so

$$\lceil x \rceil = \lfloor x \rfloor + 1 - \lfloor 1 - x + \lfloor x \rfloor \rfloor.$$

Try some values to convince yourself that this works.

21-27 For the absolute value, we have $|-x| = x = |x|$, so the absolute value is even. For the floor function, we consider a value like $1/2$. The floor function of its negative is $\lfloor -1/2 \rfloor = -1$, which is equal to neither $\lfloor 1/2 \rfloor = 0$ or $-\lfloor 1/2 \rfloor = 0$. Thus the floor function is neither even nor odd.

21-28

i. If x is an integer, then $\lfloor x \rfloor + \lfloor -x \rfloor = x - x = 0$. Otherwise, $\lfloor -x \rfloor = -\lfloor x \rfloor - 1$ (this will be obvious if you try a couple x's), so the sum is -1.

ii. If x is an integer, then $\lfloor x + \frac{1}{2} \rfloor = x$, so our assertion is true. If x is not an integer, either $n < x < n + \frac{1}{2}$, $x = n + \frac{1}{2}$, or $n + \frac{1}{2} < x < n+1$. For the first case, we want our function to give back n, since x is closer to n than to $n + 1$; it does because then $n < x + \frac{1}{2} < n + 1$, so $\lfloor x + \frac{1}{2} \rfloor = n$ as desired. Similarly, for the latter case, our function chooses $n + 1$, which is indeed the closest. For $x = n + \frac{1}{2}$, there is no "closest integer." (What does our function return for this value?)

iii. Decomposing as in the hint, we have $\lfloor x \rfloor - 2\lfloor x/2 \rfloor = x - \{x\} - 2(x/2 + \{x/2\}) = -\{x\} + 2\{x/2\}$. But the fractional part of $x/2$ is always either $\{x\}/2$ (so $-\{x\} + 2\{x/2\} = 0$) or $\{x\}/2 + 1/2$ (so $-\{x\} + 2\{x/2\} = 1$), so we are done. (For example, $\{2.4/2\} = \{1.2\} = .2 = \{2.4\}/2$, but $\{3.6/2\} = \{1.8\} = .8 = \{3.6\}/2 + .5$. Play with this a little.)

21-29 For $x \geq 3$, the function is $x^2 - 8$; the smallest this gets is at $x = 3$, where the value is 1. Thus there are no solutions for $x \geq 3$. For $-2 \leq x < 3$, the function is $x^3 + 9$. The smallest this gets is $(-2)^3 + 9 = 1$. Still no intersections. For $x < -2$, the function is $x^4 - 15$; the smallest this gets is $2^4 - 15 = 1$. There are no intersections in this region either, so there are **no intersections** on the entire real line.

21-30 The shift is to the negative because to convert $f(z + 2)$ to $f(x)$, we must write $z = x - 2$, subtracting 2 from x. This is why we shift to the negative.

21-31 Compare this to the last example. Since $f(2x)$ is a horizontal shrink by 2, $f(x/2)$ is a horizontal shrink by $1/2$, which is the same as a horizontal stretch by 2!

21-32 Have fun!

Solutions to Problems

402. We must exclude all values of x which make the denominator of any fraction equal to 0. There are three fractions to consider, with denominators $2 + x$, $2 + x$, and $2 - \frac{2}{2+x}$. The first two denominators are only equal to zero when $x = -2$. The second is zero when $2 = \frac{2}{x+2}$, or when $x + 2 = 1$, or $x = -1$. The two excluded values are thus -2 and -1.

403. To find $f(4x)$, we just substitute $4x$ for x everywhere. Then $f(4x) = 2(4x)^2 - 3(4x) + 1 = \mathbf{32x^2 - 12x + 1}$.

404. This one is only a tiny bit trickier than the previous. If we are given $f(x + 1)$ and want to find $f(x)$, the thing to do is to substitute $x - 1$ for x everywhere; that makes $f(x+1) \to f((x-1)+1) = f(x)$. We thus have $f(x-1+1) = f(x) = (x-1)^2+3(x-1)+5 = (x^2 - 2x + 1) + (3x - 3) + 5 = \mathbf{x^2 + x + 3}$.

405. This is a fairly trivial extension of the previous two. To get a -9 in the parentheses, as in $f(-9)$, we need to find x such that $4x + 3 = -9$. This x is -3, by solving the linear equation. We thus have $f(-9) = 2(-3) + 1 = \mathbf{-5}$.

406. The absolute value symbol can come off in two ways. First, if $x^2 - 6x > 0$, then the equation becomes

$$x^2 - 6x = 9,$$

which by the quadratic formula has the solutions

$$x = 3 \pm 3\sqrt{2}.$$

On the other hand, if $x^2 - 6x < 0$, then the equation becomes

$$-x^2 + 6x = 9,$$

which only has the solution $x = 3$. Since this does make $x^2 - 6x < 0$, it is another solution. The equation thus has the three solutions $\mathbf{3}$ and $\mathbf{3 \pm 3\sqrt{2}}$.

407. First, $\lfloor \sqrt{3} \rfloor = 1$ and $\lfloor \sqrt{2} \rfloor = 1$, so $\{\sqrt{3}\} = \sqrt{3} - 1$ and $\{\sqrt{2}\} = \sqrt{2} - 1$. Inserting these into the equation, we find

$$
\begin{aligned}
z &= \frac{\left(\sqrt{3} - 1\right)^2 - 2\left(\sqrt{2} - 1\right)^2}{\left(\sqrt{3} - 1\right) - 2\left(\sqrt{2} - 1\right)} \\
&= \frac{-2 - 2\sqrt{3} + 4\sqrt{2}}{1 + \sqrt{3} - 2\sqrt{2}} \\
&= -2,
\end{aligned}
$$

and clearly $[z] = [-2] = \mathbf{-2}$.

408. We have $[\pi] = 3$, so we take the top branch to find $f(\pi) = \pi + 2$. We then have $f(f(\pi)) = f(\pi + 2)$. Since $[\pi + 2] = 5$, which is not divisible by 3, we take the lower branch to get $\pi + 2 - 1 = \pi + 1$. We then find that $f(f(f(\pi))) = \pi$, with four f's we get $\pi + 2$ again, and with five f's we are back down to **$\pi + 1$**.

409. The absolute value equality is equivalent to "either $3y + 7 = 2y - 1$ or $3y + 7 = -(2y - 1)$." Solving the two equations yields the two solutions **−8** and **−6/5**.

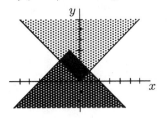

410. The easiest way here is just to carefully plot the two graphs and read the results off the plot. (Can you plot the second graph by transforming the first, rather than just using point-by-point plotting?) As shown below, the area in which we are interested is a rectangle whose sides are found by the Pythagorean Theorem to be $3\sqrt{2}/2$ and $5\sqrt{2}/2$. The area is the product, or **15/2**.

411. Here graphing and solving algebraically are about the same difficulty, so let's try algebra. If x is nonnegative, we have $2x - 2 = -2x + 2$, so that $x = 1$, which is a good solution because it is itself nonnegative. If x is negative, we have $-2x - 2 = 2x + 2$, with the solution -1. This is negative, so it is consistent with the conditions. For both $x = 1$ and $x = -1$, the corresponding y value is 0, so the point solutions are $(\mathbf{1, 0})$ and $(\mathbf{-1, 0})$.

412. Since the graph is symmetric both vertically and horizontally, we expect $|x|$ and $|y|$ to enter. Trial and error leads us to the solution $4|x| + 6|y| = 24$, or $2|x| + 3|y| = 12$. (Try some points to see how this works.)

413. Let $x = a + p$, where a is an integer and $p = \{x\}$, and $y = b + q$ similarly. We will work backwards from what we are trying to prove, being careful that all of our steps are reversible. We immediately convert what we want to prove to

$$2a + \lfloor 2p \rfloor + 2b + \lfloor 2q \rfloor \geq a + b + (a + b) + \lfloor p + q \rfloor.$$

(Do you see why?) Canceling $2a + 2b$ from both sides, what we wish to prove becomes

$$\lfloor 2p \rfloor + \lfloor 2q \rfloor \geq \lfloor p + q \rfloor.$$

But each of these terms is either 0 or 1, since $0 \leq p, q < 1$. The left side of the equation can thus be either 0, 1, or 2. If the left side is 1 or 2 we are done, since the right side is at most 1 no matter what. If the left side is 0, we have $2p < 1$ and $2q < 1$, so $p + q = (2p + 2q)/2 < (1 + 1)/2 < 1$, so the right side of the equation is also 0. Thus, whatever the left side of the equation is, the right side cannot be greater, and we are done.

Chapter 22

Inequalities

Solutions to Exercises

22-1 For example, $3 < 5$ yields $-17 < -15$ by subtracting 20 from both sides, and $3 < 5$ and $-1 < 0$ yield $2 < 5$. Play with some others.

22-2 If x is negative, then $-x > x$ and $x > y$ implies $-x > x > y$, not $-x < y$ as desired. If x is positive, $x > y$ only implies $-x < y$ if $x > |y|$, in which case $-x < y < x$, as desired. If $|y| > x$, then $y < -x$ must be true (since $y > x$ cannot be). If $x = 0$, then $-x = x$, so it doesn't work.

22-3 If both sides are negative, then we can multiply through by -1, reversing the inequality; reciprocate both sides, reversing the inequality sign again since both sides are now positive; and multiply back through by -1, reversing a third time. The three reverses mean that we must reverse the inequality (the first two cancel out but the third stays). Note how we can use what we know about positives to prove it for negatives: If x and y are positive and $-x < -y$, then $x > y$, so $1/x < 1/y$, so $-1/x > -1/y$.

22-4 The lines all have slope $1/4$, and have the y-intercepts $1/4$, $-1/4$, $-3/4$, and $-5/4$, so they can easily be graphed, as at right.

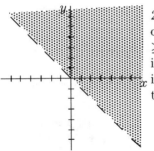

22-5 The line passes through $(0,0)$ and has slope -1, so is easily drawn; it should be dashed out since we have a $>$ rather than a $\geq$. To figure out which half of the plane is correct, we substitute in a point on one side, like $(1,0)$. This gives $0 + 1 > 0$, which is true, so it is in the half which satisfies the inequality, rather than the half which violates it. We shade this half.

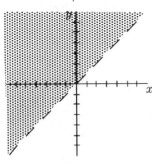

22-6 This line passes through $(0,0)$ again, but has slope 1; the point $(1,0)$ is now in the wrong half though, since $1-0 \not> 0$. Thus we shade the *other* half. The boundary line is again dashed.

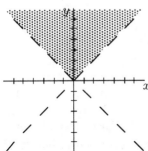

22-7 Any point which satisfies both inequalities must be in the shaded region for each; thus the simultaneous solution takes the form of the quarter-plane where the two solution regions overlap. The boundaries are again dashed, since they are not in the solution sets of the individual inequalities.

22-8 Shown is the case where we have $x + y \geq 0$ instead of $x + y > 0$. The boundary line corresponding to the $x + y > 0$ half-plane has to be colored in in the valid region, since it is now a solution. However, the point $(0,0)$, where the solid and dashed lines meet, stays out, since it still does not solve the other inequality; this is represented by the empty circle at the point. If both lines were colored, we would be able to include the point $(0,0)$.

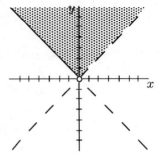

22-9 The quadratic instantly factors to $(x + 3)(x + 2) < 0$. Thus the two individual terms are $x + 2$ and $x + 3$; these must have *opposite* signs for the product to be negative. We draw the two one-variable inequalities $x + 3 > 0$ and $x + 2 > 0$ and take all points which are in one but not the other. Since the inequality is strict, the values -2 and -3 are *not* part of the solution set, so we leave them as open circles.

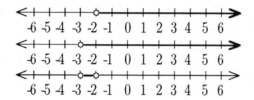

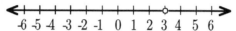

22-10 Again, the quadratic factors, yielding $(x - 3)^2 > 0$. But the only place where a square, like $(x - 3)^2$, is not greater than 0 is where it equals 0! The only x for which the inequality is not satisfied is thus $x = 3$. The inequality is satisfied on the whole real line except for this point, as shown.

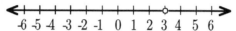

For the second one, the inequality is $(x - 3)^2 < 0$, which is never true because a square cannot be negative! The solution is empty.

22-11 This should represent an interval from -3 to 6 which includes the point -3 but excludes the point 6. It should thus have an open circle on the right end and a closed one on the left, as shown.

22-12 The given expression factors into $(x^2 - 3)(x^2 - 2) \geq 0$, or $(x - \sqrt{3})(x + \sqrt{3})(x - \sqrt{2})(x + \sqrt{2}) \geq 0$. This will be satisfied if either all four terms are positive, two are positive and two negative, or all four are negative. Given your quadratic experience, it should be easy to plot the four relevant inequalities ($x - \sqrt{3} > 0$, etc.) and read the answer off using the fact that an even number of the factors must be positive. In interval notation, we get:

$$(-\infty, -\sqrt{3}] \cup [-\sqrt{2}, \sqrt{2}] \cup [\sqrt{3}, \infty).$$

22-13 The plot is shown below; the interval notation is $(-\infty, -9/2) \cup (-3/2, \infty)$.

22-14 The steps clearly work in reverse so the initial inequality must be true.

Solutions to Problems

414. Rearranging the two inequalities, we have $y \geq 1$ and $3y \leq -1$. Thus $y \geq 1$ and $y \leq -1/3$. Clearly, there is no y that satisfies both of these so the **empty set** is the solution.

415. Subtracting 1 from each side, we have $2/z - 1 = (2 - z)/z \geq 0$. Both of these terms $((2 - z)$ and $z)$ are positive only when $0 < z < 2$. The above expression is 0 when $z = 2$ and undefined when $z = 0$. Thus, the final solution is $\mathbf{0 < z \leq 2}$. (Why didn't we just multiply both sides by z?)

416. From the second inequality we have $x > 0$ since $6/x$ is positive only if x is positive. From the first we have $(x + 6)(x - 5) \geq 0$, so $x \geq 5$ or $x \leq -6$. Only the former satisfies $x > 0$, so the solution to the problem is $\boldsymbol{x \geq 5}$.

417. Completing the square, we have $-t^2 + 60t + 700 = -[t^2 - 60t + (60/2)^2] + 700 + 30^2 = -(t - 30)^2 + 1600$. Since the first term in this sum is the negative of a square, its maximum is 0. Thus, the maximum height is $\mathbf{1600}$, and it occurs when $t = 30$.

418. Since everything is positive (why can't x be negative?), we can square both sides to get $x < 4x^2$; then dividing by x gives $1 < 4x$, and dividing by 4 gives $1/4 < x$, which is the answer.

419. The quotient will be maximized if a is as large as possible and b as small as possible. Thus we take $a = 5.1$ and $b = 3$, so $a/b = 5.1/3 = \mathbf{1.7}$.

420. We can write the first inequality as $|x| \geq 2$, which means that $x \leq -2$ or $x \geq 2$. The second may be expanded as $-3 < x - 1 < 3$, or $-2 < x < 4$. The only integer overlap between these two ranges is $x = 3$ and $x = 2$. (Draw the plots if it helps you see this.) Hence there are **two** integer solutions.

421. The given equality expands to $-3 \leq \frac{n}{3} - 2 \leq 3$. Then adding 2 to all sides gives $-1 \leq \frac{n}{3} \leq 5$, and multiplying by 3 yields $-3 \leq n \leq 15$. The possible values for n are thus $-3, -2, \ldots, 15$. To figure out how many are in this range, subtract the start from the end and add 1 to get $15 - (-3) + 1 = \mathbf{19}$.

422. Start with the given inequality $x < a$. Since x is negative (given), we can multiply both sides by x and reverse the inequality sign to get $x^2 > ax$. We can similarly multiply both sides by a and reverse the inequality to get $ax > a^2$. Combining these yields the desired $x^2 > ax > a^2$.

423. We have $x < x - y$ and $x + y < y$. Subtracting x from both sides of the first and y from both sides of the second yields $0 < -y$ and $x < 0$, which means that x and y are negative.

424. Since everything is the same, we can take reciprocals straight through and reverse the inequalities to see that $1 < \frac{d}{c} < \frac{b}{a}$. Moreover, multiplying through in this inequality by $\frac{b}{a}$ yields $\frac{b}{a} < \frac{bd}{ac} < \frac{b^2}{a^2}$. Thus $1 < \frac{d}{c} < \frac{b}{a} < \frac{bd}{ac}$, and we just need to place $\frac{b+d}{a+c}$. We compare it to $\frac{d}{c}$:

$$
\begin{array}{ccc}
\dfrac{b + d}{a + c} & ? & \dfrac{d}{c} \\
cb + cd & ? & da + dc \\
cb & ? & da
\end{array}
$$

$$\frac{c}{d} \quad ? \quad \frac{a}{b}.$$

Comparing this to the given information, we know the question mark is a $>$, and $\frac{b+d}{a+c}$ is greater. If we then compare $\frac{b+d}{a+c}$ to $\frac{b}{a}$ in the same way, we find that $\frac{b+d}{a+c} < \frac{b}{a}$. Thus we can fit it in the hierarchy:

$$1 < \frac{d}{c} < \frac{b+d}{a+c} < \frac{b}{a} < \frac{bd}{ac}.$$

425.   Put all terms on one side with a common denominator:

$$\frac{x^2 + 2x + 1}{x} \leq 0.$$

Thus, $(x+1)^2/x \leq 0$. Since the numerator is a perfect square, it is always positive. Thus, the fraction is only negative when the denominator is negative, or $x < 0$.

426.   We want the minimum value of $3x^2 + 6x + k$ to be 4. To find the minimum, we complete the square to get $3(x+1)^2 - 3 + k$. The minimum value is attained when the square term is 0, and then the value is just $-3 + k$. Setting this equal to 4, we find that $k = 7$.

427.   Since r is positive, we can divide it out without changing the sign to get $p > q$. Clearly none of the choices covers all possible pairs (p, q) with $p > q$. (For example, $(3, 2)$ disproves the first, second, and fourth; and $(3, -4)$ disproves the third.)

428.   We have $3^{20} > 2^{5x}$, and taking fifth roots on both sides leaves $3^4 > 2^x$. But $3^4 = 81$, so this is $81 > 2^x$. The largest power of 2 less than 81 is $64 = 2^6$, so $x = 6$.

Chapter 23

Operations

Solutions to Exercises

23-1   Division is **not** distributive. For example $6/(2+1) \neq 6/2 + 6/1$.

23-2   Let a be the identity. Thus, $ab = b$ and dividing by b yields $a = 1$. Since $1(b) = b(1) = b$, **1** is the identity.

23-3   Under addition, the identity is 0, so the inverse of 2 is the number we must add to 2 to get 0, or -2. Under multiplication, the identity is 1, so the inverse of 2 is the number which we must multiply by 2 to get 1, or $1/2$.

23-4   Though ideally they might be so, neither love nor friendship is transitive. For example, even though A is B's friend and B is C's friend, A might not be C's friend.

23-5   Equality, congruence, and similarity are equivalence relations, while perpendicularity (not transitive), $\geq$ (not symmetric), and $<$ (not symmetric) are not.

Solutions to Problems

429. $3 \star 2 = 2(3) - 2^3 = -\mathbf{2}$.

430.   Since $A \# B = (1/A + 1/B)/(A + B) = [(A + B)/AB]/(A + B) = 1/AB$, we have $(3\#5)/(5\#7) = (1/15)/(1/35) = \mathbf{7/3}$.

431.   Since $3@a = (3 + a)/(3 - a) = 3$, we have $3 + a = 9 - 3a$, so $a = \mathbf{3/2}$.

432.   Since $(a \star b)^n = (a^b)^n = a^{bn} = a \star (bn)$, we find $(a \star b)^n = a \star (bn)$. The other choices are all false.

433.   Let x be the identity element. Thus, $a \# x = a + ax = a$, so $ax = 0$ and if x is an identity, then $x = 0$. However, $0 \# a = 0 + 0(a) \neq a$. Hence, 0 is not an identity, so there is **no identity** for this operation.

Chapter 24

Sequences and Series

Solutions to Exercises

24-1   The first sequence is arithmetic, since each term is separated from the previous one by a fixed amount: $1 + 1 = 2$, $2 + 1 = 3$, and so on. For the same reason, the third is also arithmetic, with the common difference being 7. The second sequence is not arithmetic; the difference between the first two terms is 2, between the second two is 3, between the third two is 4, and so on. There is no common difference.

24-2   We have

$$\text{Sum} = \frac{n}{2}\left[(a) + (a + (n-1)d)\right] = \frac{\text{\# terms}}{2}(\text{first term} + \text{last term}).$$

24-3   To use the formula of the previous example, we only need the number of terms, since we already have the first and last terms. We can find n using the facts that $a = 8$, $d = -3$, and $a + (n-1)d = -10$. We find that $n - 1 = 6$, so $n = 7$. Thus the sum is

$$\frac{7}{2}\left[8 + (-10)\right] = -\mathbf{7}.$$

24-4   Since we aren't given the first and last terms, it's easiest to apply the original formula:

$$\frac{n}{2}\left[2a + (n-1)d\right] = \frac{100}{2}\left[2(-101) + (99)(2)\right] = 50(-202 + 198) = -\mathbf{200}.$$

24-5   With what we know, this is easy. There are k terms, the first term is 1, and the last term is k. Thus the sum is

$$\frac{k}{2}(k + 1) = \frac{k(k + 1)}{2}.$$

24-6 By the formula we derived for the sum of the first n integers, she would have $64 \cdot 65/2 =$ **2080** grains.

24-7 We have $a = 1$, $r = 2$, $n = k + 1$, so the sum is

$$1 + 2 + 4 + \cdots + 2^k = \frac{1 - 2^{k+1}}{1 - 2} = 2^{k+1} - 1.$$

(For example, straight adding gives $1 + 2 + 4 + 8 + 16 = 31 = 32 - 1$.) The woman asked for $1 + 2 + 4 + 8 + \cdots + 2^{63} = 2^{64} - 1$ grains. Because $2^4 = 16 > 10$, this is greater than 10^{16} grains, and even at $1,000,000 = 10^6$ grains per loaf, this is still 10^{10}, or *ten billion loaves!* And this is only a lower bound; using $2^{10} = 1024 > 10^3$, we can improve the bound: $2^{64} = 16 \cdot 2^{60} > 16 \cdot 10^{18}$. This new bound corresponds to sixteen trillion loaves. The king could not possibly pay her.

24-8 Summing the terms $x^{k-1} + x^{k-2} + \cdots + 1$ as a geometric series with $a = 1$, $n = k$, and $r = x$ yields

$$\frac{1 - x^k}{1 - x} = x^{k-1} + x^{k-2} + \cdots + 1,$$

and multiplying through by $(x - 1)$ yields the desired factorization.

24-9 Since the terms in an arithmetic series uniformly increase or decrease, they cannot tend to 0. The only way they *can* tend to 0 is if they all are 0! Thus the only convergent arithmetic series is the eminently uninteresting $0 + 0 + 0 + \cdots = 0$.

24-10 If $r = 1$, the series looks like $a + a + a + \cdots$, which diverges unless $a = 0$.

24-11 For the first one, we are adding up 1 eight times, so we let a dummy variable do the counting: $\sum_{i=1}^{8} 1$.

For the second, we need to decrease 13 by some multiple of $1/2$. The total number of terms is

$$\frac{13 - \frac{1}{2}}{\frac{1}{2}} + 1 = 26.$$

One way to do the sum is $\sum_{j=0}^{25} (13 - \frac{j}{2})$.

For the third, it is easy to get the squares, but we also need to bring in the alternating sign. This is done by raising -1 to the correct power, since the powers of -1 alternate in sign and don't affect things in any other way. Thus the sum can be written $\sum_{k=1}^{8} (-1)^{k-1} k^2$. Do you see why the exponent of -1 must be $k - 1$ instead of k? Would $k + 1$ work as well?

24-12 Let's do this just like we did the other $\sum$ problems: for each value of k, write down the value of the expression. The sum thus becomes

$$\sum_{j=1}^{4} j + \sum_{j=1}^{4} 2j + \sum_{j=1}^{4} 3j + \sum_{j=1}^{4} 4j.$$

We thus have to evaluate each of the sums in j, to get

$$(1+2+3+4)+(2+4+6+8)+(3+6+9+12)+(4+8+12+16) = 10+20+30+40 = 100.$$

24-13 The only difference between this one and the last is that now the limits of summation are different for each of the four sums:

$$\sum_{j=1}^{1} j + \sum_{j=1}^{2} 2j + \sum_{j=1}^{3} 3j + \sum_{j=1}^{4} 4j.$$

This is really no problem at all if we stay calm and expand the sums straightforwardly, obtaining

$$(1) + (2 + 4) + (3 + 6 + 9) + (4 + 8 + 12 + 16) = 1 + 6 + 18 + 40 = 65.$$

24-14 For the first one, we need to subtract the number of the term we want from 11 (for example, for the first term we want $11 - 1 = 10$), so the expression is $\{11 - n\}$. For the second, we need to divide 2 by 2^n, where n is the number of the term, so the expession is $\{2/2^n\}$, or $\{2^{1-n}\}$.

24-15 For each one, we can write down terms by just substituting $n = 1$, 2, 3, and so on. The first one thus becomes $1 \cdot 2 = 2$, $2 \cdot 3 = 6$, $3 \cdot 4 = 12$, and so on; the second is $1/1 = 1$, $1/2$, $1/6$, $1/24$, $1/120$, $\ldots$; and the third is 1, 8, 27, 64, 125, $\ldots$

24-16 This can be done by just substituting in numbers. The first three terms are 1, 1, 1. The next term is the sum of these three, or 3. The next is $3+1+1 = 5$, the next $5+3+1 = 9$, then $9 + 5 + 3 = 17$, 31, $\ldots$

24-17 In an arithmetic sequence, the first term is always a and each term is d more than the last. Thus we can define any arithmetic sequence as $\{x_n\}$, where

$$x_1 = a \qquad \text{and} \qquad \text{for any } n > 1, \ x_n = x_{n-1} + d.$$

Similarly, for a geometric sequence the first term is a and each term is equal to the previous term multiplied by r. The recursive formulation is thus

$$x_1 = a \qquad \text{and} \qquad \text{for any } n > 1, \ x_n = rx_{n-1}.$$

24-18 We want three numbers x, y, z such that 3, x, y, z, 4 is an arithmetic sequence. We have $a = 3$, $n = 5$; we just need to find d. But we know that $4 = 3 + (5 - 1)d$, which yields $d = 1/4$. Thus $x = 3 + 1/4 = \mathbf{13/4}$, $y = x + 1/4 = \mathbf{14/4}$, and $z = y + 1/4 = \mathbf{15/4}$.

24-19 Consecutive terms in a geometric series will be ar^{n-1}, ar^n, ar^{n+1}. The geometric mean of ar^{n-1} and ar^{n+1} is $\sqrt{ar^{n-1}ar^{n+1}} = \sqrt{a^2r^{2n}} = ar^n$.

24-20 We want two numbers x, y such that 3, x, y, 4 is a geometric sequence. We have $a = 3$, $n = 4$, so $4 = ar^3 = 3r^3$. This yields $r^3 = 4/3$, so $r = \sqrt[3]{4/3} = \sqrt[3]{36}/3$. Thus $x = 3(\sqrt[3]{36}/3) = \sqrt[3]{\mathbf{36}}$ and $y = rx = \mathbf{2\sqrt[3]{6}}$.

Solutions to Problems

434. Given the usual a as the first term and d as the common difference, the 31st and 73rd terms are $a + 30d$ and $a + 72d$, respectively. Setting these equal to 18 and 46, we have

$$a + 30d = 18$$
$$a + 72d = 46.$$

Subtracting the first from the second yields $42d = 28$, so $d = 2/3$; substituting this back in then gives $a = -2$. The sixth term is thus $-2 + 5(2/3) = \mathbf{4/3}$.

435. We have $ar = 4$ and $ar^5 = 16$; dividing the second equation by the first yields $r^4 = 4$, so $r = \sqrt{2}$, and $a = 4/\sqrt{2} = 2\sqrt{2}$. Thus the fourth term is $ar^3 = 2\sqrt{2}(\sqrt{2})^3 = \mathbf{8}$.

436. We can split the fraction up, obtaining

$$\sum_{n=0}^{\infty}\left(\frac{3^n + 5^n}{8^n}\right) = \sum_{n=0}^{\infty}\left(\frac{3^n}{8^n} + \frac{5^n}{8^n}\right)$$
$$= \sum_{n=0}^{\infty}\left(\frac{3}{8}\right)^n + \sum_{n=0}^{\infty}\left(\frac{5}{8}\right)^n.$$

Each of the $\sum$'s we now have is just an infinite geometric series with $a = 1$; for example,

$$\sum_{n=0}^{\infty}\left(\frac{3}{8}\right)^n = 1 + \frac{3}{8} + \left(\frac{3}{8}\right)^2 + \cdots$$

The sums of the individual series are thus

$$\frac{1}{1 - \frac{3}{8}} = \frac{8}{5}$$

and

$$\frac{1}{1 - \frac{5}{8}} = \frac{8}{3}.$$

The total sum is thus $\frac{8}{3} + \frac{8}{5} = \mathbf{\frac{64}{15}}$.

437. This is simply a geometric series with first term 1, ratio x. Thus the sum is $1/(1-x)$. Setting this equal to 4, we immediately find $x = \mathbf{3/4}$.

438. We have $a = -59$, $d = 3$, and $n = 40$, so the sum is $\frac{40}{2}(2(-59) + (40-1)(3)) = (20)(-118 + 117) = \mathbf{-20}$.

439. We want the geometric sequence $a = 8$, ar, ar^2, ar^3, ar^4, ar^5, $ar^6 = 5832$. Using the first and last terms we find that $r^6 = 5832/8 = 729$, so $r = 3$. The fifth term in the sequence is $ar^4 = 8 \cdot 3^4 = 8 \cdot 81 = \mathbf{648}$.

440. To add up the series, we can just split it into two infinite geometric series, $1/7 + 1/7^2 + 1/7^3 + \cdots$ and $1/7^2 + 1/7^4 + 1/7^6 + \cdots$ Convince yourself that the sum of these gives back the original series. Each can be summed with our basic infinite geometric series formula, $a/(1-r)$. The first gives

$$\frac{\frac{1}{7}}{\left(1 - \frac{1}{7}\right)} = \frac{\frac{1}{7}}{\frac{6}{7}} = \frac{1}{6};$$

the second,

$$\frac{\frac{1}{7^2}}{\left(1 - \frac{1}{7^2}\right)} = \frac{\frac{1}{49}}{\frac{48}{49}} = \frac{1}{48}.$$

The sum of the series is $1/6 + 1/48 = 9/48 = \mathbf{3/16}$.

441. After the first row, we have just written the number 1, after the second row, $1+2 = 3$ numbers, after the third, $1+2+3 = 6$ numbers, and so on. Thus after the seventeenth row we have written $1+2+3+\cdots+16 = 16 \cdot 17/2 = 136$ numbers. The next number, the first one on row 17, is thus 137, and the last one on that row is $136 + 17 = 153$, since the row has seventeen terms. The sum is $137 + 153 = \mathbf{290}$.

442. The sum of the first three terms is $a + ar + ar^2$ (easier to ignore the formula, since the expression is simple enough already), which should equal $7a$, yielding $1 + r + r^2 = 7$. Solving the quadratic $r^2 + r - 6 = 0$, we find that r equals either 2 or -3; we take the 2 since negatives are excluded by the problem. We should then have $a + ar + ar^2 + ar^3 = 45$; substituting $r = 2$ gives $15a = 45$, and $a = \mathbf{3}$.

443. The sum of the first n odd numbers is $\frac{n}{2}(2 + (n-1)(2)) = n^2$, which should equal 900. Thus $n = \mathbf{30}$.

444. Let the geometric sequence be a, ar, ar^2, $\ldots$, and the arithmetic sequence be 0, d, $2d$, $\ldots$ The sequence formed by summing corresponding terms is 1, 1, 2, $\ldots$, and we immediately see that $a = 1$. Using the second and third terms, we then find that $r + d = 1$ and $r^2 + 2d = 2$. Using the first equation to obtain $d = 1 - r$ and substituting in the second, we get $r^2 - 2r = 0$. Since $r \neq 0$, this means that $r = 2$, so $d = -1$. Now the sum of the first ten terms of the composite series is just equal to the sum of the sums of the two separate series, or

$$(0 - 1 - 2 - \cdots - 9) + (1 + 2 + 4 + \cdots + 2^9).$$

The arithmetic part is the negative of the sum of the first nine integers, or $-9(10)/2 = -45$. The geometric is the sum of the first ten powers of 2, which we have seen should equal $2^{10} - 1 = 1024 - 1 = 1023$. The sum is $1023 - 45 = \mathbf{978}$.

445. We split the sum into two series. First,

$$1 - \frac{1}{2} - \frac{1}{4} - \frac{1}{8} - \cdots = 1 - \frac{1/2}{1/2} = 0.$$

What's left over is

$$2 \cdot \frac{1}{8} + 2 \cdot \frac{1}{64} + \cdots = \frac{2/8}{1 - (1/8)} = \frac{2}{7},$$

which is the answer since the other part summed to 0. (Make sure you see that adding these two gives the original series.

446. The book prices form the arithmetic sequence a, $a + 2$, $a + 4$, etc. The price of the middle, or 16th, book, is $a + 15(2) = a + 30$. The price of the book at the extreme right is $a+30(2) = a+60$. Let the price of the "adjacent" book be $a+2k$; then $a+30+a+2k = a+60$, so $k = 15 - a/2$. If the book is to be adjacent to the middle book, we must have k equal to either 14 or 16; but k cannot be 16, since that would require a to be -2. Since they don't, unfortunately, pay you to take books, the book in question must be the the book to the **left**.

447. The first element of the 21st set is one more than the last element of the 20th, which is $1+2+3+\cdots+20 = 210$. Thus the first element of the 21st set is 211, and its last element is $210 + 21 = 231$. Thus the sum of its elements is

$$
\begin{aligned}
211 + 212 + 213 + \cdots + 231 &= 21(210) + (1 + 2 + \cdots + 21) \\
&= 4410 + \frac{21 \cdot 22}{2} \\
&= 4410 + 231 \\
&= \mathbf{4641}.
\end{aligned}
$$

Note how easy the sum is when we get rid of the 210 which is common to all terms.

448. The sum of the first n terms is always $\frac{n}{2}(2a + (n - 1)d)$, so we have

$$\frac{n}{2}(2a + (n - 1)d) = an + dn^2/2 - dn/2.$$

Thus $d/2 = 3$, so $d = 6$, and $a - d/2 = 2$, so $a = 5$. The rth term is thus

$$a + (r - 1)d = 5 + 6(r - 1) = \mathbf{6r{-}1}.$$

Another clever way to attack this problem is by noting that the rth term is $S_r - S_{r-1}$, where S_n is the sum of the first n terms. Try using this fact to arrive at the above answer. [Special thanks to Kai Huang for this clever approach.]

449. There are obviously the same number of terms in the top and bottom, since for each term k in the top, a $k + 1$ corresponds in the bottom. The ratio is equal to

$$\frac{\frac{\#\text{ terms in top}}{2}(\text{first term in top} + \text{last term in top})}{\frac{\#\text{ terms in bottom}}{2}(\text{first term in bottom} + \text{last term in bottom})},$$

but since the numbers of terms are the same, the first terms cancel and we are left with

$$\frac{\text{first term in top} + \text{last term in top}}{\text{first term in bottom} + \text{last term in bottom}} = \frac{1 + 199}{2 + 200} = \frac{200}{202} = \frac{\mathbf{100}}{\mathbf{101}}.$$

450. We can get the series $32 + 16 + 8 + 4 + 2 + 1$ by taking 2 to successively smaller powers, from 5 down to 0. This looks like

$$\sum_{i=0}^{5} \frac{32}{2^i} = \sum_{i=0}^{5} 2^{5-i}.$$

All we then need is to get the alternating sign, which just comes in as $(-1)^i$, so the sum is written

$$\sum_{i=0}^{5} (-1)^i 2^{5-i}.$$

As an exercise, try writing the same sum with i ranging from 1 to 6 rather than from 0 to 5.

451. We have $11 + 13 + \cdots + 49$. We find the number of terms from $11 + (n - 1)(2) = 49$, so $n = 20$ and the sum is $10(11 + 49) = \mathbf{600}$.

452. As stated in the text, the middle term should be the average of its neighbors, so $2x + 2 = [(4x - 1) + (2x - 3)]/2 = 3x - 2$, and $x = \mathbf{4}$.

453. This is a tiny bit tricky, since one-digit numbers contribute only 1 digit, two-digit numbers 2, and so on. Thus we treat each type separately. The 9 one-digit numbers each contribute their 1, for a total of 9 digits; there are $852 - 9 = 843$ to go. The 90 two-digit numbers from 10 to 99 each contribute 2 digits, for a total of 180; $843 - 180 = 663$ to go. The 900 three-digit numbers from 100 to 999 contribute 3 digits each, for 2700 digits. Oops... this goes over the limit of 852. Thus all the remaining 663 are three-digit numbers, so $221 \ (= 663/3)$ are used. We add these 221 to the last two-digit, 99, so that the last number used is $99 + 221 = \mathbf{320}$.

454. The easy way is to use the properties that terms of arithmetic and geometric series are the arithmetic or geometric means of their neighbors. Thus, since a, b, c is an arithmetic sequence, we have $b = (a + c)/2$. Also, since $a + 1$, b, c and a, b, $c + 2$ are geometric sequences, we have $b = \sqrt{(a + 1)c} = \sqrt{a(c + 2)}$. Squaring our three expressions for b yields $(a^2 + 2ac + c^2)/4 = ac + c = ac + 2a$. The second equality yields $c = 2a$. Substituting this into the first equality gives $a^2 + 4a^2 + 4a^2 = 8a^2 + 8a$, which gives $a^2 = 8a$, so $a = 8$. Then $c = 16$, and $b = (a + c)/2 = \mathbf{12}$.

455. We will proceed by induction. For the base case, $F_1 = 1$ and $F_2 = 2$ are relatively prime. Now we do the inductive step, assuming that F_k and F_{k-1} are relatively prime, and proving from this that F_{k+1} and F_k are relatively prime. Since $F_{k+1} = F_k + F_{k-1}$, the numbers F_{k+1} and F_k are relatively prime if and only if $F_k + F_{k-1}$ and F_k are. But we know that F_k and F_{k-1} are relatively prime by the inductive assumption; then $F_k + F_{k-1}$ and F_k are also, since any common divisor would simultaneously divide F_k and F_{k-1}, violating the assertion that these are relatively prime. Thus F_k and F_{k+1} are relatively prime, and we are done by induction.

456. The probability of someone losing on their roll is the sum of the probabilities of getting an 8 or a 9, namely $5/36 + 4/36 = 9/36 = 1/4$. We find the probability Doug dies, since otherwise we would have to separately consider the probabilities of A, B, and C dying. He dies the first time through if A, B, and C all do not roll 8 or 9 (probability 3/4 each) and then he does roll 8 or 9. This happens with probability

$$\frac{3}{4} \cdot \frac{3}{4} \cdot \frac{3}{4} \cdot \frac{1}{4}.$$

Doug dies the *second* time through if all players survive the first time through, then A, B, and C survive the second time through, then Doug rolls 8 or 9. This happens with probability

$$\frac{3}{4} \cdot \frac{3}{4} \cdot \frac{3}{4} \cdot \frac{3}{4} \cdot \frac{3}{4} \cdot \frac{3}{4} \cdot \frac{3}{4} \cdot \frac{1}{4}.$$

And so on. Each time through, a new factor of $\left(\frac{3}{4}\right)^4$ comes in, since that corresponds to all four players surviving for an entire round. The answer is thus an infinite geometric series with first term $\frac{3}{4} \cdot \frac{3}{4} \cdot \frac{3}{4} \cdot \frac{1}{4}$ and common ratio $\left(\frac{3}{4}\right)^4$, for a sum of

$$\frac{\frac{27}{256}}{1 - \frac{81}{256}} = \frac{27}{175}.$$

As stated above, this is the probability that Doug *dies*. The probability that he *lives*, which we are asked to find, should be $1 - \frac{27}{175} = \mathbf{\frac{148}{175}}$.

Chapter 25

Learning to Count

Solutions to Exercises

25-1 This number should be the exclusive number plus 2, since the only change is adding the start and end points. Thus there are 273, or $317 - 45 + 1$. In the same way, the number of integers between a and b is $b - a + 1$.

25-2 For each child, Horatio has a separate choice among the 5 M&M colors, so for the three children, there are $5 \cdot 5 \cdot 5 = \mathbf{125}$ ways to do the choosing.

25-3 Since the number must be odd, the last digit should be 1, 3, 5, 7, or 9, a total of 5 choices. The first digit must be 2, 3, 4, 5, or 6, for 5 choices. The second and fourth digits can be chosen in 10 ways each (anything from 0 to 9), and the third digit is already set. Writing the number of choices for each digit in that digit's position, we have

$$5 \cdot 10 \cdot 1 \cdot 10 \cdot 5 = \mathbf{2500}$$

such numbers.

25-4 Since the k contributions are all independent, and for the jth factor there are $(e_j + 1)$ choices, the multiplication principle tells us that the total number of choices is

$$(e_1 + 1)(e_2 + 1)(e_3 + 1) \cdots (e_k + 1).$$

25-5 Direct testing yields the divisors as 1, 2, 3, 4, 6, and 12, for a total of 6. The prime factorization of 12 is $2^2 3^1$, so consideration of the factorization yields $(2+1)(1+1) = 3 \cdot 2 = \mathbf{6}$.

25-6 We can factor 1,000,000 as $10^6 = 2^6 5^6$, so it has $(6+1)(6+1) = (7)(7) = \mathbf{49}$ factors.

25-7 This indeed gives all the possibilities, since any sequence of colors may be given out. It also does not overcount, since a given sequence of colors can only be given out in one way.

25-8 For the first letter, there are 26 choices, for the second 25, for the third 24, for the fourth 23. The total is thus $26 \cdot 25 \cdot 24 \cdot 23 = \mathbf{358800}$.

25-9 Let us use the method of filling in the blanks. We first put our 5 in the middle digit, with 1 possible choice, to get

$$\_\,\_\,\underline{1}\,\_\,\_.$$

We then have four choices left for the last digit, 1, 3, 7, and 9:

$$\_\,\_\,\underline{1}\,\_\,\underline{4}.$$

Of the possible first digits, 4, 5, and 6, only 5 has been ruled out, so we have

$$\underline{2}\,\_\,\underline{1}\,\_\,\underline{4}.$$

Now, since the remaining two digits can be anything but the three digits already taken, we have

$$\underline{2}\,\underline{7}\,\underline{1}\,\underline{6}\,\underline{4} = \mathbf{336}$$

as the final product. Note that we were "lucky" that the restrictions on the first and last digits did not overlap. If the range under consideration had been from 20000 to 69999, then if the last digit had been 3, the first digit would have had an additional restriction. The problem would thus have to be broken into two cases: "last digit 3" and "last digit anything else." Do you have any idea how we would do this?

25-10 In the first half of the alphabet are the vowels a, e and i, so we can choose the two vowels in $3 \cdot 2$ ways (3 for the first, then 2 for the second). We can choose the consonant in 10 ways (13 letters in the first half minus 3 vowels), and then the two unspecified letters can be chosen in $10 \cdot 9$ ways, since three letters of the 13 are taken. The total is thus $3 \cdot 2 \cdot 10 \cdot 10 \cdot 9 = \mathbf{5400}$ such "words."

25-11 We can choose one person for the first seat in n ways, then one of the remaining $n - 1$ to go second in $n - 1$ ways, then one of the remaining $n - 2$ in $n - 2$ ways, and so on until we choose the kth one in $n - k + 1$ ways. (Note that there will be $n - k$ left *after* we pick the kth one, so there must have been $n - k + 1$ before we pick it. The kth one could thus have been picked in $n - k + 1$ ways.) The total number of ways is thus

$$n(n - 1)(n - 2) \cdots (n - k + 1).$$

25-12 First, $3! = 3 \cdot 2 \cdot 1 = \mathbf{6}$. Second, $7! = 7 \cdot 6 \cdot 5 \cdot 4 \cdot 3 \cdot 2 \cdot 1$, and multiplying out gives **5040**. Third, $_7P_3 = 7!/4! = 5040/24 = \mathbf{210}$, and fourth $_5P_4 = 5!/1! = (5 \cdot 4 \cdot 3 \cdot 2 \cdot 1)/(1) = \mathbf{120}$.

25-13 We simply expand the factorial out to see

$$\begin{aligned} n! &= n(n-1)(n-2) \cdots (n-k+2)(n-k+1)(n-k) \cdots (3)(2)(1) \\ &= n(n-1)(n-2) \cdots (n-k+1)(n-k)! \end{aligned}$$

25-14 We get a factor of 2 for each of the 50 even numbers less than or equal to 100, then another for each of the $100/4 = 25$ multiples of 4, then another for each of the $100/8 = 12.5 \rightarrow 12$ multiples of 8, another for each of the $\lfloor 100/16 \rfloor$ multiples of 16, another for the 3 multiples of 32, and another for the single multiple of 64. The total is

$$50 + 25 + 12 + 6 + 3 + 1 = \mathbf{97}.$$

25-15 There are 4! ways to do it in a line, so 3! ways to do it in a circle, so $3!/2 = \mathbf{3}$ ways to do it on a keychain.

25-16 Babies are pretty clearly distinguishable. The playpens are also distinguishable. Thus, each baby can choose her playpen as an independent choice, so there are $2 \cdot 2 \cdot 2 = \mathbf{8}$ different possibilities. On the other hand, if the playpens are indistinguishable, then each configuration has a "mirror" configuration: $(ab)(c)$ and $(c)(ab)$, for example, where each parentheses represents a playpen and each letter a baby. These two cases are the same for each pair, so we need to divide our total by 2, and there are only **4** choices. (These four choices can be easily made clear: each baby alone in one playpen or all three together. In some ways, indistinguishability simplifies things.)

25-17 Since the rattles are indistinguishable, the **4** choices are $(3)(0)$, $(2)(1)$, $(1)(2)$, and $(0)(3)$, where the first parentheses contain the number given to Sara and the second the number given to Lara. How would this change if babies were identical? If rattles were not?

25-18 If we make sure and *not* pick *Anne of Avonlea*, there are 7 books to choose from, for $7 \cdot 6 \cdot 5$ arrangements. The total number of arrangements is $8 \cdot 7 \cdot 6$, so the number *with Avonlea* is

$$8 \cdot 7 \cdot 6 - 7 \cdot 6 \cdot 5 = 7 \cdot 6 \cdot (8 - 5) = 7 \cdot 6 \cdot 3 = 126.$$

Unlike tougher problems of this type, this one can also be done relatively easily by a direct method. Choose *Avonlea*, then choose its position, first, second, or third, in 3 ways, then choose books for the other two positions in $7 \cdot 6$ ways, for a total of $3 \cdot 7 \cdot 6 = \mathbf{126}$. If you try to use this to do the Europe example, however, you will find it very complicated: how many of the countries are included? Which ones? and in what positions? The subtraction method is much simpler.

25-19 The number with no repeated letter is $26 \cdot 25 \cdot 24 \cdot 23$, and the total number is $26 \cdot 26 \cdot 26 \cdot 26$. Thus the fraction with at least one repeated letter is

$$\frac{26 \cdot 26 \cdot 26 \cdot 26 - 26 \cdot 25 \cdot 24 \cdot 23}{26 \cdot 26 \cdot 26 \cdot 26}.$$

25-20 If the order of attack mattered, then by what we have already done Ulysses could make his choice in $11 \cdot 10 \cdot 9 \cdot 8$ ways. However, since it does not, we need to divide out by the number of ways these four can be arranged (GA-AL-LA-MS, AL-LA-GA-MS, etc.), which we know is 4!. Thus the choice can be made in $\dfrac{11 \cdot 10 \cdot 9 \cdot 8}{4 \cdot 3 \cdot 2 \cdot 1} = 11 \cdot 10 \cdot 3 = \mathbf{330}$ ways.

25-21 They do indeed, since

$$\frac{5!}{3!\,2!} = \frac{5 \cdot 4 \cdot 3 \cdot 2 \cdot 1}{3 \cdot 2 \cdot 1 \cdot 2 \cdot 1} = \frac{5 \cdot 4 \cdot 3}{3 \cdot 2 \cdot 1}$$

and

$$\frac{11!}{4!\,7!} = \frac{11 \cdot 10 \cdot 9 \cdot 8}{4 \cdot 3 \cdot 2 \cdot 1}.$$

25-22 Suppose we wish to choose k things from a set of n. As before, if we wanted to choose them *in order*, we could do it in

$$n(n-1)(n-2)\cdots(n-k+1)$$

ways. However, if the order does not matter, we need to divide out by the number of ways to rearrange the k objects, or $k!$. This yields

$$\frac{n(n-1)(n-2)\cdots(n-k+1)}{k!} = \frac{n(n-1)(n-2)\cdots(n-k+1)\,(n-k)!}{k!\,(n-k)!}$$

$$= \frac{n!}{k!\,(n-k)!}.$$

25-23 If one person must be on, we just need to pick two more people from the remaining four. We can do this in $\binom{4}{2} = 4 \cdot 3/2 \cdot 1 = \mathbf{6}$ ways.

25-24 The number of ways to choose 0 objects from a group of n is $\binom{n}{0} = \frac{n!}{0!n!} = \mathbf{1}$.

25-25 She must pick 2 bolts from 6 and 2 nuts from 8; she can do this in

$$\binom{6}{2}\binom{8}{2} = \frac{6 \cdot 5}{2 \cdot 1}\frac{8 \cdot 7}{2 \cdot 1} = (15)(28) = \mathbf{420}$$

ways.

25-26 This does hold generally, because

$$\binom{n}{k} = \frac{n!}{k!\,(n-k)!}$$

and

$$\binom{n}{(n-k)} = \frac{n!}{(n-k)!\,(n-(n-k))!} = \frac{n!}{(n-k)!\,k!}.$$

25-27 The word RAMANUJAN has 9 letters, with 2 N's and 3 A's. The number of ways to rearrange it is thus $9!/2!3! = 9 \cdot 8 \cdot 7!/(2 \cdot 3 \cdot 2) = 6 \cdot 5040 = \mathbf{30240}$.

MINIMIZATION has 12 letters, with 4 I's, 2 M's, and 2 N's, so it can be rearranged in $12!/4!2!2!$ ways. Simplifying the factorials yields **4989600**.

25-28   Based on our work so far, the general formula is trivial to prove. We can rearrange the word in $n!$ ways, and we then need to divide out all the ways to rearrange each letter, to get

$$\frac{n!}{k_1! \, k_2! \cdots k_j!}.$$

25-29   The previous answer was $\frac{8!}{2!\,3!}$, and the new answer is

$$\binom{8}{3}\binom{5}{2}3! = \frac{8!}{3!\,5!}\,\frac{5!}{2!\,3!}\,3! = \frac{\mathbf{8!}}{\mathbf{2!\,3!}}.$$

25-30   The method we first used is better, making the general result very obvious. With the second method, we would have to write down a string of combinations and show how they cancel.

Solutions to Problems

457.   For each question there are two choices, so for all five there are $2^5 = \mathbf{32}$ choices.

458.   This is most easily done by counting the wrong thing and subtracting. The number 2^{95} has $(95 + 1) = 96$ factors, all of which are powers of 2. The number of factors which are *smaller* than 1,000,000 may be found by finding the largest one which is smaller. We have $2^{10} = 1024 > 10^3$, so $2^{20} > 10^6 = 1,000,000$. But $2^{19} = 1024 \cdot 512$ is clearly smaller than 1,000,000, so this is the largest. The number of factors smaller than a million is thus $19 + 1 = 20$ ($2^0, 2^1, \ldots, 2^{19}$), and there are $96 - 20 = \mathbf{76}$ greater than a million.

459.   We are asked to evaluate $101!/99!$. But remember that $101! = 101 \cdot 100 \cdot 99!$, so that $101!/99! = 101 \cdot 100 = \mathbf{10100}$.

460.   Let's start to write them down and see if anything good happens: $1! = 1$, $2! = 2$, $3! = 6$, $4! = 24$, $5! = 120$, $6! = 720$, ... Since 5! ends in a zero, all those following it must also end in 0! Thus the units digit is just the units digit of $1 + 2 + 6 + 4 = 13$, or **3**.

461.   We need all the sets of two teams out of a total pool of six, so there are $\binom{6}{2} = \mathbf{15}$ games.

462.   We have

$$
\begin{aligned}
\frac{\binom{10}{8}\binom{6}{2}}{\binom{7}{4}} &= \frac{\frac{10!}{8!\,2!}\,\frac{6!}{2!\,4!}}{\frac{7!}{4!\,3!}} \\[2mm]
&= \frac{\frac{10\cdot 9}{2\cdot 1}\,\frac{6\cdot 5}{2\cdot 1}}{\frac{7\cdot 6\cdot 5}{3\cdot 2\cdot 1}} \\[2mm]
&= \frac{45 \cdot 15}{35} \\[2mm]
&= \frac{\mathbf{135}}{\mathbf{7}}.
\end{aligned}
$$

463.   We have 5 lines and 2 circles. Each pair of lines may intersect in a point, for $\binom{5}{2} = 10$ intersections. Each line can intersect both circles in two points each, for $5 \cdot 2 \cdot 2 = 20$ intersections. Last, the two circles can intersect each other in two points, for 2 intersections. The total is $10 + 20 + 2 = \mathbf{32}$ intersections. (Can you draw a maximal configuration?)

464.   She needs 1 of 4 flavors and 2 of 6 toppings; she can do this in $\binom{4}{1}\binom{6}{2} = (4)(15) = \mathbf{60}$ ways.

465.   A palindrome will look like $\underline{h}\,\underline{t}\,\underline{h}$. The digit $\underline{h}$ can be chosen in 9 ways, since it can't be 0. The digit $\underline{t}$ can be chosen in 10 ways. The total number is thus $9 \cdot 10 = \mathbf{90}$.

466.   Even numbers alternate between being divisible by 2 and not 4 and being divisible by 4: 2, 4, 6, 8, 10, 12... Thus the product of any two consecutive even numbers must be divisible by 8. Remember that $a!/b! = a(a-1)(a-2)\cdots(b+1)$. If a is even, then a and $a-2$ are even, so they cannot both be in the product; b must equal $a-2$, and $a - b = 2$. If a is odd, then $a-1$ and $a-3$ are even, so b is at least $a-3$, and $a-b$ is at most 3. If $b = a-3$, then $a!/b! = a(a-1)(a-2)$, and all powers of two come from the $(a-1)$ term. Thus if we make $a-1$ divisible by 4 but not 8, we attain the maximum value of **3**. (To better follow this discussion, consider $a = 7, 6, 5,$ and 4 and find the smallest b satisfying the restrictions for each.)

467.   We first factor 480 into $2^5 \cdot 3 \cdot 5$. The total number of factors would be $(5+1)(1+1)(1+1) = 24$, but the odd factors may not have any powers of 2, so of these there are only $(1+1)(1+1) = \mathbf{4}$.

468.   Let the number of people be n, so that the total number of handshakes is $\binom{n}{2} = n(n-1)/2$. For this to be odd, there must be only one factor of 2 in the product $n(n-1)$; otherwise the 2 in the denominator would cancel one 2, but others would remain to make the number even. Since either n or $n-1$ must be even, whichever is even must be divisible by 2 and not 4. Thus the pairs 49-48 and 48-47 are ruled out, since 4 divides 48. The next smaller pair, 47-46, works fine, since 2 only divides 46 once. Thus $n = \mathbf{47}$.

469.   Since no two of the points lie on a single line, each pair of two points determines a distinct line. The total number of lines is thus equal to the number of pairs of points, or $\binom{12}{2} = 12 \cdot 11/2 = 6 \cdot 11 = \mathbf{66}$.

470.   The white chips can either be adjacent, have one red between them, or have two reds between them. These **three** are the only ways it can be done! Try it with dimes and pennies. (Remember, two setups which can be rotated into one another are considered the same in circular problems.)

471.   The key here is to realize that the books which must be together may be treated as a single unit. Within that unit, the books may be in 2 different orders (AB or BA), but we can account for that by simply multiplying by 2 at the end. We thus have 4 books (one is our two-book unit), and these can be arranged in $4! = 24$ ways. Multiplying by 2 then yields **48**. (Make sure in your mind that all configurations are counted, and that none is counted twice!)

472. Let's consider as different cases the possible numbers of prime factors which an integer could have. If it has one prime factor p, then to have 12 divisors it must be of the form p^{11}. But even for $p = 2$, p^{11} is much larger than 100, so there is no contribution from this case.

If the number has two prime factors p and q, then we need to consider the ways of factoring 12 into two numbers: $2 \cdot 6$ and $3 \cdot 4$. Thus the number can be pq^5 or p^2q^3, decreasing the exponents by 1 as discussed in the text. Now p and q must be different. Trying $q = 2$, $p = 3$, pq^5 yields 96, a valid answer, and p^2q^3 yields $9 \cdot 8 = 72$, which is also fine. However, all other choices of p and q yield answers greater than 100, even letting $p = 2$, $q = 3$ (since q is taken to higher powers than p).

If the number has three prime factors p, q, and r, then we need to consider only the one way of factoring 12 into three numbers which aren't 1: $2 \cdot 2 \cdot 3$. Thus the number will be of the form pqr^2. Here we have more possibilities, which we explore by trial and error. Letting $r = 2$, $q = 3$, $p = 5$ gives $5 \cdot 3 \cdot 4 = 60$. Letting $r = 2$, $q = 3$, $p = 7$ gives 84. These two are the only possibilities with $r = 2$, since the next higher, $q = 5$ and $p = 7$, gives a result bigger than 100. We then move on to $r = 3$; here the only solution which is small enough is $5 \cdot 2 \cdot 3^2 = 90$.

We have thus explored all the possible cases, and the sum of all the answers thus obtained is $96 + 72 + 60 + 84 + 90 = \mathbf{402}$.

473. No matter what, there will be 4 playoff games. A different result for each will lead to a completely different outcome, since a player is out who would otherwise have been in. Thus the games may be considered independent, and each contributes 2 outcomes, for a total of $2 \cdot 2 \cdot 2 \cdot 2 = \mathbf{16}$ outcomes. Write down some possible outcomes to better understand why the seemingly related games are actually "independent."

474. For each of the 3 elements of A, we choose any of the 4 elements of B, for $4 \cdot 4 \cdot 4 = \mathbf{64}$ functions.

475. Suppose we list all the palindromes: $\{1001, 1111, 1221, \ldots, 9889, 9999\}$. Notice that if we add the first and the last, we get 11000. The same holds if we add the second and the next-to-last, and so on. Each such pair always sums to 11000. (Can you prove it?) So how many pairs are there? There are ten palindromes starting with each digit from 1 to 9, so there are 90 palindromes. Hence, there are 45 pairs and our desired sum is $(45)(11000) = \mathbf{495000}$. [Special thanks to Lauren Williams for this solution.]

476. Since $12 = 2^2 \cdot 3$, we need to find the number of 2's and 3's which divide 20!. For the 2's, we get 10 multiples of 2, 5 multiples of $4 = 2^2$, 2 multiples of $8 = 2^3$, and 1 multiple of $16 = 2^4$, for a total of $10 + 5 + 2 + 1 = 18$. For the 3's, we get 6 multiples of 3 and 2 multiples of $9 = 3^2$, for a total of $6 + 2 = 8$. Now the twos must come in packets of 2^2 to make 12's, and we have 9 such packets. The 3's are used individually to make 3's, and there are 8 of them. Since 8 is the smaller of 8 and 9, we can thus make **eight** 12's.

477. Insight #1: Each locker is switched once for every divisor it has! Since the lockers start closed, we can immediately see that those open at the end will be those with an odd number of divisors. But which numbers have an odd number of divisors? If a number is factored as

$$p_1^{e_1} p_2^{e_2} \cdots p_k^{e_k},$$

then if any of the e_i is odd, the product $(e_1 + 1) \cdots (e_k + 1)$, which gives the number of divisors, will be even, since the factor $(e_i + 1)$ is even. Thus to have odd divisors, all the exponents must be even. Insight #2: If all the exponents are even, then the number is a perfect square! Thus at the end, the only lockers open will be the perfect squares 1, 4, 9, ...

Chapter 26

Statistics and Probability

Solutions to Exercises

26-1 The sum of the 12 scores is $12(82) = 984$. The sum of the 10 scores upon removal of the highest and lowest is $10(84) = 840$. Thus, the highest and lowest have sum $984 - 840 = 144$. Since the highest is 98, the lowest is $144 - 98 = \mathbf{46}$.

26-2 The first group's scores have sum $25(84) = 2100$, while the second group's scores have sum $20(66) = 1320$. Thus, the 45 scores have sum $2100 + 1320 = 3420$, so the average is $3420/45 = \mathbf{76}$.

26-3 Since there are 3 ways to draw a ball and 2 ways to draw a yellow, the probability is $\mathbf{2/3}$.

26-4 There are 52 ways to draw a card. The number of ways to draw a black is 26, so the probability is $26/52 = \mathbf{1/2}$. The number of ways to draw a spade is 13, so the probability is $13/52 = \mathbf{1/4}$. The number of ways to draw a spade face card is 3 (jack, queen, or king), so the probability is $\mathbf{3/52}$. The number of ways to draw any face card is 12 (J, Q, K in all four suits), so the probability is $12/52 = 6/26 = \mathbf{3/13}$. The number of ways to draw the ace of spades is 1, so the probability is $\mathbf{1/52}$.

26-5 The total number of 4 digit numbers is $9 \cdot 10 \cdot 10 \cdot 10 = 9000$ (9 choices for the first digit, since 0 is excluded, 10 for the others). The total number with no digits repeated is $9 \cdot 9 \cdot 8 \cdot 7 = 4536$. The probability is thus $4536/9000 = 2268/4500 = 1134/2250 = \mathbf{63/125}$.

26-6 The probability of putaway is 0.6, so the probability of return is 0.4. Since the initial spike and the second spike can be considered independent (if we ignore volleyball reality), the probability of first a return, then a putaway, is $(0.4)(0.6) = \mathbf{0.24}$.

26-7 The probability that a red is chosen first is $3/6 = 1/2$. Once the red is chosen, there are 3 green and 2 red left, and the probability that a green is chosen next is $3/5$. Thus the total probability is $\left(\frac{1}{2}\right)\left(\frac{3}{5}\right) = \mathbf{\frac{3}{10}}$.

26-8 The probability of red first, green second is 3/10; the probability of green first, red second is 3/10. Thus the total probability is $(3/10) + (3/10) = 6/10 = 3/5$. Does it matter if the balls are chosen simultaneously or one after the other?

26-9 We just need to write down the ways to attain various rolls.

> 2: 1-1, for probability **1/36**.
>
> 3: 1-2, 2-1, **2/36**.
>
> 4: 1-3, 2-2, 3-1, **3/36**.

And so on. From 2 to 12, the numbers of ways to attain the rolls are 1, 2, 3, 4, 5, 6, 5, 4, 3, 2, 1, and the probabilities are just these values divided by 36.

26-10 If the odds of an event are 2 : 1, the probability of it happening is $1/(2+1) = 1/3$. If the odds of an event are 1 : 2, the probability of it happening are $2/(1+2) = 2/3$. The event with **1 : 2** odds is thus more likely.

26-11 The probability of getting the 1 is 1/6; the probability of not getting it is 5/6. The odds are thus 5/6 : 1/6, or **5 : 1**.

26-12 The probability of winning is 10%, and the probability of not winning is 90%, so the odds are 90 : 10, or **9 : 1**.

26-13 The probability of winning is 7/100, of losing 93/100, so the odds are **93 : 7**.

26-14 We multiply each outcome by its probability and add them up, to get $2(0.43) + 3(0.06) + 0(0.51) = 0.86 + 0.18 + 0 = $ **1.04** points.

26-15 Again, we multiply each outcome by its probability and add, to get $(0)(1/2) + (1)(1/3) + (10)(1/6) = (1/3) + (5/3) = $ **\$2**. Buying at \$2.50 would lose 50 cents on average.

Solutions to Problems

478. In the first five games, he scores a total of $5(18.6) = 93$ points. If his average is to be 20 points per game after 6 games and x is the number of points he scores in the sixth game, we have $(93 + x)/6 = 20$, so $93 + x = 120$ and $x = $ **27**.

479. The first 2 have sum $2(9) = 18$ and the last 5 have sum $5(16) = 80$. Thus, all 7 numbers have sum $18 + 80 = 98$, and the average is $98/7 = $ **14**.

480. The group has sum $30(42) = 1260$. Excluding 82 and 44, the remaining 28 numbers have sum $1260 - 82 - 44 = 1134$, so the average of these is $1134/28 = $ **40.5**.

481. From the arithmetic mean we have $(x + y)/2 = 12.5$, so $x + y = 25$. From the geometric mean, we get $\sqrt{xy} = 12$, so $xy = 144$. Squaring $x+y$ yields $(x+y)^2 = x^2+y^2+2xy$. Thus, $25^2 = x^2 + y^2 + 2(144)$ and $x^2 + y^2 = 625 - 288 = $ **337**.

482. To find the new average after the teacher doubles the last score, we must find the sum of the first five tests and twice the sixth test, then divide this sum by 7 since there are 7 scores added. We are given that the sum of the first five scores is $5m$. To determine the sixth test score, we subtract this from the given sum of the first six scores, $6n$. Thus, the sixth test score is $6n - 5m$. Hence, the new average is $\left(5m + 2(6n - 5m)\right)/7 = (\mathbf{12n-5m})/\mathbf{7}$.

483. In how many ways can I get a result I want? There are 5 such results: $\heartsuit\diamondsuit$, $\heartsuit\clubsuit$, $\heartsuit\spadesuit$, $\diamondsuit\clubsuit$, $\diamondsuit\spadesuit$. How many total possible outcomes are there? I can pick two cards in $\binom{4}{2} = 6$ ways. Thus the probability is **5/6**.

To be more clever, we could have noted that there was only one way not to get a red card, so $6 - 1 = 5$ ways to get at least one red.

484. How many ways are there to buy 2 tickets? Since there are 20 total tickets, there are $\binom{20}{2} = (20)(19)/2 = 190$ ways. To count how many ways there are to win, we count how many ways there are to *lose* and subtract: there are 18 losing cards, so there are $\binom{18}{2} = (18)(17)/2 = 153$ ways to lose. Thus there are $190 - 153 = 37$ ways to win, and the probability of winning at least one prize is **37/190**.

485. The probability that blue is drawn from the blue urn is $2/6$ (2 blue, 6 total); the probability that blue is drawn from the black urn is $11/15$; the total probability is $(2/6)(11/15) = \mathbf{11/45}$.

486. This one can best be done on straight common sense. If the pairing is done strictly at random, Camilla is equally likely to be paired with all 19 other students, so that the probability of being paired to any one in particular, including Cameron, must be **1/19**.

487. One boy and one girl can be chosen in $3 \cdot 4 = 12$ ways, since there are 3 boys and 4 girls. The choice can be made neglecting sex in $\binom{7}{2} = 21$ ways. The probability is $12/21 = \mathbf{4/7}$.

488. Just remember that the odds of $7 : 15$ translate to a $15/(15+7) = 15/22$ probability that Car Naggy wins, which is a **7/22** probability that the horse loses.

489. If it rains on $20\% = 1/5$ of the days, it should have rained for 30 days after $30 \cdot 5 = \mathbf{150}$ days.

490. The probability of getting a hit, a hit, a miss, and a miss, *in that order*, is $\frac{3}{10}\frac{3}{10}\frac{7}{10}\frac{7}{10} = \frac{441}{10000}$. We can just multiply this by the number of possible orders in which the hits can come. This is simply the number of ways to choose two of the four at-bats to be hits, or $\binom{4}{2} = 6$. The total probability is thus $6(441/10000) = 3(441/5000) = \mathbf{1323/5000}$.

491. The numbers may be chosen in $9(9) = 81$ ways. The product is not a multiple of three only if neither number is a multiple of 3. This occurs in $6(6) = 36$ ways, so there are $81 - 36 = 45$ ways to pick numbers whose product is a multiple of 3. Thus, the probability is $45/81 = \mathbf{5/9}$.

492. This problem could be very involved if a smaller number were substituted for 28. However, as it stands, the only two possibilities greater than 28 are 29 and 30. There is only 1 way to get 30 (all 6), and there are 5 ways to get 29 (one 5, four 6's), while there are 6^5 ways to roll the dice. Thus the probability is $(1 + 5)/6^5 = 6/6^5 = 1/6^4 = \mathbf{1/1296}$.

493. The seating can be done in 7! = 5040 ways, as we have 8 people arranged in a circle. If we insist on alternate seating, we need to be careful. To pin things down, we assume that the first boy is seated, which fixes the position of the table, so we don't have to worry about rotations of the table.

Then the other three boys can be seated in the three boy seats in 3! = 6 ways, and the girls can be seated in the four girl seats in 4! = 24 ways, for a total of $6 \cdot 24 = 144$ ways. The probability is thus $144/5040 = 72/2520 = 36/1260 = 18/630 = \mathbf{1/35}$.

494. The number of ways to get exactly 6 in the correct envelopes can be found by just choosing those 6 in all possible ways, for $\binom{8}{6} = \binom{8}{2} = 28$ ways. The other two can then be stuffed incorrectly in only one way. (Why is that important?) The total number of ways to distribute the letters into the envelopes must be 8! = 40320. Thus the probability is $28/40320 = 7/10080 = \mathbf{1/1440}$.

495. After putting the 1 in the first set, there are 4 spaces left in that set and 5 in the other. The 2 is equally likely to be in any of these spaces, so there is a **4/9** chance it will be in the same set as 1.

496. First, we find the probability of getting an 8 or 9 in one roll. For 8, there are 5 ways; for 9, there are 4. The probability is thus $9/36 = 1/4$.

Now the probability that Doug survives is just equal to one minus the probability that he dies. He dies if the others don't roll an 8 or a 9 and he does. This has probability $(3/4)^3(1/4)$. Thus,

$$P(\text{Doug survives}) = 1 - \left(\frac{3}{4}\right)^3 \left(\frac{1}{4}\right) = \frac{\mathbf{229}}{\mathbf{256}}.$$

497. In the old rules, one gets out of the pit 1/6 of the time, since there are 6 doubles rolls and 36 total rolls. In the new rules, one gets out on any double or triple, which means that of the $6 \cdot 6 \cdot 6 = 216$ total rolls, only the $6 \cdot 5 \cdot 4 = 120$ which have no duplicates will leave you in the pit; the other $216 - 120 = 96$ will get you out. In the new rules, then, one gets out $96/216 = 4/9$ of the time. This is $(4/9)/(1/6) = 24/9 = \mathbf{8/3}$ times as often as under the old rules.

498. We play the case game for the six possibilities of Bullwinkle's larger number.

Bullwinkle's larger number is 1 with probability 1/36, since only the roll 1-1 will do it. In this case, Rocky is greater than or equal with probability 1. The probability for this case is thus 1/36.

Bullwinkle's larger number is 2 with probability 3/36, as the rolls 1-2, 2-1, and 2-2 are all OK. In this case, Rocky is greater than or equal with probability 5/6, for a probability of 15/216.

Bullwinkle's larger number is 3 with probability 5/36: 3-1, 3-2, 3-3, 2-3, 1-3. In this case, Rocky is greater than or equal with probability 4/6, making 20/216 for this case.

Bullwinkle's larger number is 4 with probability 7/36. In this case, Rocky is greater than or equal with probability 3/6, for 21/216.

Bullwinkle's larger number is 5 with probability 9/36. In this case, Rocky is greater than or equal with probability 2/6, to get 18/216.

Bullwinkle's larger number is 6 with probability 11/36. In this case, Rocky is greater than or equal with probability 1/6, making 11/216.

The total probability is found by adding the probabilities for all the cases, to get

$$\frac{6 + 15 + 20 + 21 + 18 + 11}{216} = \frac{\mathbf{91}}{\mathbf{216}}.$$

499.   Let the probability of seeing a car in 5 minutes be p. Then the probability of not seeing a car in 5 minutes is $(1 - p)$, and the probability of not seeing a car for the entire 20 minutes is thus $(1 - p)^4$. But from the given information, the probability of not seeing a car for the entire 20 minutes is also 16/625, so that $(1 - p)^4 = 16/625$. Thus, $1 - p = 2/5$, and $p = \mathbf{3/5}$.

Chapter 27

Sets

Solutions to Exercises

27-1 The first one is just the positive even integers less than 10, so we can rewrite it as $\{\, x \mid x$ is an even integer, $0 < x < 10 \,\}$. The second is clearly {John, Paul, George, Ringo}.

27-2 The union of A and itself is the set containing all elements in either A or A, and no others. Thus it is just A again. The relation $A \cup A = A$ would hold for any set A for the same reason.

27-3 To ensure that A and B have no common elements, let A be the set $\{1, 2, 3, \ldots, 8\}$ and B be $\{9, 10, 11, \ldots, 17\}$. Clearly the union, $\{1, 2, 3, \ldots, 17\}$, has 17 elements. In any case where A and B have no common elements, the union should have the sum of the numbers of elements in A and B, since there are no elements in common.

27-4 This one is just like the previous one, except when we count up all the elements in A and B, we have counted 6 elements twice. Thus we need to get rid of the duplicate copies, reducing the total number of elements from 17 to $17 - 6 = \mathbf{11}$. To see this more clearly, let A be $\{1, 2, 3, \ldots, 8\}$ and B be $\{1, 2, 3, 4, 5, 6, 9, 10, 11\}$. Do you see that the conditions of the problem are satisfied? Do you see why the union has 11 elements?

27-5 This one is just like the previous. When we combine the two, we will have $a + b$ elements, but we need to get rid of x duplicates, leaving $\boldsymbol{a + b - x}$ elements.

27-6 The only obvious subset of {Barbie} is {Barbie} itself. But there *is* another set which is wholly contained in {Barbie}, namely the empty set $\varnothing$. Thus {Barbie} has $\mathbf{2}$ subsets.

27-7 We now have the possibilities $\varnothing$, {Barbie}, {Ken}, and {Barbie, Ken}. There are $\mathbf{4}$ subsets.

27-8 Getting worse now; we need to be careful to get all possible combinations. So we first take all those with no elements, then with one, and so on: $\varnothing$, {Barbie}, {Ken}, {Starshine},

{Barbie, Ken}, {Barbie, Starshine}, {Ken, Starshine}, and {Barbie, Ken, Starshine}. In all, **8**.

27-9 The empty set Ø has only one subset: itself.

27-10 We need to figure out what is changing in the sum. Only the bottom component of the "n choose something" terms is changing from term to term; this bottom ranges from 0 to n. Thus we can write the sum as $\sum_{k=0}^{n} \binom{n}{k}$, and the identity is

$$\sum_{k=0}^{n} \binom{n}{k} = 2^n.$$

27-11 For $n = 1$ we have

$$\binom{1}{0} + \binom{1}{1} = 1 + 1 = 2 = 2^1.$$

No big deal... could be a coincidence. For $n = 3$ we have

$$\binom{3}{0} + \binom{3}{1} + \binom{3}{2} + \binom{3}{3} = 1 + 3 + 3 + 1 = 8 = 2^3.$$

The odds that this is luck are diminishing. For $n = 5$ we have

$$\binom{5}{0} + \binom{5}{1} + \binom{5}{2} + \binom{5}{3} + \binom{5}{4} + \binom{5}{5} = 1 + 5 + 10 + 10 + 5 + 1 = 32 = 2^5.$$

Are you convinced? You shouldn't be. For example, maybe it only works for odd numbers. Try a couple of evens to make sure our argument didn't have some odd-number loophole.

27-12 You'll have to do this yourself.

Solutions to Problems

500. We need all sets which include 1, 2, and some subset of $\{3, 4, 5\}$. The number of such sets is just the number of subsets of $\{3, 4, 5\}$, or $2^3 = \mathbf{8}$.

501. This set may be written in several ways. One easy way to do it is to realize that it is the union of $A \cap B$ and $A \cap C$, or $(A \cap B) \cup (A \cap C)$. It could also be written, for example, $A \cap (B \cup C)$, since it is also the intersection of A with the other two sets.

502. One way to do it is as in the text: the union has all the elements in either A or B, or $15 + 12 = 27$, but then has 8 duplicates, leaving only $27 - 8 = 19$. We can also draw a Venn diagram, as shown. We first enter 8 into the intersection, then put the remaining 7 and 4 in A and B respectively. We can then count the union by counting all the numbers in both circles, for $8 + 7 + 4 = \mathbf{19}$.

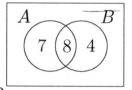

503. This number is 5 choose 3, from the chapter on counting. Evaluating, we have $\binom{5}{3} = \mathbf{10}$.

504. We want $\binom{N}{6} = 11\binom{N}{3}$, or

$$\frac{N(N-1)(N-2)(N-3)(N-4)(N-5)}{720} = 11\frac{N(N-1)(N-2)}{6}.$$

Simplifying, we have

$$(N-3)(N-4)(N-5) = 120 \cdot 11.$$

Without multiplying anything out, we observe that $120 \cdot 11 = 12 \cdot 11 \cdot 10$, so if we let $N - 3 = 12$, everything falls into place. Thus $N = \mathbf{15}$.

505. This is perfect for a Venn diagram. Working from the inside out, we place 4 in the center (4 students taking all three languages). Since 11 people take Czech and Polish, we enter $11 - 4 = 7$ into the space for $(C \cap P) \cap \overline{G}$, since 4 people are already counted in the "all three" space. Similarly, we put $9 - 4 = 5$ into the "C and G but not P" space (can you put this in set notation?). We can then enter $30 - 7 - 4 - 5 = 14$ into the "C only" space, since that is the number of Czech-speakers who are not yet accounted for.

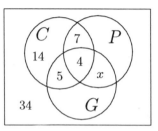

At this point we have a problem, since we don't know how many to put into the $(G \cap P) \cap \overline{C}$ space. To keep going, we just use x; then $20 - 7 - 4 - x = 9 - x$ goes into the "Polish only" space and $15 - 4 - 5 - x = 6 - x$ into the "German only" space. We also enter 34 outside all the language spaces, for the 34 students who aren't taking any language.

All we have left to do is to use the final constraint, which is that there are 75 total students. Adding up all the numbers in the Venn diagram, we see that there are

$$34 + (9 - x) + 7 + 4 + x + 14 + 5 + (6 - x) = 79 - x$$

total students; setting this equal to 75 yields $x = 4$. Thus there are 4 students taking Polish and German, but not Czech. The total number of students enrolled in Polish and German is this 4 plus the number taking all three languages, or $4 + 4 = \mathbf{8}$.

506. To choose a k-element subset which definitely contains a given element, all we really have to do is choose the other $k - 1$ elements of the subset from among the other $n - 1$ elements of the large set. Thus there are $\binom{n-1}{k-1}$ such subsets.

To choose a k-element subset which does *not* contain the element, we choose all k elements from among the other $n - 1$ elements. Thus there are $\binom{n-1}{k}$ such subsets.

Clearly there are $\binom{n}{k}$ total k-element subsets. Since every subset either contains the given

element or doesn't contain it, we must have $\binom{n}{k} = \binom{n-1}{k} + \binom{n-1}{k-1}$.

507. The first set is given by $\{3, 6, 9, \ldots, 99\}$. The second set is $\{4, 8, \ldots, 96\}$. A set is a subset of both sets if and only if all its elements are divisible by both 3 and 4; that is, are divisible by 12. Thus every desired subset must also be a subset of $\{12, 24, 36, 48, 60, 72, 84, 96\}$, a set with 8 elements. Every subset of this latter set is one of the desired subsets and every desired subset is also a subset of this set. Hence the number we wish is just the number of subsets of this 8-element set, or $2^8 = \mathbf{256}$.

Chapter 28

Prove It

Solutions to Exercises

28-1   The first requires "only if." Not every number divisible by five ends in a 5 (some end in 0), but every number which ends in 5 is divisible by 5. The second requires "if," since every human is a mammal but not every mammal is human. The third requires "only if," since every circle obeys the given property but not every figure obeying the given property is a circle. (It could be a half-circle, for instance. Tricky.) The fourth requires an "if and only if," because integers have no fractional part and numbers with no fractional part are integers.

28-2   Did you go back and review the proof?

28-3   If $x = 0$, then we have $c = 0$, which is false since we are given $c > 0$. If x is positive, then $ax^2 + bx + c$ is positive, so cannot equal 0. Hence, if $ax^2 + bx + c = 0$ and a, b, and c are positive, then x must be negative if x is real.

28-4   The problem is the first inductive step. When we remove one person from a group of two, the remaining person is indeed in a group in which everyone is the same height since that person is in a group alone. The induction fails because this one person cannot be said to be the same height as anyone else because there is no one else in the group. Hence, the two people in a group of two are not necessarily the same height. If we were able to say that in any group of two people, the people are the same height, then the proposed induction would be all right.

28-5   The maximum number of people we can serve using 2 of each dish is $2(5) = 10$. Thus, if we have **11** people, some dish must be served 3 times.

28-6   The proposed proof is incomplete because, as stated, it only covers the case in which two students sleep for the first minute, two for the second, etc. The solution does not cover those cases in which a student sleeps for 15 seconds, stays awake for 3 minutes, then sleeps for 45 seconds more, etc. There are infinitely many such cases. To cover all these cases we must find a more comprehensive approach. We do this by counting the sleeping time required for all 21 students to sleep for one minute. This is 21 minutes. We compare this to the maximum amount of sleeping time available if no more than 2 students are asleep at one time. The maximum such time is $2(10) = 20$ minutes. Since this is less than the required time, there must be some moment when more than 2 students are sleeping. This correct proof is very close in spirit to the proposed solution, but it covers every possible case rather than just one.

Solutions to Problems

508. Suppose the integer is odd. Thus n^4, $3n^2$, and n are all odd, while $4n^2$ and 4000 are even. Hence, the sum $n^4 + 4n^3 + 3n^2 + n + 4000$ is the sum of 3 odd and 2 even numbers and is therefore odd. Since 0 is even, the sum can never be 0 if n is odd. Thus we have shown n cannot be odd, so n must be even if it is an integer solution.

509. We can only say that if x is a real solution, it is negative, but we cannot say that all negative numbers are solutions. Thus the "if" part of "if and only if" fails because x is not necessarily a solution if it is negative.

510. The sum is an arithmetic series with sum $S = n(n + 1)/2$. A prime number is a number which has no factors besides 1 and itself. For all even numbers greater than 2, $S = (n/2)(n+1)$ shows that S has 2 factors greater than 1 and hence is not prime. Similarly for odd numbers, $S = n[(n + 1)/2]$ shows that S has two factors greater than one and thus is not prime.

511. There are $\binom{11}{3} = 165$ triangles, since we form each triangle by choosing 3 points. By the Pigeonhole Principle, at least $\lfloor 165/4 \rfloor + 1 = \mathbf{42}$ of them must get the same letter. If no letter is used at least 42 times, then the largest number of triangles we can label is $4(41) = 164$, so at least one letter must be used 42 times or more.

512. Since $(x/y)(y/x) = 1$, if x/y and y/x are both integers, they must both be 1 or both be -1. In the former case, $x = y$ and in the latter, $x = -y$. Thus in both cases, $|x| = |y|$.

513. The problem is how we counted the money. By saying the men each paid 14 dollars and the messenger has two, we imply that the hotel has 42 of the 45 dollars and the messenger has 2, but this is untrue. Of the 42 dollars the men spent, the hotel received 40, and the messenger received 2. If we wish to count the original 45 dollars, the hotel has 40, the messenger has 2, and the men each have 1 dollar.

514. If $x = 0$, we have $|x| + x = 0$, a contradiction to $|x| + x > 0$. If $x < 0$, we find $|x| + x = -x + x = 0$, also a contradiction. If $x > 0$, then $|x| + x = 2x$. Since $x > 0$, $2x > 0$, so $|x| + x > 0$. Thus if $|x| + x > 0$, then $x > 0$.

515. The difference between the number on a chair and the number on the chair across from it is $2n/2 = n$. If every odd numbered chair is directly across from another odd numbered chair, the difference between them, n, is even. Since n is even, $2n$, the number of chairs, is divisible by 4.

516. There are six consecutive numbers between two multiples of 7. Given any three consecutive numbers, exactly one of them must be a multiple of three. (Why?) Returning to our 6 consecutive numbers between multiples of 7, among the first 3 of these there is a multiple of 3 and among the second 3 there is a multiple of 3. Hence, there are exactly 2 multiples of three among the 6 consecutive numbers.

517. We look at the 3 lines through the origin as 6 rays with the origin as the vertex. Let one of the rays be the x-axis. Starting from the positive x-axis and moving counterclockwise all the way around the origin, we sum the angle between each successive pair of rays. Since there are 6 such angles (draw the picture and see), if each angle is greater than $60°$, then the sum of the angles is greater than $6(60°) = 360°$, a contradiction since summing the angles about a point always gives $360°$. Hence, at least one of the angles must be less than or equal to $60°$.

518. We prove this with induction. Since $1/(1 \cdot 2) = 1/(1)(1+1)$, the assertion is true for $n = 1$. Now, assume $1/(1 \cdot 2) + 1/(2 \cdot 3) + \cdots + 1/[n \cdot (n+1)] = n/(n+1)$. Adding $1/[(n+1) \cdot (n+2)]$ to each side, we have

$$
\begin{aligned}
\left(\frac{1}{1 \cdot 2} + \cdots + \frac{1}{n \cdot (n+1)} \right) + \frac{1}{(n+1) \cdot (n+2)} &= \left(\frac{n}{n+1} \right) + \frac{1}{(n+1)(n+2)} \\
&= \frac{n(n+2)}{(n+1)(n+2)} + \frac{1}{(n+1)(n+2)} \\
&= \frac{n^2 + 2n + 1}{(n+1)(n+2)} = \frac{(n+1)^2}{(n+1)(n+2)} \\
&= \frac{(n+1)}{(n+1)+1}.
\end{aligned}
$$

This completes the induction.

519. The number of distinct factors of an integer is found by first finding the prime factorization of the number. Take all the exponents of the primes in the factorization, increase them by 1, and multiply them. This gives the number of distinct factors. For example, since $60 = (2^2)(3)(5)$, 60 has $(2+1)(1+1)(1+1) = 12$ distinct factors. The product of a set of numbers is odd if and only if all the numbers in the set is odd. Thus if an integer has an odd number of factors, the exponents of all its prime factors must be even (so the exponents increased by one are all odd and their product is therefore odd). Any number in which all of the exponents in its prime factorization are even must be a perfect square because raising the factorization to the $1/2$ power leaves only integer exponents. For example, $(100)^{1/2} = (2^2 \cdot 5^2)^{1/2} = 2^1 \cdot 5^1 = 10$. Thus an integer with an odd number of distinct factors is a perfect square.

520. Among the three women, there are 3 matches played. Thus there are 3 wins and 3 losses to distribute among the women. Anyone who doesn't win one game and lose one must either win 0 games or 2 games. If all three women win either 2 or 0 games each, the total number of wins will be an even number. However, we know that the total number of wins is 3, an odd number. Thus at least one of the women must win an odd number of games, so there is someone who wins one and loses one.

521. We proceed using induction. Since $(1)^2 = 1^3$, the initial case is proved. Now, assume $(1+2+\cdots+n)^2 = 1^3 + 2^3 + \cdots + n^3$. We wish to show that this implies $[1+\cdots+(n+1)]^2 = 1^3 + \cdots + (n+1)^3$. We do this by expanding the square on the left and using the fact that $1 + \cdots + n = n(n+1)/2$,

$$
\begin{aligned}
[(1 + \cdots + n) + (n+1)]^2 &= (1 + \cdots + n)^2 + 2(n+1)(1 + \cdots + n) + (n+1)^2 \\
&= (1^3 + \cdots + n^3) + 2(n+1)[n(n+1)/2] + (n+1)^2 \\
&= 1^3 + \cdots + n^3 + n(n+1)^2 + (n+1)^2 \\
&= 1^3 + \cdots + n^3 + (n+1)^3.
\end{aligned}
$$

This completes our induction.

522. By the Pigeonhole Principle, if $3(3) + 1 = 10$ socks are taken, at least 4 of them must be the same color. If only 9 are taken, we could have 3 of each color, but by taking **10** we are certain to have at least 4 of the same color.

523. If the woman gets $k - 1$ of them correct, there is only 1 letter left and one envelope and these must match. There is no way she could put this final letter in a wrong envelope. Thus the number of letters which are in the right envelope cannot be $k - 1$. To show that she can get any other number, n, suppose she correctly puts letters 1 through n in their envelopes and puts letter $n + 1$ in envelope $n + 2$, letter $n + 2$ in envelope $n + 3, \ldots$, letter $k - 1$ in envelope k, and letter k in envelope $n + 1$. This covers all possible numbers of envelopes stuffed correctly.

524. One way to do this is to examine the factorization

$$
n^5 - n = n(n^4 - 1) = n(n^2 + 1)(n^2 - 1) = n(n^2 + 1)(n + 1)(n - 1).
$$

To show that the number is divisible by 10, we need to show it is divisible by 2 and by 5. Clearly either n or $n + 1$ must be divisible by 2, taking care of that restriction. To look at divisibility by 5, consider what n could be congruent to mod 5. If $n \equiv 0$, then it is divisible by 5 and we are done. If $n \equiv 4$ or $n \equiv 1$, then $n + 1$ or $n - 1$ is congruent to 0. If $n \equiv 2$, then $n^2 + 1 \equiv 4 + 1 \equiv 0$; if $n \equiv 3$, then $n^2 + 1 \equiv 9 + 1 \equiv 0$. But we have covered 0, 1, 2, 3, and 4, which are all the possibilities! Thus the product always contains a factor of 5, and we have already shown that it contains a factor of 2, so it must contain a factor of 10. Can you find any higher numbers which always divide $n^5 - n$?

525. Consider our connecting one point, point A, to the other 5. Since we are coloring these 5 segments with 2 colors, at least three of them must be the same color. Now, if we connect any two of these three points with that color, we form a monochromatic triangle (triangle in which the sides are all the same color) with those two points and A as vertices.

Thus we must connect these three points with the other color. However, in doing this we form a monochromatic triangle with these three points as vertices. Hence, there is no way to connect the 6 points as suggested without forming a monochromatic triangle.

Chapter 29

Parting Shots

Solutions to Problems

526. Let his second score be x. Thus the first score was $x - 3$ and the third was $x + 11$. His teacher tells him that if he scores 100 on the fourth test, the sum of his four scores will be $4(81) = 324$. Thus $x + x - 3 + x + 11 + 100 = 324$ and $x = 72$. Thus his third exam grade was $x + 11 = \mathbf{83}$.

527. Since we know the man was born in 1800s, we look for squares whose first two digits are 18. The only such square is $43^2 = 1849$. If the man is 43 in 1849, then he was born in **1806**.

528. The area of the floor is $9(12) = 108$ ft^2. The area of each tile is $4(6) = 24$ in^2. To determine the number of tiles needed, we must first determine how many square inches are in the floor. Thus we convert square feet to square inches.

$$(108 \text{ ft}^2)\left(\frac{12 \text{ in}}{1 \text{ ft}}\right)^2 = 15552 \text{ in}^2.$$

Thus the number of tiles needed is $15552/24 = \mathbf{648}$.

529. The first person calls 3 people, who in turn contact 9 people, who then call 27 more. At this point, 40 people have been notified. To contact the last 60 people, only $60/3 = 20$ of the 27 people last called need to call anyone. Thus these 60 plus the 7 of the 27 that didn't call anyone don't have to make a call. The answer is **67**.

530. Rearrange and factor as $x\sqrt{5-x} - \sqrt{5-x} = (x-1)\sqrt{5-x} = 0$, which has solutions $x = 1$ and $x = 5$. Thus the equation has **2** roots.

531. Let the long length of the pool be y and the shorter length be x, where each of these are in yards. We choose yards because the desired quantity, the area, is in square yards.

There are 1760 yards in a mile, so we have $80y = 1760$, so $y = 22$. From swimming around the perimeter, we have $22(2x + 2y) = 1760$, so $22(2x + 44) = 1760$. Solving for x, we have $x = 18$ yards. Thus the area of the pool is $22(18) = \mathbf{396}$ square yards.

532.   Since the area of each is πr^2, the sum, S, of the areas is

$$
\begin{aligned}
S &= 1^2\pi + \left(\frac{1}{2}\right)^2 \pi + \left(\frac{1}{4}\right)^2 \pi + \cdots \\
&= \pi\left(\frac{1}{1} + \frac{1}{2^2} + \frac{1}{2^4} + \frac{1}{2^6} + \cdots\right) \\
&= \pi\left(\frac{1}{1 - 1/4}\right) = \frac{4\pi}{3}.
\end{aligned}
$$

533.   This is an exercise in factoring, as r and $r + 1$ are common factors of $f(r)$ and $f(r-1)$.

$$
\begin{aligned}
f(r) - f(r-1) &= r(r+1)(r+2)/3 - (r-1)(r)(r+1)/3 \\
&= \left[\Big(r+2-(r-1)\Big)(r)(r+1)\right]/3 \\
&= 3r(r+1)/3 = \mathbf{r(r+1)}
\end{aligned}
$$

534.   First, we factor $x^2 - 5x + 6$ as $(x-2)(x-3)$. If this number is prime, one of these factors must be 1 or -1, otherwise the number will have two different nontrivial (i.e. not 1) factors and hence will not be prime. Thus our possibilities for x are 1, 2, 3, and 4. We can immediately exclude 2 and 3, as our expression is 0 for these two values; however, for 1 and 4 the expression equals 2, a prime number. Thus the answers are **1** and **4**.

535. x is the perfect square of $\sqrt{x}$. Thus the next larger perfect square is the square of $\sqrt{x} + 1$, or $(\sqrt{x} + 1)^2 = \mathbf{x + 2\sqrt{x} + 1}$.

536.   This is a good brain-teaser. Number the chains 1 through 6. You may be tempted to cut a link of chain 1, add chain 1 to chain 2, then weld shut. Then cut open the end of chain 2, add chain 3, and so on. This results in a cost of \$1.25. There is a better way. Cut open all four links of chain 1. Use one link to connect chain 2 and 3, then weld this link shut. Use the next free link to connect the other end of chain 3 to chain 4 and so on. This way, we only cut and weld 4 links, for a cost of **\$1.00**.

537.   Let the side of square S be s. Thus the length of rectangle R is $1.1s$ and the width is $0.9s$. Thus the area of S is s^2 and the area of R is $0.99s^2$. Thus the ratio of the areas of R and S is $0.99s^2 : s^2 = \mathbf{0.99 : 1}$.

538.   To find the answer, we find the largest integer which has a four-digit square and the smallest positive integer that has a four-digit square and conclude that every number in between has a four-digit square, and that these are the only four-digit squares. Since

$100^2 = 10000$, the largest integer with a four-digit square is 99. Since $961 = 31^2 < 1000 < 32^2 = 1024$, the smallest positive integer with a four-digit square is 32. Thus the integers from 32 to 99 have four-digit squares. There are $99 - 32 + 1 = \mathbf{68}$ such integers.

539.   The ratio in weights of the balls equals the ratio in volumes. The ratio of volumes is the cube of the ratio of the diameters. Thus

$$\left(\frac{8 \text{ inches}}{12 \text{ inches}} \right)^3 = \frac{80 \text{ pounds}}{x \text{ pounds}}.$$

Hence, $80/x = 8/27$, and $x = \mathbf{270}$ pounds.

540.   The original triangle has area $bh/2$. If we remove x from the base in the new triangle and add m to its altitude, the area is $(b-x)(h+m)/2$. Since the area of the original triangle is twice that of the new one, we have $(b - x)(h + m)/2 = (bh/2)/2$. We solve this equation for x by first multiplying by 4, then dividing by $(h + m)$, yielding $2b - 2x = bh/(h + m)$. Thus $2x = 2b - bh/(h + m) = (2bh + 2bm - bh)/(h + m)$, and finally $x = \dfrac{\boldsymbol{b(2m + h)}}{\boldsymbol{2(h + m)}}$.

541.   The committee can have 2, 3, or 4 senior partners, who can be chosen in $\binom{4}{2}$, $\binom{4}{3}$, or $\binom{4}{4}$ ways, respectively. Thus there are a total of $6 + 4 + 1 = 11$ ways of choosing senior partners. As for the junior partners, we can choose one of the three in 3 ways, or not choose any, leaving us 4 options. Thus there are $11(4) = \mathbf{44}$ ways to form the committee.

542.   The triangle formed by connecting the midpoints of the sides of a triangle is similar to the original triangle and has half the perimeter of the original triangle. Thus the sum of all the perimeters is

$$3a + \frac{3a}{2} + \frac{3a}{4} + \cdots = 3a \left(1 + \frac{1}{2} + \frac{1}{4} + \cdots \right) = 3a \left(\frac{1}{1 - 1/2} \right) = \mathbf{6a}.$$

543.   There are 100 positive integers, 101 negative integers, and 0, for a total of 202 integers. The sum of these is -101, because all the other negative integers cancel with their positive counterparts in the sum. Thus the average is $(-101)/202 = \mathbf{-1/2}$.

544.   If the lines are all parallel, we attain 0 intersections. If they all pass through a single point, we attain 1 intersection. To show that 2 and 3 intersections are impossible, consider the 3 shown diagrams of 3 and 4 lines intersecting in 2 and 3 points. Where can the next line be added so as not to increase the number of intersections? Nowhere. All numbers from 4 to 10 can be the number of intersections. Try to show that these are all possible. (Use parallel lines for many of them; for example, to attain 5 intersections, draw three parallel lines, then draw two lines which intersect at a point on one of the original 3 lines.) Thus the answer is $2 + 3 = \mathbf{5}$.

545.   Initially, the car contains $6(0.1) = 0.6$ quarts of antifreeze. Adding x quarts of pure antifreeze, we have $0.6 + x$ quarts of antifreeze in $6 + x$ quarts of solution. Since the solution must be 20%, we have $(0.6 + x)/(6 + x) = 0.2$, or $0.6 + x = 1.2 + 0.2x$. Thus $0.8x = 0.6$ and $x = 3/4$.

546.   The first 9 pages consume 9 digits. The next 90, from 10 to 99, consume 180 digits. Thus you have $999 - 9 - 180 = 810$ digits left. Since the rest of the pages will use three digits, you can number $810/3 = 270$ of them. Thus you have numbered $99 + 270 = $ **369** pages.

547.   Since the length of the train is in feet and the time they pass each other is in seconds, we convert the speeds to feet per second. Thus

$$20 \, \frac{\text{miles}}{\text{hour}} \cdot \left(\frac{5280 \text{ feet}}{1 \text{ mile}} \right) \left(\frac{1 \text{ hour}}{3600 \text{ seconds}} \right) = \frac{88}{3} \text{ ft/s}.$$

Since 40 mph is twice as fast, it is $176/3$ feet per second. The time it takes for the trains to pass each other is the time from when the fronts first meet until the tails are just leaving each other. During this time, the fronts of the trains are racing away from each other at a rate of $88/3 + 176/3 = 88$ feet per second. In 30 seconds, they must be exactly the sum of the lengths of the two trains apart, since their tails are at the same point and the trains are pointing in opposite directions. Thus if the length of the second train is x, we must have $30(88) = 1000 + x$. Thus $x = $ **1640** feet.

548.   We employ our multiplication to cancel technique here. Since $z = \frac{x}{y}$ and $z = \frac{4y}{x}$, multiplication of these two will cancel the x's and y's, leaving $z^2 = 4$. Thus the possible values of z are $\pm$**2**.

549.   Note that this is not one of those clever manipulations we discussed earlier. We can see this immediately by noting that we are asked to find $2x + 3y$ rather than some nice symmetric quantity like $x + y$ or $x^2 + y^2$. Looking at the second equation, we see that we can factor it as a difference of squares, so $x^2 - y^2 = (x - y)(x + y) = 21$. Since we know $x + y = 7$, we can substitute that value in this equation to yield $x - y = 3$. Adding these gives $2x = 10$, so $(x, y) = (5, 2)$ and $2x + 3y = $ **16**.

550.   Let cost be c and the number of units be n. Since the two are linearly related, then for some m and b we have $c = mn + b$. We are given that $c = 40$ when $n = 10$, so $40 = 10m + b$. Similarly we have $c = 70$ when $n = 20$. Thus $70 = 20m + b$. Now, we solve these for m and b. Subtracting the first equation from the second gives $10m = 30$, so $m = 3$ and $b = 10$. Thus $c = 3n + 10$. For 25 units the cost is $3(25) + 10 = $ **85** dollars.

551.   The sum of the interior angles of a polygon with n sides is $180(n - 2)$. The angles of the polygon in the problem are the first n terms of an arithmetic sequence with first term 160 and common difference -5, since 160 is the largest angle. Thus the nth angle is $160 - 5(n - 1) = 165 - 5n$, and the sum of these angle measures is given by $\frac{n}{2}(160 + 165 - 5n)$.

Since this equals our expression $180(n - 2)$ above, we have

$$\frac{n}{2}(160 + 165 - 5n) = 180(n - 2)$$

$$325n - 5n^2 = 360n - 720.$$

Thus rearranging and dividing by 5 gives $n^2 + 7n - 144 = (n - 9)(n + 16) = 0$. Since n must be positive, we have $n = \mathbf{9}$.

552. Since the product of the powers of the exponents increased by 1 in the prime factorization of an integer determine the number of factors, we consider the prime factorization of the integer. If there is only one prime factor, it must be of the form a^{76} to have 77 factors. Since 2^{76} is far greater than ten million, there are no such integers which satisfy the problem. Numbers which have two prime factors must have the form $a^6 b^{10}$, so they have $(6 + 1)(10 + 1) = 77$ factors. Both $2^6 3^{10}$ and $2^{10} 3^6$ are valid solutions of this form. Since $2^{10} 5^6 = 2^4(1000000) = 16000000 > 10000000$, there are no more solutions of this form. Since 77 only has two nontrivial factors, there are no solutions with more than 2 prime factors or with different exponents than above. Hence, there are only **2** such integers.

553. Let $N = 10t + u$, where t and u are the digits of N. Thus the number formed by reversing the digits is $10u + t$ and this number subtracted from N yields $9t - 9u$. Thus the positive perfect cube which is the difference of these two numbers is divisible by 3. Since the only perfect cubes which are less than 100 (and hence can possibly be expressed as the difference of 2 two-digit numbers) are 1, 8, 27, 64, the perfect cube in this problem must be 27, as it is the only one divisible by 9. Thus $9t - 9u = 27$ and $t - u = 3$. The pairs of digits which satisfy this are $(t, u) = (3, 0); (4, 1); (5, 2); \ldots (9, 6)$. Thus there are a total of 7 such pairs and hence **7** such N.

554. We are asked to find two numbers which differ by two whose product is a power of two. Any prime factor of one of two numbers is also a factor of the product of the numbers. Since the only prime factor of the product of our two numbers is 2, the only prime factor of either of our numbers is 2. Thus both of our numbers are powers of 2, so we are looking for two numbers which differ by 2 and are both powers of 2. The numbers 2 and 4 satisfy this, but no other pairs of positive numbers do. We must not overlook the pair -2 and -4, for their product is 8, so they fit the criteria as well. Thus there are **2** solutions, $(12, 3)$ and $(6, 3)$.

555. Let the people be A, B, C, D, E and the instruments be V, W, X, Y, Z. Let person A play V and W, B play W and X, C play X and Y, D play Y and Z, E play Z and V. Thus if A chooses V, E must play Z, so D must play Y, so C must play X, and B must play W. Similarly, if A chooses W, B must play X, C must play Y, and so on. Thus A's choice determines everyone else's. Since A has 2 choices, Sam can form his band in **2** ways.

556. To begin with, $384x^2 - x^8 = x^2(384 - x^6)$. Thus we desire to find x^2 and x^6. We have $x^2 = 2 + \sqrt{2} + 2 - \sqrt{2} + 2\sqrt{(2 + \sqrt{2})(2 - \sqrt{2})} = 4 + 2\sqrt{2}$, and $x^6 = (x^2)^3 = 64 +$

$3(16)(2\sqrt{2})+3(4)(8)+16\sqrt{2} = 160+112\sqrt{2}$. Thus $x^2(384-x^6) = (4+2\sqrt{2})(224-112\sqrt{2}) = 224(2+\sqrt{2})(2-\sqrt{2}) = \mathbf{448}$.

557. Any two distinct (i.e. different) segments which intersect on the circle cannot possibly intersect inside the circle. Thus no two segments in the question share an endpoint. Since there are 17 points from which to choose endpoints and each segment must have 2 endpoints, the maximum possible number of segments is **8**, which corresponds to 16 endpoints. We must show that this is possible. If we number the points in order from 1 to 17 and connect point 1 to point 9, point 2 to point 10, etc., we will have the desired 8 segments.

558. Since $2^{2x} - 3^{2y} = (2^x)^2 - (3^y)^2$, we can factor this as the difference of squares, yielding $(2^x - 3^y)(2^x + 3^y) = 55$. Since each of the factors on the left of this are integers, they must be $(5, 11)$, or $(1, 55)$. Note that the first factor must be the smaller, as it is the difference of two positive numbers, while the second factor is the sum of these numbers. Trying $(5, 11)$, we have $2^x - 3^y = 5$ and $2^x + 3^y = 11$. Adding these yields $2(2^x) = 16$, so $2^x = 8$ and $x = 3$. Thus $y = 1$. Trying $(1, 55)$ as above, we find that $2(2^x) = 56$, which has no integer solutions. Hence $(\mathbf{3}, \mathbf{1})$ is the only solution.

559. We simplify the radical expression as much as possible. First, $\sqrt{33 + \sqrt{128}} = \sqrt{33 + 8\sqrt{2}}$. Letting this equal $x + y\sqrt{2}$, we have $x^2 + 2y^2 = 33$ and $xy = 4$, from which we find that $(x, y) = (1, 4)$. Note we don't use $(-1, -4)$, as the positive value is required. Thus $\sqrt{33 + \sqrt{128}} + \sqrt{2} - 8 = 1 + 4\sqrt{2} + \sqrt{2} - 8 = -7 + 5\sqrt{2}$. The reciprocal, upon rationalizing, is $7 + 5\sqrt{2}$. Thus $N < 7 + 5\sqrt{2}$. Since $1.4 < \sqrt{2} < 1.5$, we have $7.0 < 5\sqrt{2} < 7.5$, so $14 < 7 + 5\sqrt{2} < 15$. Hence, the largest such N is **14**.

560. Let the two polygons have m and n sides, respectively. Thus the interior angles have ratio

$$\frac{180 - 360/m}{180 - 360/n} = \frac{n(180m - 360)}{m(180n - 360)} = \frac{n(m - 2)}{m(n - 2)} = \frac{3}{2}.$$

To determine all integers which satisfy this equation, we solve for one variable in terms of the other. Remember what follows here; it is an important problem solving technique. Getting rid of denominators, we have $3mn - 6m = 2mn - 4n$. Solving for m gives $m(n - 6) = -4n$, so $m = -4n/(n - 6)$. Since m and n must be positive integers, the expression $-4n/(n - 6)$ must be positive, so $n < 6$. Also, this expression must be an integer. Since it is an integer for $n = 3$, 4, and 5, we have **3** solutions in positive integers, namely $(m, n) = (4, 3)$; $(8, 4)$; $(20, 5)$. Note that although m is an integer for $n = 2$, this is not a solution to the problem, as no 2 sided polygon exists.

561. This is essentially a proportion problem. Since there are 60 minutes in the face of a clock and 360 degrees, our problem becomes determining how many minutes are between the minute and hour hand of the clock. Since the time is 3:20, the hour hand is $20/60 = 1/3$ of the way from the hour 3 to the hour 4, or 1/3 of the way from the minute 15 to the minute 20. Thus it is at minute $15 + 5/3 = 16\frac{2}{3}$. Since the minute hand is at 20, the hands are $20 - 16\frac{2}{3} = \frac{10}{3}$ minutes apart. Since there are 6 degrees per minute, this corresponds to

an angle of

$$\frac{10}{3} \text{ minutes} \cdot \frac{6°}{1 \text{ minute}} = \mathbf{20°}.$$

562.   Let the volume of each of the two jars be V. Thus the amount of alcohol in the first is $pV/(p+1)$ and the amount of water is $V/(p+1)$. Similarly, there is $qV/(q+1)$ alcohol and $V/(q+1)$ water in the second. Thus when mixed the ratio of alcohol to water is

$$\begin{aligned}
\frac{\frac{pV}{p+1} + \frac{qV}{q+1}}{\frac{V}{p+1} + \frac{V}{q+1}} &= \frac{\frac{p}{p+1} + \frac{q}{q+1}}{\frac{1}{p+1} + \frac{1}{q+1}} \\
&= \frac{[p(q+1) + q(p+1)]/[(p+1)(q+1)]}{[q+1+p+1]/[(p+1)(q+1)]} \\
&= \frac{p+q+2pq}{p+q+2}.
\end{aligned}$$

563.   The player who chooses from among 7 sticks will always lose. If he chooses x sticks, the other player chooses $6-x$ sticks, and the first player is left with only 1 stick. Similarly, the player choosing from among 13 sticks will always lose, for if he chooses x sticks, the other player chooses $6-x$, leaving our first player with 7. From above, this player loses since he is choosing from among 7 sticks. Continuing in this manner, we find that the player choosing from 19, from 25, from 31, from 37, from 43, from 49, and from 55 is the loser. Thus if Bill takes **4** sticks, leaving Ted with 55, Bill will win. Try this game (or some variation of it) on your friends. If you go first in this game, you should always win. In this example, Bill takes 4, then every time Ted takes x, Bill takes $6-x$.

564.   First, we need the 4 corner posts. To make one 20 foot length of the fence, we need one corner, then a post every 2 feet, for a total of $20/2 = 10$ posts. Since the last of these is also a corner, we have 9 posts which are not corner posts. For a 12 foot width of the field, we need $12/2 = 6$ posts, one of which is a corner. Thus we need the 4 corners, plus 9 for each of the lengths and 5 for each of the widths, for a total of **32** posts.

565.   Since the face of a clock has 60 minutes and 360°, 10° corresponds to $10°(60 \text{ minutes}/360°) = 5/3$ minutes. Thus we seek the time when the hour hand is 5/3 minutes from the minute hand. Let the minute hand be at x minutes. Thus the hour hand is $x/60$ of the way from hour 4 to hour 5, or from minute 20 to minute 25. Hence, the hour hand is at minute $20 + (5)(x/60) = 20 + x/12$. The first time the two hands are 10 degrees apart, the minute hand will be before, i.e. at a smaller minute, than the hour hand. Thus we have $x + 5/3 = 20 + x/12$, or $11x/12 = 55/3$, so $x = 20$. The first time the hands are 10° apart is **4:20**.

566.   The minimum occurs when none of the lines intersect within the circle. This divides the circle into 5 regions as shown. The maximum occurs when each segment intersects all the others at distinct

points within the circle as shown, dividing the circle into 11 regions. Thus the desired answer is $5 + 11 = 16$.

567. To get an expression involving just x, we multiply the final two expressions in the equality, yielding

$$\left(\frac{2}{x}\right)^2 = \left(\frac{y}{3}\right)\left(\frac{x}{y}\right) = \frac{x}{3}.$$

Thus $4/x^2 = x/3$ and $x^3 = \mathbf{12}$.

568. Let the altitude be a. Thus the bases are $a + r$ and $a - r$ for some r. The area is then $a(a + r + a - r)/2 = a^2$. Since the area is a^2 and we know nothing of the value a, we cannot conclude that the area is rational or irrational, so **none** of the choices are correct.

569. Let the numbers be x and y, respectively. Hence, $3.7(10)^{18} > x > 3.6(10)^{18}$ and $3.5(10)^{14} > y > 3.4(10)^{14}$. Thus $3.7(10)^{18} \cdot 3.5(10)^{14} = 1.295(10)^{33} > xy > 3.6(10)^{18} \cdot 3.4(10)^{14} = 1.224(10)^{33}$. Both of these limits have 34 digits, so the product xy has **34** digits.

570. Since the least common multiple of two numbers times the greatest common factor of the two is the product of the two numbers, we have (LCM)(GCF)=10! 18! 12! 17!. Writing the two numbers in terms of common factorials they are $18(10! \, 17!)$ and $12(11)(10! \, 17!)$. Since the GCF of 18 and 12(11) is 6, the GCF of our two numbers is $6(10!)(17!)$. Thus $(\text{LCM})(6)(10!)(17!) = 10! \, 18! \, 12! \, 17!$, so LCM$=(18! \, 12!)/6 = (18! \, 12!)/3!$. Thus the desired product is $(18)(12)(3) = \mathbf{648}$.

571. Solving for y and z in terms of x, we have $y = bx/a$ and $z = cx/a$. Thus

$$
\begin{aligned}
\frac{x}{a} &= \frac{xyz}{x + y + z} \\
&= \frac{x(bx/a)(cx/a)}{x + bx/a + cx/a} \\
&= x^2 \frac{bc/a^2}{(a + b + c)/a} = x^2 \frac{bc}{a(a + b + c)}
\end{aligned}
$$

Thus $x = a(a + b + c)/abc = \mathbf{(a + b + c)/bc}$.

572. Since the roots of the equation are the same, the discriminant of the equation is 0. Thus $4b^2 - 4ac = 0$, or $b^2 = ac$. Thus $a/b = b/c$, so the terms a, b, c form a geometric sequence.

573. We seek the smallest n such that $10^{1/11} 10^{2/11} \cdots 10^{n/11} > 10^5$. Thus $(1 + 2 + 3 + \cdots + n)/11 > 5$. Since $1 + 2 + \cdots + n = n(n + 1)/2$, we have $n(n + 1)/22 > 5$, so $n(n + 1) > 110$. Thus $n^2 + n - 110 = (n + 11)(n - 10) > 0$. This has solution $n > 10$ or $n < -11$. Since $n > 0$, we must have $n > 10$, so the smallest possible value of n is **11**.

574. Any line through the center of a square bisects the area of the square. Indeed, if a line passes through the center of a square, it divides the square into two congruent pieces in which one is a 180° rotation of the other. You should try to prove this fact. In order for any line to bisect the area of a square, it must pass through the center of the square. (Why?) The center of the given square is $(1/2, 1/2)$. The equation of the line then is $(y - 1/2)/(x - 1/2) = 6$. The y-intercept is the point where $x = 0$, so $y - 1/2 = 6(-1/2)$, so $y = -5/2$ and the y-intercept is $(\mathbf{0}, \mathbf{-5/2})$.

575. We must consider the cases of a convex and a concave quadrilateral separately. In the first figure, we note that the sum of the four angles of $ABCD$ is $360°$. If all of these are acute, the sum is less than $4(90°) = 360°$. Thus the angles

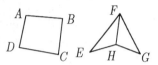

cannot all be acute. Since none are right, one must be obtuse. For the case of $EFGH$, we draw HF. Since reflex angle EHG is greater than $180°$, the two angles EHF and GHF cannot both be acute, or their sum will be less than $180°$. Since neither of these are right, at least one must be obtuse.

576. Since the equations have real roots, their discriminants must be nonnegative. Thus $a^2 - 8b \geq 0$ and $4b^2 - 4a \geq 0$. From the second we have $a \leq b^2$, so the minimum b allows the smallest possible a, and hence the smallest possible sum $a + b$. Putting this in the first inequality gives $0 \leq a^2 - 8b \leq (b^2)^2 - 8b$, so $b^4 - 8b \geq 0$. Since $b^4 - 8b = b(b^3 - 8) = b(b - 2)(b^2 + 2b + 4) \geq 0$, the solution set for b is $b \geq 2$ or $b \leq 0$ (note that the final term is positive for all positive b). Since we are given $b > 0$, the smallest possible value of b is 2, so $a^2 \geq 8b$ and $a^2 \geq 16$. Thus the smallest possible positive value of a is 4, and the smallest possible value of $a + b$ is **6**.

577. Let $BP = x$. Thus we have

$$\frac{AB + BP}{PC + CD} = \frac{BP}{PC}$$

$$\frac{b - a + x}{(c - b - x) + (d - c)} = \frac{x}{c - b - x}.$$

Getting rid of the denominators, we have $(b - a + x)(c - b - x) = (d - b - x)(x)$. Hence, $-x^2 + (a - 2b + c)x + (b - a)(c - b) = -x^2 + (d - b)x$. Thus $(a - b + c - d)x = -(b - a)(c - b)$. Since $OP = OB + BP = b + x$, we have

$$OP = \frac{b(a - b + c - d) - (b - a)(c - b)}{a - b + c - d} = \frac{\mathbf{ac - bd}}{\mathbf{a - b + c - d}}.$$

578. Two hexes together make a total of 10 vertices. The third can make 13 vertices as in A, or it can make 14 vertices, as in the two figures in B. There is no way to add a hex to A to add less than 3 vertices to make a 15 vertex figure, and no way

to add a hex to either of the figures in B to add fewer than 2 vertices to make a 15 vertex figure. Thus there is no way to make a 15 vertex figure. All larger numbers of vertices can be attained from the base cases 13, 14, 16, and 19. Two of these are shown; try to make the other two. To these, we can easily tack on hexes to add multiples of four to the number of vertices. Thus all integers greater than **15** can be attained.

579. For each of the k triangles, we can form a group of 4 points by adding any one of the other $n-3$ points to the 3 which form the triangle. Thus for each of the k triangles, there are $n-3$ groups of 4 points which contain the triangle. Since there are $n-3$ groups for each of the k triangles, there are at most $k(n-3)$ groups of 4 points which contain at least one of the k triangles. Note that there are not exactly this many groups, because some of the groups of points may be counted for more than one triangle and hence we have overcounted.

580. Since we know the roots are real and different, the discriminant cannot be negative or 0. Thus the discriminant is greater than 0, or $p^2 - 32 > 0$. Now, since we are asked to prove something regarding the sum of the roots of the quadratic, we note that $r_1 + r_2 = -(p/1) = -p$. Thus $p^2 = (r_1 + r_2)^2$, and our inequality is $(r_1 + r_2)^2 - 32 > 0$. Adding 32 to both sides and taking square roots gives $|r_1 + r_2| > 4\sqrt{2}$.

581. Using our definition of $\{x\}$, we have $x + y - \lfloor x + y \rfloor = x - \lfloor x \rfloor$, so $y = \lfloor x + y \rfloor - \lfloor x \rfloor$. Since both $\lfloor x + y \rfloor$ and $\lfloor x \rfloor$ are integers, y, as the difference of these, must be an integer also.

582. Since x is between 0 and 1, we have $x^a < x$ for positive a if $a > 1$ and $x^a > x$ if $a < 1$. Also, for $0 < a, x < 1$, we find $x^a < 1$. Since $x < 1$, we have $x < x^x < 1$. Thus $x^{(x^x)} > x$, so $z > x$. Since $x < x^x$ and $x < 1$, we find $x^x > x^{(x^x)}$ (make sure you follow this), so $y > z$. Hence, in increasing order, the quantities are $\boldsymbol{x, z, y}$.

583. Multiply the first by 3 and the second by 2 and subtract to cancel the constant terms. Thus we have

$$6x^2 + 15xy + 9y^2 = 6$$
$$12x^2 + 16xy + 8y^2 = 6.$$

Subtracting yields $-6x^2 - xy + y^2 = 0$. We wish to factor this as $(ax + y)(bx + y)$ Thus $ab = -6$ and $a + b = -1$. Hence, the factorization is $(-3x + y)(2x + y) = 0$, so $y = 3x$ and $y = -2x$ are solutions. From the first solution, we have $2x^2 + 5xy + 3y^2 = 44x^2 = 2$, so $(x^2, y^2) = (1/22, 9/22)$, and $x^2 + y^2 = 5/11$. From the second solution, $2x^2 + 5xy + 3y^2 = 4x^2 = 2$, so $(x^2, y^2) = (1/2, 2)$, and $x^2 + y^2 = 5/2$. Thus the maximum value of $x^2 + y^2$ is **5/2**.

584. Since $9^2 + 12^2 = 15^2$, $\triangle BCP$ is a right triangle with right angle at P. You should be able to quickly recognize this because the given lengths are in the ratio $3 : 4 : 5$. Next, we draw XY through P such $XY \perp AD$ and $XY \perp BC$. Drawing AP, we note that it is the hypotenuse of right triangle APY. To find the legs AY and PY, we find the lengths BX (which equals AY) and PX (which subtracted from the width yields

PY). Since $\triangle PXB \sim \triangle CPB$, we have $PX/PB = PC/CB$, so $PX = (9/15)(12) = 36/5$. Similarly, $XB/PB = PB/BC$, so $BX = 48/5$. Thus $AY = 48/5$ and $PY = AB - PX = 14/5$. From the Pythagorean Theorem, (or remembering that 7-24-25 is a Pythagorean triple), we find $AP = \mathbf{10}$.

585.   Let the weight of a coin in bag i be $x_i + 1$. Thus all the x_i are 0, 1, or 2. We do this because the way the problem involves 1, 3, 3^2, and 3^3 as the numbers of coins hints at a solution involving base three numerals (remember this as a general technique). Thus from the given information we have $(x_1 + 1) + 3(x_2 + 1) + 3^2(x_3 + 1) + 3^3(x_4 + 1) = 95$, so $x_1 + 3x_2 + 3^2 x_3 + 3^3 x_4 = 55$. Considering the bounds on the x_i, we realize that these make up the base three representation of 55. since $55 = 2001_3$, $(x_1, x_2, x_3, x_4) = (1, 0, 0, 2)$. The weights of the coins are these increased by 1, so the weights of a coin in each bag, in order from bag 1 to bag 4, are $\mathbf{2}$, $\mathbf{1}$, $\mathbf{1}$, and $\mathbf{3}$ ounces.

586.   Instead of working with the trapezoids, let's look at triangles CDE, CFG, and CAB. From the given information we have $[CDE] : [CFG] : [CAB] = 1 : 2 : 3$. Thus the ratio of corresponding sides is the square root of this, or $CD : CF : CA = 1 : \sqrt{2} : \sqrt{3}$. Hence, if we let $CD = x$, $CF = x\sqrt{2}$ and $CA = x\sqrt{3}$, so $CD/FA = x/(CA - CF) = x/(x\sqrt{3} - x\sqrt{2}) = 1/(\sqrt{3} - \sqrt{2}) = \sqrt{2} + \sqrt{3}$.

587.   Collecting all variables on one side and factoring, we have $a^2 - b^2 + bc - ac = (a - b)(a + b) + c(b - a) = (a + b)(a - b) - c(a - b) = (a + b - c)(a - b) = 0$. Thus $a = b$ or $a + b = c$. From the first, there are 25 solutions, because a and b can be any of 5 integers, and for each of these we have 5 choices for c, for a total of $5(5) = 25$ triples. For the second, we consider each value of c separately for solutions to $a + b = c$. For $c = 1$ there are no solutions, and for $c = 2$, the only solution is $(1, 1, 2)$, which has already been counted in the case $a = b$. For $c = 3$ we have 2 new solutions, $(1, 2, 3)$ and $(2, 1, 3)$. For $c = 4$ we have 2 new solutions, $(1, 3, 4)$ and $(3, 1, 4)$, and one which has already been counted, $(2, 2, 4)$. Finally, for $c = 5$, there are 4 new solutions, $(1, 4, 5)$; $(2, 3, 5)$; $(3, 2, 5)$; $(4, 1, 5)$. Thus there are a total of $25 + 2 + 2 + 4 = \mathbf{33}$ solutions.

588.   Let $AE = AF = x$. We divide the quadrilateral into trapezoid $EHDF$ and triangle EHC by drawing EH perpendicular to CD as shown. Since $EH = 1$ and $FD = 1 - x$, we have $[EHDF] = (DH)(EH + FD)/2 = x(2 - x)/2$. Also, $[EHC] = (CH)(EH)/2 = (1 - x)(1)/2$ (since $DH = AE = x$, $HC = 1 - x$). Thus

$$[EFDC] = [EHDF] + [EHC] = \frac{x(2 - x)}{2} + \frac{1 - x}{2} = \frac{1 + x - x^2}{2}.$$

To maximize this, we complete the square in the numerator and find that

$$[EFDC] = \frac{-(x - 1/2)^2 + 5/4}{2} = \frac{5}{8} - \frac{(x - 1/2)^2}{2}.$$

Thus the maximum area is $\mathbf{5/8}$, which occurs when $x = 1/2$, or when E and F are midpoints.